WHEN THE GODDESS CALLS

VOLUME 4

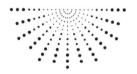

TINA PAVLOU

authors
AND CO.

CONTENTS

TINA PAVLOU

THE GREAT AWAKENING OF 2020

> *No one saves us but ourselves. No one can, and no one may. We ourselves must walk the path.*

*W*elcome to the Fourth Edition of When The Goddess Calls, this volume is being written while the outside world is in chaos, fear-mongering and scarcity, however; in my world and all the Goddesses that are by my side, it has been one of the greatest events in our lives. Instead of worrying and utilising energy from the past; myself and the Goddesses from The Goddess Rooms, The Temple have taken this time to go within to create, to release, to grow, to take ourselves back to our inner being of who we truly are. We have been embracing our divine feminine, connecting with our sexuality, our sensuality, connecting with our core and together we have been on an adventure of self-discovery.

February 27th, 2020, it's my birthday - I'm in the Gold Coast launching Volume 3 of When the Goddess Calls with such excitement for the future, so much happiness, so much joy! The vibration and frequency of the Gold Coast and of Australia is so high; I am feeling amazing like I never have before.

> *When you notice how PERFECT everything is, you will tilt your head back and laugh at the sky.*

As I sit preparing for the book launch dressing in my Camilla dress that was gifted to me, placing my crystal headpiece onto my crown chakra; I finally felt in my heart true completeness, and I saw the magic that I was creating with women around the planet. I felt so humbled, and I wiped the tears of joy from my eyes. Fast forward two weeks as I left Australia and flew into Dubai, I was told there was a virus, a deadly virus that was killing thousands of people and that I had to return home to the UK. I checked in with Creator to find out what was truly going on, and I was shown the truth.

> *Be a LIGHT unto yourself. Be your own confidence. Hold to the truth within. You yourself, as much as anybody in the entire universe, DESERVE your love and affection.*

I landed back on the March 17th 2020 and as I returned I could feel the fear energy in the UK, all over social media people were scared, scared for there families, scared for their livelihoods, scared for how they were going to pay their bills, scared to go near any other humans; and families were told to separate. As I entered my home, I went into the Theta state, cleared my home and downloaded it with hope, joy, happiness and released all radiation. I found lockdown to be a time that I could enjoy my home. I woke up on the March 18th with my beautiful Guide standing next to me with a message; the time is now – this is the time you've been waiting for, stand in your light, be a beacon - shine your light bright for they will come!

> *Teach this triple truth to all: a generous heart, kind speech, and a life of service and compassion are the things which renew HUMANITY.*

I was told to introduce 'Mantras in pyjamas' with an essential oil, so I chose Young Living Believe. I began going online every morning and singing mantras from Lord Ganesh, Kali Ma, Lakshmi, Saraswathi and other Goddesses. I cleared everyone in my group of fear, and I downloaded them with hope and love. Every morning I cleared their houses, and I helped them find their inner power and tap into their inner Goddess.

Fashion your LIFE as a garland of beautiful deeds.

Around the world more and more people began to join my group, there had been times when I just wanted to lay in bed with the blankets over my head, but I knew that people needed me - they were my inspiration - we were all in this together. My beautiful assistants Michelle, Rochelle and Claire supported me with my dream of awakening and helping others. This was the time of great growth for thousands of people, many jumped in as an opportunity to earn money, many jumped in as an opportunity to help others, many took this as an opportunity to rest, and many took it as an opportunity to chill, some for the first time in their adult life!

> *Three things cannot be long hidden: the sun, the moon, and the truth.*

I call this the great awakening of 2020 - my belief is that there is a virus out there, a common cold, severe flu but if your immune system is strong; if you drink your greens and eat the right food you will not become ill; you will become strong, and any virus cannot be attached to your body as any virus can only be attached to the feeling of unworthiness. This is another reason why Theta healing is so important as we can release these beliefs and teach you what it feels like to live in the energy of plenty, to live without fear, to live without feeling unworthy and to teach your body what it feels like to be worthy and deserving.

> *If your respectful by habit, constantly honouring the worthy four things will increase – long life – beauty – happiness and strength.*

MY TRUTH

This is my truth; I speak with truth, and I speak with honour. I believe the virus, and the epidemic is man-made from the higher powers who wish to take out the monetary system for control over the humans on this planet. It is to take away freedom, no more cash in hand jobs, no more helping others behind closed doors, no more money in your children's piggy banks where they learn the value of money or in their birthday cards; everything that you do on the monetary system will be transparent. I have many books especially by the author Sylvia Brown who predicted this, that money would be out of circulation by 2021, and I believe this too.

> *To keep the body in good health is A DUTY...otherwise,*
> *we shall not be able to keep our mind strong & clear.*

I have seen not only the greatest awakening but also the greatest division. The veils dropped and to be able to see the truth about every human and which vibration they live, in lack and fear or abundance and love. There is no judgement on this, only growth and for us to be in compassion for the people who are living in fear, who are not awake and who attack us for having the beliefs that we do. Over the last six months, there is a different topic of debate where everyone is falling out, and I know this to just be an illusion to continue to divide the public. People reporting other people for not wearing masks reminds me of the old schoolbooks of the Gestapo, history is repeating itself, how human behaviour is still recycling itself - we are the greatest experiment. Some people choose not to speak out and stay in their bubble, some people react in anger and fighting in the streets, and some people are choosing just to stay in their comfort bubble turning blind eyes; there is no judgement on any choice you make. Your vibration is unique to you and what is playing out in your world is coming from your subconscious; many of our fears are being triggered by our ancestor's beliefs that we carry in our subconscious.

> *HAVE COMPASSION for all beings, rich and poor alike; each has their suffering....*

In Theta healing we have a wonderful world relations course which teaches us about love and that we can put a stop to hatred as it doesn't matter what the colour of your skin is or your religious beliefs are. We are all the same, and we are all one. The experience and the experiment are just to learn to love. Did you know that you can change any belief and any feeling in your body and subconscious by connecting to Creator in our wonderful world of Theta healing? In the last six years, I have been teaching Theta healing and taught healing from around the world. I am so blessed to be able to teach in The Goddess Rooms and now online, so we can reach thousands of more people.

I have been using the Young Living essential oils, and, in my opinion, I have found them to be the highest vibrational essences on this planet. As I hold the bottles of oils in my hands, I feel the vibration of the fairies and the elementals of the second plane of existence. So, when using my essential oils, my favourite is Abundance and White Angelica, which are a blend of some of the most delicious oils grown around Europe and North America. Working with Theta healing this expands my consciousness beyond the human mind and to quantum realms.

I can see beyond the veils and connect with trees, feel their energies, and connect with the flowers using flower essences on a daily basis. Wearing my crystals from the First plane, the Fourth plane working with my Ancestors, Fifth plane working with Goddesses, Masters and Angels, the Sixth plane I've been working with my tones and the Laws of the Universe and The Seventh plane is the Creator Of All That Is; these are the seven planes of existence which I tap in and tune into daily. I have connected with the Abundance of light codes, which I now incorporate into my unique healing modality.

> *I AM Creatrix, I AM Abundance, I AM Sovereignty, I AM Queen, I AM Priestess, I am Goddess, I am Warrioress this is my daily mantra.*
>
> *All that we are is the result of what we have THOUGHT. The mind is everything. What we think, we become.*
>
> — *WHEN THE GODDESS CALLS*

THE TEMPLE

The Goddess Rooms is a beautiful sanctuary where we run courses that Women and Men come to learn many things such as Theta healing, Angelic reiki, Red tent, Sacred Feminine classes/dance, Children's workshops and meditation and we now introduce bespoke healing. The Goddess Rooms is a community of the highest frequency, and anything or anyone who is not heart lead is always removed by the Goddess in one way or another.

> *The way is not in the sky. The way is in the HEART.*

I am blessed to introduce a bespoke healing that we have created here with two of our Goddesses Julie and Jan, and they are called the Fae Healers. Here at the Goddess Rooms, we offer monthly packages of flower essences and homeopathic remedies that all the Goddesses have now been taking since the beginning of lockdown to help support them and release any old fears that arise and for their families too as we have children.

> *Health is the greatest GIFT, contentment the greatest WEALTH, faithfulness the best RELATIONSHIP.*

SELF CARE & MAGIC

The magical techniques of self-care.

Here in the Goddess Rooms, we create lifestyles, and I invite you into my daily Goddess self-care ritual. The magical ways to pamper, soothe and care for your body and spirit. Each morning as I awake, I recall my dreams in my journal book at once, I make myself my greens with freshwater, and I switch on my diffuser. Every morning I tune into the best oils that will support my wellbeing, I place the oils into the diffuser, I breathe and meditate and then shower or bathe in oils. The first thing I do in the morning is make my bed, a made bed clears out the junk in the brain, and for me, I can see the rest of the day in clear focus. I sing my mantras, and I continue to drink my juices in the morning. I do not eat any food until midday as I cleanse my body out by drinking or using fresh herbs.

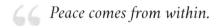 *Peace comes from within.*

I place the oils all over my body to lift my vibration, and I place my white angelica onto my crown chakra. I repeat my affirmations I AM THAT I AM, I pull out a daily oracle card, I connect to Creator, I clear my home and set my intentions for the day. I give Mother Earth a healing and all living souls including animals I send unconditional love every morning. I do my stretching, or I walk my dog on the beach when all the time I am in gratitude and creating. I eat healthy food, anything that has a soul I will not eat. I am a vegetarian, and I do not eat dairy. I am conscious of anything that goes in or on my body. True self-love is knowing that your body is a beautiful temple and your muscles have memories. I dance to my Goddess music, I have a massage, reflexology, and Angelic Reiki once a week. I make it my number one priority to take care of my mind, my body, and my spirit first so that I can serve humanity. I ask the universe a question every day…How may I serve?

When the mind is PURE joy follows like a shadow that never leaves. You are the miracle.

People are nervous about changes around their friends and families but staying authentic to who you are in your heart and spirit can be an ongoing challenge. It is so easy to go back to the old programming and conditioning, but I promise once you truly fall in love with yourself and find your true self-worth, you will never abuse your body or another living thing again. Questions I ask myself, what am I thankful for in the Spring, what am I thankful for in the Summer, what am I thankful for in the Autumn and what am I thankful for in the Winter and as I walk, I am always connected to the Creator, and I say thank you, thank you, thank you. Working with the Law of Attraction, the more gratitude you have, the more you will be given to be grateful for. I find wearing the oils of Bergamot and Ylang-Ylang bring me clarity and confidence with inner peace and serenity, and I remain calm throughout my day. I love to wear Rose or Jasmine when I feel I need to be open to receiving love. I love to wear lavender when I need to find balance, and when I need to find emotional balance. I turn my phone off at night now, and my dreams have become light and airy, no radiation or electromagnetics vibrating into my frequency.

Setting boundaries is an important part of self-care, helping you to keep balance and whole. They protect you from people claiming your time but wearing frankincense also emanates the air of boundaries. Loving my inner child is essential; I love to write in my gold book, my wishes and my desires, my manifestations, and my gratitude each day. I have earnt the name of the Queen of Abundance as I am a master manifestor in the highest and best and I now teach this in my one to one packages or in my Sensual goddess online courses.

> *However many holy words you read, however many you speak, what good will they do if you do not ACT upon them?*

Nutrition is so important to regulate your hormones; for memory and mental clarity, you must listen to your body's needs. It is also so important to clear out your body with a cleanse; I do these every 6 weeks. I bath and shower with oil and body scrub each day. I take care of my aura; my home is cleaned with non-toxic products; even my clothing liquid is non-toxic added with essential oils. Toxic cleaning products can damage your lungs, and this includes some perfumes. The media are advertising designer fragrances which are toxic to your skin; did you know an essential oil takes 22 seconds to go into your bloodstream. Can you imagine what a toxic fragrance that you buy from a general store does to your body.... but the great thing is more and more people are awakening now so its easier. There are many studies and research articles that you can read for yourself and see the truth of this. Make the body alkaline as no disease can thrive in an alkaline body. Herbs and minerals that cleanse your body are wormwood walnut extract, oregano oil, olive leaf (kills yeast) charcoal kills parasites, colloidal silver kills all kinds of parasites and yeast but do not take this all the time. Thyme can kill any yukky parasite too, but the easiest thing is fresh juice, carrots, celery, a little beetroot, garlic and ginger is one of the best cleanses in my opinion. Noni juice and eucalyptus are great for anti-bacterial and fungal.

> *BELIEVE nothing, no matter where you read it, or who said it, even if I have said it, unless it agrees with your own reason and your own common sense.*

My favourite is the flower essences and my homeopathic remedies; each month I am taking a different remedy and flower essence. I was downloaded and shown a flower and the name of a flower and shown to take it as an essence. I spoke to Jan about this; one of our Fae healers and she had never heard of this before, so she went out to investigate and found the flower in a local garden and asked the owner of the garden if she could have a cutting. She went home and created the essence that I had spoken about, this essence is related to the Goddess Isis, and as I held the finished product in my hand, I was downloaded and gifted new information that I will be sharing in my Sensual Goddess courses. I take this flower essence every day; we call it the Mother, it is very powerful - the first week I took it I was so angry, it was releasing abuse that I had encountered over the last year. This lasted for a few days, and I started to feel and see with new eyes. I also want to share how much I have fallen in love with myself over the last 6 months I'm not afraid to go out of my home without any makeup or paint my toenails or have to have my eyebrows waxed or my roots done ...quick, quick get to the hairdressers. I no longer want eyelashes placed over my eyelashes I am embracing my inner goddess, my inner warrior my inner creatrix, my inner priestess, my inner Queen.

> *The way to happiness: live simply, give much, fill your life with LOVE.*

Who do I serve, and what do I do? I have created the most amazing courses, the Sensual Goddess online and on our retreats I coach one to one and in groups empowering women to find there real sensual inner goddess, inner witch and inner beauty and to connect to their sacred feminine and awaken to the power within there sexual energy. I coach holistic goddesses to awaken and set up their businesses so that they too can spread their light.

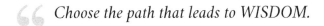 *Choose the path that leads to WISDOM.*

I am unapologetic to who I am; I am love, I am a woman of substance, and through my challenges and my lessons in life, I have grown into a truly beautiful woman. I am a sage, the wise woman and through my knowledge, my learnings and my challenges I help women release their shame and their guilt through the subconscious and the physical from womb healing to light language. I am grateful for every aspect of myself who went through every challenge. I thank the younger Me's, for the younger Me's have enabled me to help humanity rise. Do I look back on myself, on my past, do I feel regret remorse…NO? My body is too pure to allow anything of low vibrations.

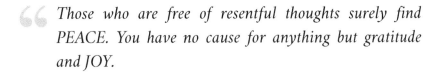 *Those who are free of resentful thoughts surely find PEACE. You have no cause for anything but gratitude and JOY.*

No-one should carry shame, guilt or trauma in their body and this is my expertise to help people release the trauma, to help you fall in love with you, to help your business grow so you can help other souls, to help your relationship with your lovers, your husbands, your mother and father and your best friends. Everything starts with you; every emotion starts with you, and your subconscious creates your outer world. Do you live in fear, or do you live in love? It is impossible to be in my company and walk away in the energy of fear – I truly empower people to believe in themselves, to believe in their missions and to heal their wounds. Everything that is going on in your life is being filtered by your wounds, clear your wounds, and you see truth. My name is Tina Pavlou; I am the creator of The Goddess Rooms and the Number one bestselling book series, When the Goddess Calls. I invite you to join us to step onto your spiritual path. I do not care where you have come from or where you've been; I truly believe when you release all your old programming, you will shine bright like a diamond…until we meet again in the next volume. God bless *xx*

> *If you propose to speak, always ask yourself, is it true, is it necessary, is it KIND?*

ABOUT THE AUTHOR

Tina Pavlou is a Clairvoyant and an intuitive Coach and Mentor.. a Seer into the Spiritual realms, who works with the Seven Planes of Existence and the Spiritual Laws; a Theta Healing® Instuctor, an Angelic Reiki Master and teacher, a Suara Sound Therapist and a Divine FEMININE Taoism Sexual Energy Teacher from Kent in England.

Tina specialises in empowering people to live their best lives by giving them the spiritual tools to do so.

After experiencing the Dark Night of the Soul, she made it her passion to help as many people as she could, so they would never have to experience as much suffering and pain as she had.

It is impossible to be around Tina without feeling anything other than positivity and love as she vibrates on such a Divine, Goddess high frequency. Her passion is just love.

CONTACT DETAILS

EMAIL: Pavloutina@yahoo.co.uk

WEBSITE: tinapavlou.com

2

LECKRANEE BURTHOO-BARAH

I was born on the 07th of August 1977, in a public hospital of Mauritius to a young mother of 17 years old. My brother was born 2.5 years after me, he is my best friend, and we have a very solid bond.

My childhood was a fairly happy one. I was an outdoor child, collecting wildflowers, rocks, seashells, and having dogs as pets. My life as a child was pretty good; I had loving parents, an amazing brother, and friends.

But my mother remained to date a very dominant figure in my life. My mother gave me the responsibility of being a caretaker for my brother. She strongly believed in physical punishment as part of parenting to teach obedience, discipline, success, and achievement.

Nevertheless, I love my mother to the moon and back, because now being in the space where I am in life, I can understand being married at 15 years and being a young mother, with all responsibilities and expectations of being a homemaker, would not have been easy. By having the awareness and not holding anything against my mother, I have shifted my limiting beliefs.

As a child I was very studious, my mother was very demanding from both me and brother, to study hard, learn quickly, and to make something good out of our lives. But she was harder on me because I remember she would always say, "I want to you have the opportunities that I did not have. The power of a woman lies in her ability to make money".

Childhood passed very quickly, but adolescence hit me hard. I was lost most of the time, my body was changing, and my mother would not talk about any girl stuff to me. My father was distancing from me as well. I could not comprehend what was happening! At that time, there was no access to the internet, social media like these days, so information was either from school, teachers, friends, television, or parents.

I started getting interested in boys, at a very young age, 11 years old, which was considered as sinful by my parents. I received my first love letter at 11 years old, and it fell into the hands of my mother; hell broke loose! She told me she is getting me educated to be an independent woman, not be with boyfriends. Needless to mention, I was physically punished for this.

As I was growing up, my father started being strict with me, I remember he would always tell my mother, "Girls should be controlled, anything can happen to them". I would not understand what it meant, nor I was given any explanation about it.

Summer vacations, I would insist on spending at my grand-mother's place because all my cousins would be there or at my aunties' place. My father was not very happy with the idea, but my mother would agree from time to time.

When I look back to what my father was really scared of was abuse. It did happen to me several times, which I understood when I turned 15 years old. I did not understand at that time what it was; for me, it was love. Because the more my father was distancing from me, the more I was looking for that love in other men. Being in the space where I am in life now, I under-stand my father was struggling to be with his daughter as much I wanted it, but the lack of understanding a daughter was there.

My mother was very supportive in getting me educated, throughout my secondary education, she would ensure that I took tuitions so that I achieved good marks. But my father did not take any interest in my studies. He never asked, "what you going to do when you grow up".

To be honest, I never knew what I wanted to become as an adult; all I knew was I wanted to be a working woman because my mother wanted me to. It was so strongly built in me; I wanted to be good at school because I knew my mother would like it. It was her way of giving me, love. I was slowly replacing my parents with my teachers because they would understand, praise, encourage, and nurture me, which I lacked at home. I would play the victim with my teachers to get their attention; however, I was a very good student. I was very studious and hardworking because I wanted to be the teachers favourite.

Going out with friends have always been a "no-no" for my parents because "a girl from a good family does not go out". I heard this zillions of times until I gave in and never asked again if I could go out. But all I knew was the day I turned 18 years old I would be earning money, and I would run away from here. I would go very far where no one knew me, and start a new life! I kept on repeating in my mind that my mother was right, and a woman can only be free if she made money, it was my motivation mantra!

During school days and time, I would do whatever I wanted, but once I was home, I would study hard. Studying became a passion rather than an obligation because it was the only way I could exist at home, together with watching TV. Very young, I learned how to live a double life unknowingly; at home, pleasing my parents doing whatever makes them happy and at school pleasing my teachers. I was accepted that way, so it did not bother me, but now I know that it was a limiting belief!

In 1990, I sat for my School Certificate exams for the first time, (Mauritius follows the British Curriculum), the results were not brilliant. My mother was so upset with me, it was obvious she physically punished me for it, but she allowed me to repeat my School Certificate. Whatever her way was, I owe her for the life I have. It was not the best way, but that is all she knew. She wanted her daughter to get out of the dogma which was so ingrained in our culture "Girls are a burden which is passed on to someone else through a marriage".

I passed my School Certificate on the second attempt with a brilliant result; a Grade 1. I was third among all students who took part in the examinations in Mauritius. My teachers were so proud, and my mother was over the moon. It was a Saturday when the results were out, but we could only receive the official papers on Monday. I can still see it clearly. My elder cousin was at my place on that day, and she congratulated my father on my passing. My father was fuming, and he said "What congratulations, for what?", my cousin told him about my result, and he immediately answered, "Where is the result slip to prove it, she is a liar, and all of you are believing her, I need to see the proof of her result".

It was heartbreaking, the whole scene. My mother answered him back, and a whole argument about it broke out, which I did not understand. I answered back to my father, and my mother slapped me. On that night I cried myself to sleep, not knowing that my beliefs "I am not good enough" and "I am not worthy" got reinforced again.

There are so many incidents that happened before this one, where I felt it would have better if I was not born. All the complaints my mother was getting from others, for me being a "girl out of control" in their terms. I was born to shake up the baseless societal requirements of being a girl. I was expressing it in my actions, and I was very vocal. Physical punishment became a small part of it.

For my young self, physical punishment, slut-shaming (I prefer not to go into details), and other cruel statements and words were another way of me becoming stronger and bolder. The anger in me became my loyal friend, my motivator, my way of living. The more resistance I was experiencing, the better I was feeling, because deep inside of me, I knew I could overcome anything. I could show the world how powerful I am, that I will be on top one day and no one could touch me. I was working one goal – liberation! So I did not care how it happened.

Since I had a very good result in my second attempt with my School Certificate, my father wanted me to stop my studies and join teaching training to become a teacher. I was against it. I was fully supported by my mother, who wanted me to complete my Higher School Certificate. My father was very clear that he will not provide additional money, and my mother needed to find ways in whatever is given to her in the house budget to manage.

We did manage it. I completed my Higher School Certificate in 1997 with brilliant results. The challenge was it would not be possible for me to land a good-paying job because the work market in Mauritius was saturated. My father refused to finance my education further, and the University was very far from where I was living. My mother told me she did not have any means to pay my university fees.

The bitterness of the estranged relationship with my father was getting worse every year; my mother told me to start working. We were staying in the same house, but I was not on talking terms with my father, I had lots of resentment for him. At this point, resentment became my other good friend after anger.

One of my school teachers told me there is a newly set up institution very close to where I was living, and they were offering 2-year diploma courses at affordable prices. I went to check the prices and discussed it with my mother. She agreed to manage it but on one condition, since the institution had both boys and girls as students she did want any single complaint, judgment, criticism from my dad or anyone else that I am getting too close to boys. If there was one single complaint, my course would be stopped immediately. I agreed and promised I would never do anything to hurt my mother. To be honest, not all of them were kept!

I enrolled for a Diploma in Business Administration, specialising in Marketing in mid-1997, and completed with Grade A in mid-2000. My father was not happy with our decision of me getting further education; he was watching over me like a hawk, looking for that single mistake so that it ends. It did happen several times, now understanding that the Universe always has our back, I managed to graduate!

My graduation ceremony is one of the most hurtful events. Both parents were invited to the ceremony, but my mother already warned me that my father would not come and if she informed him, he would create a scene out of it. So, I agreed with my mother, and she invited her brother to accompany us for the occasion. Looking at all my friends, accompanied by both their parents and being photographed by the professional photographer in a perfect family frame, my heart broke into million pieces, knowing I didn't deserve this happiness.

Our graduation ceremony was covered by the media, and the next day my picture appeared in the national newspaper receiving my diploma from the Minister of Education. I remember it was a Sunday, and the phone at home could not stop ringing with congratulation messages from those who saw the picture. It was probably one way of the Universe compensating for what I missed on that day!

I started working for one of the banks in October 2000 as a finance assistant in their offshore department after some temporary jobs. I was finally a working woman, the dream I always asked for. I was happy. I was finally making money, and my mother was very proud of me. I felt a burden was lifted from my shoulders after the odds on the way. However, my father did not make it easy for me. He would complain of my office attires, that my short corporate skirts show too much skin, and that men in the office would think I am from a "bad" family. I had to deal with it every day, and the disgust in his eyes would boil inside me. The anger inside of me never got lesser but increased with each confrontation with my father.

In April 2001, my mother's brother, who resides in the UK asked my mother if she would like me to move to the UK. I would not deny I did mention to my uncle a couple of times I want to leave Mauritius because being in this emotional turmoil was draining me. I was so happy when my mother accepted my uncle's offer.

My flight to the UK was booked for the beginning of June 2001. My father got to know about me leaving in the morning when we were leaving to go to the airport. There was a big argument with my mother, which is why his permission was not asked. It went on and on for hours until we left. I finally landed in the UK, and I already had in my mind that I would get a diploma, it would be easy for me to look for a job and I could do my certification from the Association of Chartered and Certified Accountants(ACCA) while working, which I have always dreamed of. Unfortunately, my uncle broke the news to me, stating that if I want to stay in the UK, it would be advisable to undertake a health care course as they are in great demand. After 3 to 4 years, I could think about something else if I wanted to. He made it very clear if I decided to do anything other than what he had in mind for me, I would be not be supported!

After spending more than 6 months in the UK and enrolling myself in the health care courses to be trained; one morning, I woke up and decided to come back to Mauritius. I was not happy at all. The way I was treated, and also the way people would react to me; I felt at the mercy of others. I felt stuck, and I could barely sleep or function. I would sit for hours in the parks thinking about what I should do. The weather was not helping, it was cold, and it would always rain. I was getting sick all the time with a cough or the flu.

Once I returned back to Mauritius, my relationships with my parents were the same; nothing had changed. I was jobless. I started applying for jobs every single day, any job. I was very harsh and hard on myself; I needed a rush of anger and adrenaline to make it happen, it had to happen. In the end, this was the only way I learned to move forward, through feeling worthless and not good enough!

Thanks to Universe, I landed myself a job with one of the biggest accounting and audit firms at the end of 2001. I joined them as an assistant auditor in their offshore section. I could finally enrol for an ACCA course as this was one of the requirements when joining the firm. Back to work to earn my living, my father angry again, my mother dealing with the toxic father-daughter relationship again. Fallouts were frequent, fueling my anger, but at this point, my anger was my motivator to grow, to progress, to make more money, because I knew money could get me my freedom!

Maybe you are thinking, why can she not just go and live on her own as she is making money now. Well unfortunately in our culture, girls are not allowed to stay on their own. If they are single, they stay with their parents irrespective of their age, the only time they are allowed to leave their parents' home is when they get married.

Many of you will be asking, what happened to my love life? All I am talking about is my career. I did date a couple of guys; I fell in love for entertainment. Yes falling in love was a process for me – I see a guy, I like the guy, I date the guy, the guy cheats on me, the guy leaves me, I am heartbroken, but being heartbroken was another motivation, it allowed me to have a boost of adrenaline, to stay focused on my career. It went on for a while because there was no way I was settling down, being tied up in marriage, stuck to serve a husband chosen by my parents, having kids, and being doomed forever. I was scared to death of the word "marriage"; it felt like capital punishment that I would not be able to endure; it would take away my career and once my career was over, I would be done with life!

My times at the audit and accounting firm lasted for nearly 5 years. I did complete more than 50% of my professional certification from ACCA. My relationship with my father was getting better, we were not on talking terms, but it was less toxic. There would be fallouts here and there; I guess I had grown up as well, so I would deal with them differently. It was much better than what it used to be!

My thirst for being bigger in my career where I would make more and more money was growing every day. I was looking for other opportunities. This was when one of my good friend's sister, who was working in an offshore company told me about a vacant position in her company. After submitting my CV, and being called for an interview, I got an offer that I accepted as I was making twice what I was making within my current job as an "Internal Auditor and Client Accountant" at the accounting and audit firm.

In February 2006, I joined the new company (which I later found out was a chain of companies) as "receptionist/assistant accountant", where 50% of my time I would cover as the receptionist, and the remaining 50% I was assigned to assist one of the finance managers with bank reconciliation.

On my first day I met one of the directors, a Portuguese South African who had been staying in Mauritius for quite a while. He asked what I had been doing before joining his company, and I told him. After the meeting, he told me that he had something more exciting for me, and he will find someone else to do the job I was employed for.

So, I was offered to be the assistant of the same Finance Manager. I enjoyed my work, lots of learning about international businesses and dealing with suppliers from Asia and Europe. Three months down the line, the finance manager submitted his resignation. So, a new replacement was being searched for. Since I already knew the process and was familiar with the reporting side as well, I was offered to be the replacement with a lesser salary of the finance manager because I needed to prove my abilities. Someone else took over my work, and I filled in for the finance manager as the financial accountant.

The South African division was expanding rapidly, and I was asked to report to the South African division's CFO directly. It had been six months in my new role; I had been putting all my energy, time, and efforts passionately into my job. One morning I received a call from the CFO, asking me if I would be interested in a short trip to South Africa to meet the team I was working with. Did I accept it, yes of course I did!

A wonderful short trip to South Africa opened the doors of opportunities for me, there was no looking back. In one year, I was known to everyone in the company in Mauritius and South Africa. My work was recognised and appreciated. My salary increased by more than 100% of what I was initially making. Trips to South Africa became frequent, my team was expanding, and I was officially invited to the board meeting of the group. Yes, I was very proud of myself, I was finally making it big. My ego was boosted with each achievement, each increase in pay, each bonus I was earning. I could finally prove to the whole world who I was! The girl who was always made to feel unworthy was now making lots of money, and she had an amazing career with foreign trips. How does it get better than this?

Over the years, my relationship with my fathe⌐
We were still not talking to each other, ⌐
decreased a lot. The day he knew how much I ⌐
his mind, he had nothing to say. My mother ⌐
pride, that all her efforts and sacrifices were worth it, her
daughter became the woman she always wanted to!

Where is my brother in life, you all might be wondering? Well,
he grew up, and he was working. We are very close since childhood, so every turn in my life, he was supporting me, sometimes
even answering my father on my behalf. He is very proud of me.
My brother taught me how to drive; he said "having your
driving license will be better for you. You can dedicate more
time to your work and your success".

In March 2008 I had enough savings, I was eligible for bank
loans, and as I was earning a very good salary, I decided to get
my car. My brother helped me to find a good one, did all the
paperwork for me for registering and insuring the car. Finally,
my life was complete, earning my living, being able to afford
whatever I desire, and single life was perfect! I thought from
here that I would just flow with life, I would probably meet
some hot hunk down the road and settle down.

In 2008, there had been lots of management changes in my
company. The CFO I was reporting to left the group and moved
somewhere else, I lost contact with him, which saddened me as
he was my mentor. My work also changed a lot. In October
2008 I received a missed call from a number which was not in
my contact list. I returned the call; it was the CFO with whom I
was working with previously. He moved to Dubai in April 2008

rking as the Finance Manager in a big construction company. He wanted me to join his finance team in Dubai as soon as possible.

On the same day, I received an email from him with the job offer and my role in his team. The only thing I knew about Dubai at that time was there was a 7 stars hotel on the sea which looked like a boat's sail. I discussed it with my brother, since working for an insurance company, he knew about the middle east.

My brother told me that night in these exact words:

"Do not think twice about it, take the offer, Dubai is one the most amazing place to be. It is very developed and advanced. Many people are praying for this kind of opportunity, and it came to you without asking. Pack your bags. This place is not for you, people don't understand you here and they never will. You have always been looking for an opportunity to leave Mauritius, and the opportunity is here!"

I did not discuss this new opportunity with my mother because deep inside my heart, I knew she would talk me out of it. I resigned from my current position and told my mother I am going to Dubai on a short assignment in 1 month. She did not ask me much about what is happening; she just told me to do what you feel is right for you.

On the 12th of November 2008, I landed on the land of Aladdin as my brother and I used to call the middle east. It was a new experience for me, the place itself, with all those tall buildings, fast-driving cars, and so many nationalities working together, like little robots. Soon I became one of the robots. I met a couple of nice people, dated a couple of guys, and fell in love with them. The liberation I felt here was priceless, away from my small island.

From time to time, I would miss my mother's food as I did not know how to cook. Soon Dubai became home, where I felt safe, grounded, a big part of my existence. I went for a quick trip to Mauritius in January 2009 for my brother's wedding. My mother knew that I was not coming back so soon. I stayed for seven days and left soon after the ceremonies were over.

Dubai was teaching me every day. Driving was a struggle in the beginning. I got a lost couple of times, and I would sit in my car and cry. I thought I would never make it through, it was too difficult for me, I felt unsupported, but there is something in this place that kept me going. I got myself a pink GPS the same year, and I named the voice in it "Emily". "Emily" became my best friend. On Fridays, I would take my car and drive around with no destination just to get used to the roads. It worked! I met someone at my place of work, and we were together for 4.5 years until we parted ways as he wanted to settle down. He was an amazing soul who respected me like no other man on this planet.

In 2009, the global recession happened, and Dubai was no indifferent. My company was navigating through, but it was getting more and more challenging. The company decided to close business in the middle east in 2011. People were being laid off; I was worried I would have to go back to Mauritius, which I didn't want to. I was so happy to be on my own, having the freedom and independence, taking care of myself, being in relationships where I did not have to explain myself.

My boss left the company in 2011. I was asked to stay back by the management to assist in the wind-up. I was given an increase in salary and other benefits, with the right to look for another job. I finally got another job in a commodity trading company as Chief Accountant, in January 2013 and joined in March 2013. Since it was a multinational company, I was travelling to Europe for seminars and workshops. I was very pleased that I got to stay in Dubai.

On holidays, I would travel to other countries. I visited Nepal, India, Turkey, France, Switzerland, and Oman, rather than going to Mauritius, I just could not get my heart to agree. Maybe because of the life experiences I have been through. I always had this feeling, that if I go there, I might be stuck, and I will never get another opportunity to leave. The thought would bring a cold sweat, I promised myself, as long as it is not an emergency, I would not go to Mauritius.

However, in 2012 my father was very ill, and I decided to visit him because I did not want to live with the guilt if something more serious happened and I did not do anything. When I met my father, he did not recognise me, and he had lost so much weight. At that time, I decided I could not stay angry at him forever. We just talked, and the energy between us was much more positive than it used to be. But something was missing, it was not genuine; it was like a formality rather than love. Maybe time and distance had filled the gap in our relationship, and it was not possible to reach out to each other, or maybe it was ego and pride that did not allow us to get any closer! Anyway, I had to prove to the man who had rejected me, slut-shamed me, and made me feel good for nothing, that I made it without him!

From 2014 to 2016, life had huge lessons for me; I never saw it coming! In 2014, I was offered a role as Group Financial Controller by the same CFO who offered me the job in the construction company. I was very happy that I would be working with him once more as he has always been my mentor. I learned so much from him, and we were also close as I had given him a "big brother" figure in my life. At that time, I did not know about co-dependency! He was filling the gap that my father never did!

In 2015, I met someone, a causal relationship that came with so many life lessons, phew! I was hurting inside for so long, that I never realised that those wounds made me so vulnerable ener-getically that I attracted a narcissist. He abused me emotionally, physically, and financially, but still, I could not leave that rela-tionship; it was like an addiction, two minutes of love and plea-sure with the agreement to get abused after. Who knew an intelligent, smart, independent, self-made woman, who thinks the world is in her grip would be trapped in an abusive relation-ship with a guy who was half her age and worth! The relation-ship was bringing my downfall, but I could not see it. Everyone around was advising me to break up with him, but I didn't see any reason to do so.

In February 2016, I was laid off from my position as a Group Financial Controller, the reason that was typed in my letter redundancy was "restructuring", but I was asked to leave because I could not focus on my work like I used to. I was penniless, with credit card debt, and a car loan. I started looking for work. I landed a temporary job from March to June 2016, but unfortunately, the company could not afford to pay a salary, so I was asked to leave again. I thought it was the end of the road for me. I was in a very dark place in my life, where I did not have any support from anyone.

I could not tell my mother what was happening as she would be worried and heartbroken, though I did tell her I lost my job. All she told me was to pray, and I can still hear her words in my ears – "Only God has the power to change a curse into a blessing, have faith". I don't know how or what, but there was this little voice in my heart telling me I am being prepared for something else.

It was these moments in my life that I saw his true colours; he distanced himself obviously because I was not making any money. I was applying for all types of jobs I could find on the internet but staying at home was driving me nuts. One evening I went to a place called Gurudwara (A gurdwārā; meaning "door to the guru") is a place of assembly and worship for Sikhs. The energy of the sacred place is so smooth and calming, and they even serve nice vegetarian foods.

It was a Thursday night in July 2016, so many people were present. After prayer, I went to have some food, and this is when I saw volunteers cleaning vegetables. After I inquired, they told me that on Fridays they have lots of visitors, around 10,000 to 15,000 people because Friday is the first day of the weekend in Dubai, they serve lots of food. So, I told them I was jobless, and I would like to volunteer. It happened, and in the morning I would apply for jobs, and the remaining day till 9pm, I would be serving at the Gurudwara for 2 weeks. I did end my relationship for good during this time. I felt like I need a decluttering and cleaning, to welcome what the Universe had in store for me. Volunteering at that magical place gave lots of clarity and focus.

I did go for a couple of interviews in between, but they did not end with any offer. On the 20th of July 2016, I received a call, the person on the line introduced himself as the CFO of a group of companies. The holding company was a French entity, and he said that he has a position available that matches my profile. The interview was set up for the 24th of July 2016, and it went well. On the 26th of July 2016, I received my offer letter for a Chief Accountant. I could not believe it was happening, that finally my prayers were heard, that God was not upset with me, that God did not forget me.

It was a real blessing because here starts an amazing journey!

Work was demanding, as the French entity was making lots of business acquisitions in the United Arab Emirates. I was giving my best, working 24/7 because I had fears of losing my job; I had to be grateful for the Universe for saving me. My company was very pleased with my performance. I was even invited to a finance workshop in France by the holding company. During the same year, I approached the CEO of the company for an advance on my salary (it is a common practice in Dubai, the loan is set off against your salary month over the period agreed) so that I could repay all my debts, which happened. In August 2017, all my debts were paid off and got a 50% increase in my existing salary. How does it get better than this?

2016 brought along so much positivity to me, but I was struggling from the inside. If I was at home, I would replay the scenes of my relationship with the narcissist in my mind. I would ask myself millions of questions, how I could not see it, why I couldn't leave earlier, why I allowed myself to be in a mess, there were too many whys!

Years and years of limiting beliefs, feeling unworthy and undeserving deep inside, looking for validation, having a huge ego, and to top it all off, I had uncontrollable anger which became part of my being; I never realised how aggressive I sounded and I was!

I was always told I was a strong woman, for me being strong meant being angry, aggressive, rude, belittling others, and having a huge ego. I looked at women who could express their emotions through tears as weak. They deserve what was happening to them because I found them too emotional to my taste. My anger would always get the best of me! I was feeling like a wreck from the inside.

I was a loner for most of my life; I did not have any friends in Dubai or any social network. I thought of getting counselling, but I never went ahead with it. I felt like I needed a distraction, anything that would make my heart happy again! One of my team members advised me to adopt a pet, first I thought of a dog, but then I was living in an apartment, and a dog is demanding. So, I decided to get a cat instead, even though I'd never had a cat in my entire life.

I advertised in the cat adoption groups stating exactly my lifestyle, on the 07th of April 2017, I was contacted by a wonderful rescuer who was fostering a 4-year-old female Arabian Mau which would be perfect for my lifestyle. She asked me to come and visit the cat. On that day I was introduced to Lily. On the 09th of April 2017, I messaged the lady telling her I will take Lily on a trial adoption. As she had been fostering her for more than four years, I was not very sure if it was going to work between us. She agreed, and she advised me on what I needed to get to welcome Lily who was brought to me on the 10th of April 2017, and we officially became family.

With Lily now being part of my life, I was feeling better emotionally; Lily was my distraction. I would come home to her, and with each passing day, the hiding was less. She would wait for me at the door. We started to bond, and I felt more stable in feeling my emotions, but my anger was still there, it would burst out, and I would lash out on people.

Being a person always connected to God, I wanted to deepen my relationship through spirituality. I got connected to a couple of groups and people on social media. Not all of them worked out, but I got pretty much an idea of what I was looking for. I was looking for a connection In Dubai, where I could meet and talk. This was when I came across "Liked-minded Goddesses" around May 2017. By going through the pages on social media, I got to know about Natalia Sushkova, a Kundalini Master Teacher and Shamanic Medicine Woman who has the Red Tent in Dubai. I contacted her, and she invited me to visit her as she had an event happening, called "Samsara Games" (card reading games on the Archetypes).

When I met Natalia for the first time, I was blown away, she was wearing this beautiful white flowing dress, with forehead jewellery like a goddess. Her energy was out of this world. We played the game, which lasted for 2 hours with another lady. Natalia asked me to join her Red Tent, which I did. I was frequently going for the new moon and full moon circles.

I got to know about feminine healing, yoni eggs, yoni healing through Natalia. Before that, I did not know that we, women, carry so much of ancestral wounds in our wombs. I got my first yoni egg; it was rose quartz from Natalia, which did not stay with me for too long. With Natalia, I also discovered about shamanic plant medicines.

At the time between May to June 2017, I tried Rapé (Rapé is a complex blend of pulverised Amazonian medicinal plants, trees, leaves, seeds, and other sacred ingredients used for healing). I had also experience Ambil (a thick, black "gelatin" cooking medicine leaves which, heals the body, revives, and purifies the mind). I had visions with Ambil, and it took me straight to the jungle, it was the first time I met my grandfather (the father of my father) whom, I had never met in person as he passed away before I was born. He was sitting around a bonfire with some shamans, he looked at me, smiled and said: "I have been waiting for you, welcome home". I thought the Ambil made me high, and I was hallucinating, but my heart kept on telling me no!

It was around the end of July 2017, and I felt a slight pain in my right foot, I thought I tripped on something unknowingly, the pain was there for a week. At 2am someday in July 2017, I had an unbearable pain on the same foot, I woke up, and I felt like my foot was breaking inside. The pain was so severe that I sat on the bed, crying, not knowing what was happening. I decided to drive to the 24 hours clinic as it was too late to ask anyone. Reaching the clinic, they helped me inside and took my blood sample for testing. While waiting for the result, they gave me an IV of painkillers. I was lying on the bed, thinking of what was happening to me without comprehension. While having the IV transfusion, the pain was less, and I dozed off in the clinic. A nurse woke me up at 7am, later in the morning, and took me to the doctor who told me it's a Uric Acid attack. I did not have any clue what it was. The doctor prescribed some medication and told me to come back after a week.

Miraculously, the pain was completely gone; I was doing very well, and it was as if the pain never existed. I went to work, and life went on for a week, then I had another more 3 attacks, which happened weekly. Having IV transfusions became a routine in my life; I was asked to change my lifestyle to stop eating red meat, drinking wine, and smoking; 3 things which are not part of my life and have never been. My doctor also advised me to stop having a variety of pulses and vegetables, which were high in Uric Acid because the attacks were so severe that I had gout and crystal formation on my right toe. Now, both of my ankles were swollen, and I could not wear shoes at all. I started looking for information over the internet, and all I could find about Uric Acid and Gout is that they are autoimmune health conditions, and there are no specific medications for them.

I was scared that I would lose my legs, and it brings my career to an end. I was praying every day, I could not lose my job again, not at this point when everything in professional life was as I always wanted. The desire to fight against all the odds was part of my life, even in pain, I would come to work every day and, in the evening, I would go for IV transfusion just to calm the pain, and this was my routine for nearly 2 months. I was on a daily maintenance pill as well, and my doctor told me, this is life now, that I should not worry as many people suffer the same, as if it justified my suffering.

In September 2017, I decided to get a second opinion from another doctor. I still remember the doctor telling me "You have Gout, and only famous people suffer Uric Acid because of their lifestyle!". He told me diet would help me a lot which I was already on, and the maintenance pill was a must. The day I would miss the pill, my feet and ankles would swell, and I would not be able to walk. I was not happy at all with what was happening to me; I felt stuck once again. I had a racing mind giving the worst-case scenarios, that I would lose everything, and I would become a burden for myself. I constantly thought I was too young to be on a maintenance pill for life; there must be some other solution.

At the time, I was still an emotional wreck, and my health was not improving. I informed my mother about my situation; she advised me it's better to come back to Mauritius. I could not consider it, as I did not have savings as my excess money was being set off against the loan I had with the company I was working. I could imagine going home being penniless and being dependent on my family.

I was frequently on social media, finding a group what I can join to elevate myself spiritually. A member of one of the groups I was in, posted about "Kambo" (is a substance that comes from frog secretion which is used for healing by shamans) that she used to heal herself. Since I was already aware of these types of medicines exist, I got curious and did some research on it. There was little voice in me, telling me I need it. Living in Dubai, I knew it was impossible to have it, but I badly wanted it!

When you want something, the universe has its way of getting it to you; in ways you will never imagine. I guess my desire to have a trip with Kambo was so strong that after a week, Natalia advertised about a Kambo circle. I could not believe my eyes when I saw the post. Not losing time, I enrolled to join the circle, and information was sent to me to prepare to experience Kambo. One of the requirements was that if you are on medication, you have to stop taking them at least 3 days before taking Kambo. I stopped taking my maintenance pill, still very worried about the Uric Acid attack; fortunately, there was no attack, only swelling and pain on both of my ankles.

The circle was at Natalia's sacred space, early in the morning. I reached it on time, but with anxiety, because I did not know what to expect. Kambo is not consumed, but, administered to a person via small holes that are burned into the top few layers of their skin. On my second dot, I fainted, I had to be woken up because of the purging that happened for a straight 20 minutes.

I came back to my senses after 5 mins, and purging started, and believe me it's not pleasant at all.

After my first Kambo session, I had less swelling of my ankles, and I stopped taking the maintenance pill. I felt so clean in my gut, my vision sharpened, I was calmer, and it was bliss. The 20 minutes purging was worth it. To date I am still doing Kambo, my body knows when it needs it, the spirit of Kambo starts appearing to me.

My connection with the spiritual world kept growing every day. I felt more connected to myself and could clear my mind and be silent. I started reading a lot of material online, joint other groups on social media, it was just unfolding amazingly, and I could not complain. Other Kambo ceremonies followed, which I did, and my anger was reducing. I could let go of things that I could not control. I stopped engaging in stuff that did not matter to me. I was choosing my battles, and I could manage stress at work.

2018, life was getting better. I was feeling more in balance with myself, no more Uric Acid attacks, no more maintenance pills, and work was stable. I was promoted from the Chief Accountant to the Financial Director with another increase in my paycheck, which made it easier for me to repay the balance of my loan and start saving.

I was discovering myself every day. I started asking myself, what was life for me? Why was I was born? Where am I going from here? People around me started noticing a change in me. My relationship with my team at work was much more balanced. I had stopped shouting and screaming at them. I was proud of the progress I was making, I took a few spiritual courses online and started practising candle magic, and moon rituals for myself. I had a strong calling to have an alter, which I set up with Hekate, Kali, Ganesha, and little angels on it. My visions were getting clearer, my intuitive abilities were opening, and there was this knowledge in my heart.

On the 02nd of October 2018, I lost my father; he had a heart attack. He just left this world without any sign. I rushed home to be there for my family. My mother was in great sadness and grief. In September 2018, while we were planning our leave for the Christmas and New Year break, I decided to go on leave as well. I wanted to come home and to set everything right with my father. My heart was healing. But unfortunately, it did not happen as planned. I stayed for a week in Mauritius for my father cremation, but I did not cry, I did not have any sadness, regret, or grief. I think I was still processing it.

I came back to Dubai and did a Kambo session because my heart was so heavy. I wrapped up work and went to Mauritius for another 10 days to attend all the rituals of my father. Reflection on my life became stronger; maybe the guilt I had in my heart for not being able to mend a relationship with him. When I returned to Dubai, I did not go to work; I wanted to spend time with myself, which I did. I spent my days crying because I was revisiting the fallouts him. I could feel his presence all around me all the time. I wrote him letters every day, opening my heart to him. I went back to work after 2 weeks break, but still, there was an emptiness in me somewhere. I never knew losing a parent at 41 could be so difficult. I thought being an adult kind of makes it easier because you understand the concept of life and death, but it was not the case.

In November 2018, Natalia informed about Ayahuasca (it is a brew with powerfully hallucinogenic properties claimed to open your mind and heal past trauma, she is a feminine energy). I just read about it but did not watch any ceremony; I did not want to have any expectation even though I was scared. I had my very first Ayahuasca ceremony in December 2018; it was a 3 day ceremony. I never had an experience like Ayahuasca in my life, the power, wisdom, love of the spirit is mind-blowing. The definition of Ayahuasca is – Death, Re-birth, and Love, yes if you are asking if I died, yes I died, the big ego that I had been carrying for 41 years died.

The first day of the ceremony was not unpleasant; we were getting to know each other, so no purging. I was very tired, I wanted to sleep, but it is said not to sleep but to hold the medicine while she is doing her healing. For the first time in life, I had let go of control because I could not fight the medicine, she took me on a nice geometric ride, I was full of visions. The fact that I was out of control brought lots of fear, and when I came back home, I was thinking of not going back to the ceremony.

On the second day, I did not have to wait long to feel the effect of the medicine. The ride was rough, I was scared, I thought I would die, my whole body, mind, spirit was taken over by Ayahuasca. Hearing the Shaman's icaros was making the medicine more powerful, and I purged. As soon as I purged, I was back to my senses. Aya was gone, I felt so relieved, thinking that

I was done for the night. After 10 mins, she was back, taking over me like she was here to stay, I was rolling on the floor. The spirit of Ayahuasca asked me to lie down like a woman is about to give birth; I did because who does not listen to her. At that time, I saw myself giving birth to a black ball that went into the river I was sitting on. No, it was not a dream. I was not high on drugs; it was Aya getting rid of my suppressed emotions, my anger which I kept for so long. I was too tired to drive back home, so I stayed back at the ceremony. The next morning when I woke up, I lost 5 kg, I looked 10 years younger than my age, my face had a baby's innocence, and my heart was light.

On the third day, the last day of the ceremony, I was quite happy to go as I had in mind that I was healed already, nothing much would be happening today. Well, the spirit Ayahuasca had something else for me. As soon as I had consumed the brew, she took over me, and we went on a nice geometric ride. She asked me if I was happy with life and if I had everything I ever wanted. My answer was "Yes, I have a perfect life, I am successful, I earn good money, I am free, what more could I ask for". At that moment, Ayahuasca told me to look down, and I saw myself on the floor in the ceremony, in a fetal position in a deep state of trance. Aya told me: "Look at Leckranee, someone who does not even know who she is? What she desires from life? All she knows is that she needs to prove to the world she can make it big. She does not know where she is heading in life. She thinks money is everything in life and her ego is her best friend". At that very moment, I remember I took 5 long breaths, and I died; I stopped breathing. I was brought back into my body after 5 minutes, and I started breathing again. I came back home the next morning, but I could not sleep. My heart was breaking, and I was scared. I could see spirits in my house, my third eye was opened, and I could hardly think. I felt my whole existence had vanished somewhere. At night it was worst, I could not sleep, and I would pray all the time because I had an unexplained fear.

I was not in a position to go to work as I had not slept for days. I wanted to run away from myself. I felt like there was someone stuck in my body. It took me 2 weeks to integrate Ayahuasca, while driving to work the person stuck inside me came out, it was like having 2 persons in one body. So, I asked who she was and what does she wants. She told me she was my fears, and if I worked on my fears, I would be free! Don't even ask. I went to work on that day very disturbed. On that night, I decided to research how to integrate Ayahuasca from those who did it before. One of the interviews I saw, the person who did it, said journaling helped him a lot. So, I started journaling, the more I would write, the better I would feel better. I was feeling a happier person every day, and I started detaching myself from work (I was working 24/7). I felt there was a bigger life, but we just do not see it. We are not meant to live the way we live our lives, in hardships, struggles, stress, and diseases!

2019, I made a couple of trips back home to visit my mother; the guilt I had towards my father was gone. Something shifted in me, I did not know what, but I was a calmer and happier person. On the 06th of August 2019, on my 42nd birthday, I decided to resign from my corporate job because I was not happy. I could not deal with the fakeness of people at work, all the politics which I used to enjoy once in life, was making me feel out of place. I felt like a stranger at work, I would not engage in any political games, whereas previously I was the one who initiated them. I wanted to take a years break to travel to Europe and India; I was excited to be on holiday with myself. When I submitted my resignation on the 07th of August 2019, it did not go well with the management of the company. But my mind was made, and I would not change it for anything.

In the same month, I met Tina Pavlou during one of her free talks on Angelic Reiki ® at one of the holistic centres in Dubai. When I saw her the first time we instantly connected, she was so bubbly and loving. During that evening, I had a free meditation with her. I had Goddess Isis coming to me and whispered in my ear "You can do it", and she gave me an Arch on my hand. I decided to take Angelic Reiki® 1 & 2 with Tina. During the Angelic Reiki® workshop, Tina Pavlou introduced me to Theta-Healing®; I went on the 7th plane of existence with ease. Needless to say, Angelic Reiki® 1&2 was out of this world.

On the day we graduated for Angelic Reiki® 1&2, Tina Pavlou suggested to me to get a Basic ThetaHealing® book, which I did. Since I was on a notice period at work, I would come home at a normal time and go through my book, nothing in that book was new. I felt like I was doing some kind of revision. I would meditate, do my healing and non-interference affirmations. I manifested to do ThetaHealing® classes as soon as I am done with work for good. Tina Pavlou came back to Dubai in October 2019, for Angelic Reiki® 3&4 which I enrolled, completed, and graduated. I did not have any intention to become a practitioner or teacher of Angelic Reiki®, but whoever I had given a free session to told me that I should make it my living. I was constantly being told that I am already a healer, and I have been doing these many times. But I was not convinced enough, probably because I was not confident enough yet.

I officially left my corporate job on the 23rd of October 2019, and it was not an easy exit. I was put in a very dark place for four days. If I was not connected with the Angelic Kingdom, I would not have made it through. I had Archangel Michael with me all the time, and Tina Pavlou was with me energetically clearing me all the time, which I am abundantly grateful for. These four days came with lots of life lessons and karmic clearings of my past lives, as well as genetics.

In December 2019, I joined Basic Thetahealing®, and I said to myself, I will clear all my blocking beliefs. Then I decided to join the Advance Thetahealing® as I had plenty of time to learn and work on myself. I was swapping sessions after my classes, and everyone told me that I am good at it. By that time, I already ordered a Dig Deeper Thetahealing® book which I was using to work on myself. I then decided to join the Dig Deeper class and completed it.

During my Dig Deeper Thetahealing® class which happened in January 2020, I got to know about Vianna Stibal who was coming to Dubai in February/March 2020 for instructor classes. I heard so much about this wonderful soul, but I was not interested in teaching at that time. My teacher told me that her energy was amazing, and just by being in her presence, you will start healing yourself. So, I contacted those who were hosting her, stating that I would enrol for instructor courses for Basic,

Advanced, and Dig Deeper with Vianna Stibal, just to be in her energy. The person I talked to asked me if I was interested in doing the other instructor courses with Vianna, so I agreed, not knowing at that time that I had to complete the practitioner level. After all, my confusion was resolved; I completed my ThetaHealing® relationship class, so I was able to attend the instructor courses.

I am very blessed that I was able to attend the instructor classes, after meeting Vianna and being in all the classes for more than 18 days, I felt my vibration was higher. Last day of our class, the lockdown for COVID 19 was announced. I was not happy about it because we would not be able to meet anyone to swap sessions, and I did not know what I would do as an instructor and not being able to run classes. But the Universe knows better, during the lockdown I was working on myself a lot and surfing the internet to get more information on spirituality. I attended several online meditations, talks, and then I realised that I should start practising on others to gain my confidence online.

In April 2020, I advertised on the several ThetaHealing® groups that I would be offering "free readings" for other ThetaHealing® healers. I was contacted by many, and with each reading, I felt like I had been doing this forever. I was swapping sessions with other healers, 3 to 4 sessions a day for 2 months. It was intensive work on myself because with each session, I felt the transformation, I was becoming more positive, happier, calmer, and life seemed to be unfolding beautifully.

On the 11th of May 2020, I booked my first paid ThetaHealing® client. I got a request for paid Angel Tarot card readings, which I was doing previously for free. In less than a year, since I left my corporate job, Creator of all that is has been surprising me every single day. Today, if you ask me if I am a strong woman, my answer would yes because I deeply and completely honour, love, accept myself. I know how to be vulnerable but stay in my power.

My whole life has turned in 180 degrees, and I am still working on the process. I am walking my divinely crafted soul path. As a human, I have transformed beautifully, and I am now aware of how powerful we are and that we have the choice to bring changes in our lives. The universe is full of amazing tools whatever be thy name given, they have existed forever, it is up to us to choose whether we want to live a life of an ignorant mundane or to bloom into the magnificent, limitless being of light we are.

Do I resent my parents? No, because now I am in a space in my life, where I understand I chose them to learn the lessons. They taught me in the best way possible due to their own limiting beliefs! The day we change our mindset, everything falls into place, life is a beautiful gift of experiences that are only given to the brave ones. There is nothing more powerful than love. I can see my path unfolding to elevate myself, and along the way to guide others to do so too.

In August 2020, I am attending practitioner Intuitive Anatomy of ThetaHealing. In October, I am joining one of the holistic centres in Dubai, as a healer and teacher. I know this is just the beginning of my journey; I have a long and beautiful way to go with the Universe and Creator having my back.

ABOUT THE AUTHOR

LECKRANEE BURTHOO-BARAH

Leckranee is a beautiful soul of 43 years old who lives in Dubai, UAE, for the last 12 years. Before moving the Dubai, Leckranee was based in South Africa. She is originally from the exotic island, Mauritius. Leckranee is Hindu by religion as her ancestors migrated from India 250 years ago to settle in Mauritius. She is the proud daughter of a late civil servant and an amazing housewife. Leckranee has a younger brother, married, and settled in Mauritius.

Leckranee holds a Diploma in Business Administration, specialized in Marketing. She is also a fellow member of The Association of Certified Chartered Accountants (ACCA, UK).

Leckranee is a woman full of determination, dedication, and perseverance. She is a go-getter, hence pouring all her energy into working hard for her dreams has always been her thing. She did achieve what she dreamed of as a finance professional and was on top of the corporate ladder as a Chief Financial Officer of a EUR800 billion multinational. However, in August 2019, on her 42nd birthday, Leckranee decided to leave the corporate world to walk her soul journey.

She met Tina Pavlou in August 2019 in Dubai during one of the free evening talks in one of the holistic centre's. Well, as we all know, Tina Pavlou is a catalyst transformer for whoever meets her, and it was not different for Leckranee. Leckranee completed her certification as an Angelic Reiki® practitioner in August 2019 and a master teacher in October 2019. During her Angelic Reiki® workshop, she got to know about the Theta-Healing® technique, being of a curious nature, she decided to explore it further. Leckranee is also a certified ThetaHealing® practitioner and instructor.

Leckranee has been told by many, that she is throwing a beautiful career of 20 years out the window. Maybe she needs a life coach to bring her senses back, as at her age, many go through a midlife crisis. She has been constantly reminded that a corporate job provides a better retirement package than a yoga mat.

However, trusting the Creator of All That is, she is following her divinely crafted soul path. Leckranee has already started her work as a healer by providing 1 to 1 ThetaHealing® and Angelic Reiki® sessions. She is going to teach ThetaHealing® and Angelic Reiki® in November 2020.

Being in her natural state of a determined soul, she is continuing her self development and spiritual journey with additional ThetaHealing® modules as well as mastering Light Key Frequencies®.

Coming from a small island of only 1.2m inhabitants, Leckranee desires to inspire others through her journey by choosing to always follow her heart and trusting the Divine. She knows life is abundant, everyone has the right to abundance, and that happiness is within. With a positive mindset, a healthy lifestyle, and great energetic vibration – total harmony of body, mind, and spirit can be achieved by anyone. She was always considered as the "black sheep" in her family for being unconventional to the family traditions, she is now an inspiration to the younger generations of her own family and many others.

Leckranee's Soul Mantra:

 "Sex energy is aphrodisiac

Communication is divinity

Wisdom is enlightenment

Action is bravery

Life is unconditional love"

3

MRIDULA BOSE

*H*ave you ever wondered what it's like to be truly happy? Have you ever looked at a happy person and wondered, "Why can't I be like that?" Are there times when you feel like you don't deserve happiness? Do you feel stuck in a constant loop of fear? Fear of being judged? Fear of change, or truly finding yourself? Are you afraid of embracing your true essence? If I were to ask you to visualise your ideal life, a life full of love, joy, optimum health and wealth, what holds you back? Is it the fear of loss? Is it the fear of being unworthy or undeserving? Or are you afraid of *Happiness*? Yeah, that's a real thing because I used to be that girl. I have felt fear to the point where I couldn't function anymore; I was frozen. My emotions and feelings, my dreams and aspirations didn't matter to me anymore. I would constantly find myself in relationships that brought me more trauma and sadness. Abuse haunted me every day, so much so that I was afraid of being seen. The fear of my traumas being repeated only attracted more of it. I viewed the world in fear.

I WAS A BABY WHEN IT HAPPENED.

As a youngling, I was always drawn to things that people around me couldn't see. I was a highly sensitive empath, seer and communicator of the realms beyond what meets the naked eye. I now think that if I had the knowledge and guidance required in honing my gifts, I would have lived a vastly different life and probably would not have had to suffer the kind of traumas I have. But such is the miracle of life. The lessons we are meant to learn in this lifetime will not pass by us. And so, my life has been nothing short of colourful. There were many times I've wanted to end my life, and many more when I've prayed to forget it all and live like it never happened.

I was a baby when I first felt a man in an inappropriate manner, and even at that age, I knew what he was doing wasn't right. Little did I know that a part of my strength and will to fight back had been taken away. Children are more vulnerable and sensitive, and when they go through such harsh situations at a tender age, it tends to stick to them like glue till they have the right guidance and learning in what it means to truly heal.

Where I come from, crimes against women are seen as a thing of normalcy. I was told this by some girls when I was studying in India, "this is how it is in India, we grow up like this, and we get used to it; don't sit and cry over such small things"; just after I had been pinched and groped by a boy on the street right outside my College. But I wouldn't stop crying, not because of the indecent act, but because of what my women had to go through every single day of their lives and for thinking that this is the rest of their lives. It's unfair! So, I made a promise to myself that I would do everything in my power to *Educate* the right way. What we have lacked in our world is education, and I don't mean schooling, I mean the right kind of education where respect is taught. All my life I've heard many sayings and one of them is 'Respect is to be earned', but how do we know how to earn something when we haven't been taught it?

Just like everything else we earn in our lives we are taught, so why is respect not being taught at schools and colleges? I have met many men who respect women and a woman's sacred space, and I've met many more who don't even know what that is. "It's all in the upbringing", they say. But how do you raise a child with love and respect if you haven't experienced it? We treat others how we treat ourselves. We treat ourselves the only way we know how to. When a child has seen hate, patriarchy, sexual abuse, gender biases, assaults and other crimes against women while growing up, what are the odds that the child will grow up acting any differently? Very few have gone through injustices and come out into the light realising that life is more than just repeating the actions of our predecessors.

We all have a choice, and so did I. I had a choice to continue to spiral downwards into the darkness of my abusive past or to stand in my power and seek help. The road to healing was even tougher than I had expected, and a process that cannot be rushed. Every individual brave enough to heal their wounds has a time and process that is unique to them. Even now, as I write my story, I'm shedding layers of shame and guilt I had been holding onto for many years; I am in tears as I type. I was afraid to let my story be heard; I was ashamed of how people would see me. I did not want anyone to see me as a damaged woman, or an abused woman – these are terms we women are stamped with when we come out with our stories in my country. Men look at us differently, and women show lack of compassion because of societal pressures. Not all are the same, but the ones who do blame us for what was done to us, affects us deeply.

IT IS IMPORTANT TO REMEMBER THAT ALL OUR BODIES ARE SACRED, AND ANY ACT OF VIOLENCE AGAINST IT IS AN ACT AGAINST NATURE ITSELF.

Throughout my life, I have naturally attracted people into my life who strike conversations with me out of the blue and end up telling me their deepest pains. I've understood this as my energetic boundaries being empathic as I had seen very similar situations as theirs. As a highly sensitive empath who did not have any idea nor understanding of protecting energetic boundaries or setting them, I also used to attract narcissists into my life. These people liked to compare my life to theirs and bask in their "good luck" because I was always sulking. I was always sulking, and in fear, because I desperately needed help but didn't even know I needed it. And now I understand others who are going through the same phases because I've been there. Looking back, I thank the Universe for sending me these valuable lessons because I understand that wounded people wear many faces and narcissists are deeply wounded people who don't want to look within and do the work.

Adversity is not your enemy! Every challenge or challenging person has an underlying lesson for you and had I not experienced having my boundaries breached I would have never known that I needed healing, which led me to set healthy boundaries and be firm in my conscience. It takes a lot of strength, courage and commitment towards yourself to stand up for YOU because as an empath, standing up for others came easy to me but when I did not have my foundations firm, helping others proved to drain more energy from me than ever.

AND I PRAYED FOR THE LIGHT TO SHINE THROUGH ME.

I wanted to end my life, but I would watch the news or read the newspapers and be reminded that my women are suffering the same pain, if not worse. Somehow there was a glimmer of light in me that wanted to stay alive and strong for my women and children.

2018 was the year all my hard work in masking the many years of abuse had gone out of control. Until then, I was adept at hiding my true self, sweeping all my fears under the many layers of shame and guilt I had adorned myself with over the years.

I was told by astrologers that I had abuse written many times in my chart and that I'd have to wait a very long time to find a man with the growth and maturity to truly understand what it means to be with a woman like me. These kinds of statements haunted me for dear life and one after the other the world of men kept proving the astrologers right. I was devastated and living a lie. No one around me knew what I was going through because as humans living in the matrix, we don't open up to our fullest potential and instead give in to the hustle-bustle of our material lives; authentic human interactions tend to get lost in a series of judgements based on face value. Even your closest friends or family may not know the real you because we project onto the world many faces, some true to ourselves and some that hide our deepest pains. But not many know of the truths that lie beneath the portrayal of an "accepted" being; that being who only wears masks to save face from societal discredit.

Through my deep healings arose depression, frustration, and absolute rage against how I had been quietly living my life in lies and not respecting the power of my Divine Self. I started asking myself questions that provoked something deeper; "So what if the world knows the real me?", "So what if my society knows of the tortures I've been through?", "Why is a woman put under a shameful light when she is subject to violence at the hands of men?", "Why is it is that when a woman speaks of her abuse, she is looked down on?" "Why is it her fault?" "Why is her attitude or dress code questioned?" "Why does the action of the abuser have less value than what she wore or where she was and at what time?" "Why do people say, 'she asked for it'?" – This is how the world has defeated women, by piling on excuses, non-existent values and cynical gender disparities atop the unfair violence committed against her; by shaming her into depression or worse. "Who asks to be tortured?" – People are so quick to judge a woman's character for being abused, but they don't realise that they are influencing the younger generations to condone such gruesome acts. "Why isn't the man's actions and character shamed?" A woman who has been through a savage act like that needs to be nurtured and loved back into wholeness, not thrashed down even further. "And what of the children, how is it their fault?" – These angry questions loomed over me like a dark cloud. I didn't understand what I was going through; I couldn't get past the quest for my answers. I was so deep in rage and resentment that I was sleepless, unable to function normally, and had pains in different parts of my body; it felt like my energy was being sucked out. I had so much anger and un-forgiveness in my heart that my chest felt heavy, and I would often feel like I was gasping for air. I had gained weight, started losing hair, and felt like there was no purpose in life if only to suffer. I used to pray for my life to end.

But I knew in my heart that I wasn't a bad person; I knew that the collective conscience was wrong and that whatever had happened to me wasn't my fault; I just couldn't get past the actual memory of it all. I was completely out of balance. My body was screaming for help! I didn't know how to get past the feeling of being forced. The memories of it all were haunting me.

I made a conscious decision to get myself some much-needed help.

THERE IS WISDOM IN YOUR BODY.

From a very young age, I've been more drawn to the spiritual aspects of life and healing than any other medicines, and I've always known that our present problems are a result of our constant negative self-talk, our chakra imbalances, energy blocks, past hurts and many more. Energy and Universal sciences, and the 'hidden arts' were what drew me in to seek guidance that gave me a deeper meaning and knowing of life. So, I began meeting people who helped me understand different aspects of my blocks, explain to me my bodily pains and help me heal them. I suffered through my healings; it wasn't easy for me. I was angrier than ever! I wanted justice; I wanted harm to come to those who had harmed me. I wanted them to feel the same hurt they had put me through. The more I resisted the light, the more ill I became. I didn't know what surrender meant until I finally 'gave up'! I became tired of spewing hateful energy against mankind and humanity; I became tired of victimising and pitying myself, and most of all, I was tired of being tired. I wanted my energy back; I yearned to live wild, free and happy.

The realisations of my past had hit me only in the year 2018. I had been hit real hard. 11 years before that I was living in India and going through a world of problems but never once did I find myself getting defeated by it all. I was dealing with many different kinds of injustices and pushing through life's challenges like a warrior; the issues kept growing, and I kept fighting. What I didn't realise was that I gave no time to honour my body and feelings. I would shut off my emotions and move onto the next thing in life. I never gave myself permission to relax, nurture myself, or even cry. I pulled my tears back and never had a huge, loud cry – that was the kind of release I had been missing out on. I would silently cry my pains back into my body. I didn't know how to release. "Crying is for babies. Don't be so sensitive. Adults don't cry. Only emotional women cry" – growing up with these "teachings" makes you closed off from embracing your inner wisdom. There is wisdom in clearing and releasing, and crying is also a massive release. Only when you clear the air of misconceptions can you truly open yourself up to release in all your glory, and when you release those pent up emotions, you have free space to allow yourself to be healed, and healing brings up our authentic selves to understand the truth. There is wisdom in our body. All the answers to our questions lie within us, if only we awaken ourselves to it.

A GODDESS NEVER FORGETS.

I don't hate men anymore. I don't think I ever have. I've been heavily fearful of men because of my previous experiences. I have, however, done my best to mess up my relationships with men because subconsciously that's how I protected myself.

What some men do to women is on them; they may never realise the pains we go through for the rest of our lives and the consequences we've had to face as the after-effects of their brutality, but they will also never experience the true abundance and magic a woman holds.

In my land, Kerala, we celebrate the birth of a daughter. A baby girl is seen as Goddess Lakshmi, the one who brings light, purity, abundance, and all good things into the family. It is also a well-known fact in my culture that when you harm a child or a woman in her womb, you invite limitless harm unto you and your future generations to come. But that has never stopped patriarchy from shining its ugly head; it hasn't stopped men from treating us so callously. It begs the question of why. My observations and personal experiences have boiled down to one thing – access to the right kind of education by the right kind of people. There is nothing my culture cannot learn by studying our own past. We come from a rich heritage of science, arts, laws, abundance and everything else. Where the rest of the world is learning and practising what India has launched into this world, Indians are neglecting. From a tender age, girls are told not to do more things than they are told to do. I once had a lovely young woman come to me because she realised that she had a pattern of being submissive to everyone in her life and couldn't hold her ground. When I worked with her on a Theta level, she realised it was due to her not being able to fully express her wild and free-spirited side when she was younger. She was told to stay indoors and wear long dresses that made her freedom feel curbed. She was not allowed to play with boys. Now, as a 4 or 5-year-old you want to spend your hours burning the bursts of energy you've got instead of covering up and being told not go out and play. Young children don't know the specifics tagged onto different genders; they just want to have fun! By raising her to be submissive, she grew up not knowing where her identity lies. She never forgot that feeling of her right to be a child being taken away, and when she was ready to heal, she sought the kind of help that resonated with her soul.

It is through my own traumas that I have been able to and continue to help many women, men, and others who cross my path. My understanding of many of the dilemmas that people go through comes easy as I have been through it myself and from a tender age I've had to see a lot that caused me immense heartache and confusion. The ones who wronged me may have forgotten me and moved on to their next victim, but no woman can ever forget that kind of pain. No woman will ever forget the faces of those who stripped away her innocence with brute strength; no woman will ever forget that feeling, that breath huffing down on her as she grips in pain. No woman can ever forget her life force being robbed away from her. A Goddess never forgets!

I only understand now that my highly sensitive nature as a child needed more grounding and firmer boundaries as I was more vulnerable and susceptible to attracting people and situations that were beyond my age and innocence to comprehend. Growing up in a world that shows you how men can do what they want and get away with it because they are men and women are only as good as the kitchen sink, can in many ways blur your reality; the reality that you mould yourself into as you journey on with life. The truth is, when a woman is in her element, truly happy, respected and balanced, she becomes the bringer of abundance and all things good; an empowered woman brings magic into your lives. When I walk into a home or a business, I can energetically read the aura around the physical space and tell if the women there are treated well or not. You may be the richest person, but you will never know what true success and happiness feels like if you treat the women and children around you like tools. When a woman is in the Divine Feminine flow of the Universe, she embraces the Goddess within her and shines a light on all beings around her.

GUARDIANS.

Through healings, I found my light in my Guardian Angels. We all have Guardian Angels assigned to us, even before we are born on this planet. They know everything about our lives and stick with us through thick and thin. Connecting with them was a very emotional experience for me because before then, I had no idea that I was worthy of such pure unconditional love! They give me so much love every single second of my days, and they have been doing so even before I could remember. I started receiving clear messages from them about the reality of my dreams and visions. Prior to this, I had always doubted myself; doubted my visions, dreams, and my ability to see farther than the naked eye because historically I had been told to not speak of such things. Misunderstandings were of common presence in my young adult life. I started seeing passed on souls and visions of my past lives at a young age, and although at the time I was so innocent and felt like it was normal to live amongst such beings, the world around me did not share my reality. The people, particularly men, who did not understand me, wanted to dim my light and after several instances of bodily harm and mental agony, I shut off my God-given gifts completely until in 2019, through my path to embrace and live in my truth and purpose, I found my buddies I had once closed myself off to, and now they are always with me. I now know that my purpose in life is to serve, educate, create and spread the joy of Mother Earth and Creator's unconditional love and live my life in abundance.

In 2019 I set out on one of the most spectacular journeys of my life to learn powerful healing modalities, went on a spiritual retreat with 22 amazing women, and unleashed the Goddess within me. I allowed the light to shine through me and gained a community of sisterhood who share my purpose to be of service.

LESSONS IN LEARNING.

It takes time to understand oneself. To self-introspect means to look deep within and face your demons because otherwise there really isn't any growth in constantly blaming the situations that have happened, but growth comes from knowing that what happened does not define us as individuals; our past hurts have valuable lessons hidden in them and until we learn those lessons, we continue to attract the same hurts into our lives. Harsh? Trust me, if you think I'm being harsh then know that this applies to me as much as it does to you. Before I met Tina Pavlou, I did not understand how to see the underlying lessons in all the traumas. I had no clue why all that happened had to me, and I was drowning in self-hate, self-pity, self-victimisation, and mostly my fears towards men. I couldn't bring myself to fully be open to acceptance. Acceptance of that which took place, acceptance of the fact that I was in no way to blame because I had shrouded myself in blame for the atrocities committed by others. I realise now that I was only doing what I had known best. I only blamed myself because that is what is done to women from my land; we are blamed for being tortured. I also hated women who seemingly had their lives easy and had never known the kind of pains I had to endure. But pain is pain, no matter what form it takes, and everyone has their own experience of pain. Tina understood my plight and made sure that I was nurtured throughout my healing. She knew that I had it rough even without me having to say much. And she understood that my path had been so because I'm meant to learn how to love myself and help others to do the same.

To help someone is to be kind, loving, and whole within yourself first. You won't be of much help to anyone if you don't take care of yourself first. All my life, I've theoretically known all these valuable principles of life, but I didn't know how to put them to practice once life really started. The application of it all was lost to me.

In November 2019, my life took an abrupt plunge into deep healing. I flew to Bali for a Goddess retreat with Tina and her partners Joanne and Nicole, where I learnt what it really feels like to be the beautiful Goddess that I am. We women may deny ourselves the gift of our Feminine presence, but that denial is only a temporary lapse in sight. When you awaken to your true potential, you too will view yourself as the Goddess you truly are.

FINDING GRATITUDE.

We are not taught energetic connections in our classrooms. We are not taught the power of love and kindness and staying in the light. We are not taught how to protect our energies. These once profound teachings of the past are now called the "Hidden Arts". But they are not so hidden. Ancient civilisations used to use all these techniques in order to live with the flow of the Universe, and they had high regard and respect for Mother Earth and Creator (in my country and faith we call Creator, BrahmaDev). But we have forgotten the value of Creator's creations; we have neglected Mother Earth's magic. Every single object in our world, even the ones that we think don't have a life, have life. We are all intrinsically connected.

I was that annoying child who always asked questions that people seldom had answers for. That never stopped me from seeking the truth. What is truth? What I believe in becomes my truth. My truth embodies all of me and I it. My truth became my authenticity and strength.

If my spirit has taught me anything, it is that I am ever so grateful for not losing myself or losing sight of my purpose. I was 8 years old when I knew what I wanted to do, and I have been working step by step towards it. My childlike wonder and peppy attitude are attributes of myself that I am so thankful for. I was named the Happiness Ambassador of India and Happy Princess 2007 by the Happiness Guru, Dr Shelley Sykes, whom I met in Dubai at the age of 15. I was told that I was chosen to be so because of my resilience and kindness to move on and help others do the same.

I am a lover, and I love to laugh and bring laughter into the lives of those who cross my path. I appreciate myself now. I accept my gifts from the Universe wholeheartedly and happily. I love asking my Angels, "How can I be of service today?" and the answers I get every day are nothing short of wonderful. My life is a miracle, and I live in gratitude and abundance because I deserve it; I know my worth. I've seen darkness, and I've come out of it a grown woman who will not have her light dimmed ever again.

My parents are a huge source of strength for me. They may never know or understand the kind of injustices I've had to face, but they never left my side when I was spiralling. There are so many lessons we learn from our family, and I'm so grateful for the family I chose to be born into because we are resilient, beautiful and courageous.

It is important to remember that working on your healing and inner self is a process that will only grow the more you are willing to nourish it. The more I work on myself, the more clarity I get in my visions and channelling. The more I work towards healing myself and my past, the more loved I am by everyone around me because my light is visible now. Today I am stronger, healthier, and happier than I've ever been in my life and fully in love with every aspect of my body, mind and self. My inner world projects my outer reality and the people who have known me for years have seen me flourish right in front of them, so I want you to know that you CAN overcome anything in life that weighs you down right now. You are meant to lead the life you envision for yourself. Happiness is your birthright!

Let me assure you this, you may feel lost right now, but you're never lost forever. I want you to know that you were NOT created in fear. You were created in love and with utmost JOY, and you are meant to live in that essence. I want you to know that you ARE worthy; you ARE loved, protected and supported. There is beauty in this world, and you can live your true purpose.

I want you to know that I'm here for you, I have been you, I feel you, I see you, I hear you, and I'm here to help you understand that the challenges you've faced are not for nothing. Beautiful lessons and teachings lay there waiting for you to tap into.

And finally, I want you to know that if I can find my truth, my identity, my true essence and purpose, then so can you. If I can forgive and be free, then so can you! All it takes is the right kind of guidance tailored to your uniqueness.

I pray my trials and triumphs bring you hope. I pray my resilience gives you strength. I pray my growth invokes you to face your shadows and own them. I pray that this brief testament to my life's journey encourages you to seek the guidance and help that fits you well. I pray we move forward together into a world where the Divine Feminine is set free and we live in the balance of the Divine Masculine and Divine Feminine combined, because life is in all its aspects is beautiful, and we all deserve to live a joyful, balanced life. We owe it to ourselves to speak up, and we deserve to be heard. We deserve to be happy, wild, and free.

If you are ever in need of clarity, healing, finding your gratitude, or someone to talk to, I am here for you.

Mridula Bose, hailing from India, was born and raised in Dubai. She is a Lawyer practising in Dubai, an Angelic Reiki Master/Teacher, Theta Healing Practitioner, a gifted intuitive, clairaudient, clairsentient, claircognizant, clairalience, and a highly sensitive empath. She is the Happiness Ambassador of India and was given the title due to her understanding of life which showed her that shadow exists but so does light, and it is the choice between the two that we make every day that determine the course of our present and future.

As a Lawyer, she is not only passionate about getting her clients justice but also using her platform to spread the good word about Mother Nature, Sustainability and Renewable Energy, and her quest to make the world a more understanding place for women and children. She has laid out plans for starting an association that will include Lawyers from around the world who share her vision. She works for her father and feels blessed to have parents who have taken her around the world, due to which, she has always viewed herself as a child of the world.

She channels messages straight from her Guides and always brings a ray of sunshine into your life. All her life, she has sought love but found it in places that undermined her value and dimmed her light. She had no idea how special she was and how everyone's lives change because of her pure, childlike love and generosity. She was born with magic, and for a period in her life, that knowing and wisdom was lost to her. After a series of dramatic events, she unknowingly shut out her gifts and lived a life that she was "expected" to. But she continued on not knowing how to *heal* from within. The constant battles within herself led to her hitting rock bottom. She was mad at humanity for all that had happened and kept it all hidden inside because she was essentially mad at herself. But her will to break free and the deep connection she had to God led her to seek spiritual guidance and help. Through the practices of meditation, mindfulness techniques, LOA and manifestation, she grew and slowly shed her layers. When she was ready to transform, she met Tina Pavlou, who was then visiting Dubai to teach Angelic Reiki. They immediately struck a connection and knew that they had a much larger purpose together. Tina showed her what the power of love for oneself could truly do. Only when you love yourself can you truly understand the power of forgiveness. When Mridula learnt how to love herself, she made peace with her past and understood that life is more than just hatred. Through the past year, Mridula and Tina have created a remarkable sisterly bond.

Mridula is now on a path to her true purpose - teaching, connecting with Mother Nature, sharing her knowledge, and working towards her aim. She is a true believer in learning every day and sharing her joy with the world. She is committed to helping others find their way to their highest potential. The world is a better place in her eyes now as she has found love within herself.

CONTACT:

Email: msbose6667@gmail.com

in linkedin.com/in/mridulaboselaw

4

AMANDA ELLIOTT

*A*s a young girl raised in rural New South Wales Australia, I never once imagined that in 2020 I would be contributing my story to offer insight into intuitive spiritual healing. There is more to each of us than our story, and by sharing mine I seek to create positive change and inspire the beautiful women of the world to heal their past, to seek their soul nourishment and to know that there is much more available to support them. Here I am, and I invite you on a journey of healing, triumph, soulful insights, delight and much love.

My passion and enthusiasm for the Spiritual, the metaphysical and energy healing, and the opportunity for positive change are only possible due to my own personal journey of discovery. As a practitioner that works with the deepest parts of people that often even they are unaware of, the results of my work give me so much happiness and joy. I have no guilt in telling you that I benefit greatly from seeing the light come on in someone's eyes, seeing the smile on their face and them shaking their heads in a little amazement when they feel the shifts that have occurred. The clients already aware of their intuitive connections and seeking to release their restrictions and fears delight in the changes, just as I do, as my journey leads me forward to uncover new layers of insight to myself. I was that person once, the one that had body aches, medication and literal heartache due to the way my life was turning out for me. I accepted that way of being because I knew no different, and I had a load of habits and personal, ancestral, societal and DNA beliefs that kept me there. It wasn't always like it is now, and at times I wondered how I was going to find the strength to keep going. Fortunately for me, over the years I have had the most spectacular support and intervention where I have been guided to people and places that have saved me from death and further harm on more than one occasion. My journey had massive turning points to get me moving forward on my path, as without any of the interactions, the situations, the circumstances I would not be who I am today, and I enjoy who I am.

My first marriage had seemed wonderful at first. My daughter's biological father had been much older than me, and as a young woman who felt that she should have been married and had children at the age of twenty-five, I married someone much too quickly. I had the best of intentions to enjoy the many lovely qualities of this man and have a family with him. The day after we were married, he moved into a separate part of the house and being pregnant with my eldest daughter, I realised that maybe I had made a big mistake. What followed was years of sorrow as the physical, mental, verbal, financial control, and the abuse became more frequent, and there had been the arrival of my youngest daughter. After years of increasing verbal, mental and at times, physical violence; my heart was literally beating irregularly. My mental health had declined to a state where I had just decided to outlive him so I could be free of the big mistake that I had brought two children into. Of course, no one really knew what was going on except the girls and I. I was in an appointment with my General Practitioner when my youngest daughter was around two years old. He asked me how I was, and I remember saying "I am fine, I am pleased that she is growing up". He looked at me a little and asked me to take these tablets for three months and see if I felt that anything improved for me. My body ached all the time. I had already been told by another female doctor that I needed heart monitoring tests. I wore the halter monitor and kept a diary of what I was doing or what conversations I had while my heartbeat was monitored, recording any irregularities. My doctor told me that my relationship was literally killing me as it was creating heart palpitations and I broke down a little... it was becoming increasingly obvious that I had indeed made a massive mistake, not only that, I had made two beautiful children and they were sharing my mistake also. Within three months of taking medication for depression, I could not only see the trees in the proverbial forest but felt empowered enough to take action to rectify this situation for myself and my daughters. My four and two-year-old daughters were flinching at fast movements and would turn wild-eyed at loud noises.

The night before I was leaving, I had told him I was going. The police arrived at 4.00 am after a triple zero emergency call from a four-year-old girl that had wisdom way beyond her age- to tell them that she needed the police as Daddy was hurting Mummy. They arrived over an hour after her call, and we lived fifteen minutes out of town. The police officer was calm as I told him that if I told him the truth, then my husband would have to be arrested for attempted rape, attempted murder and grievous bodily harm. I just wanted to get away with my daughters. I had no blood, and no visible bruising the police wrote down. I left out the part where my husband had deliberately thrown me multiple times, headfirst into a brick wall as he verbalised to me that the bruising wouldn't show. Or how I begged him to let me live as I was the mother of his children, as he held my neck between his knees and then ankles and kept squeezing that lock manoeuvre that I had only seen on action films. This was all while he was naked and visibly sexually aroused. I left out the part where I somehow managed to gently wake my daughter and smile while the closed door to her room was visibly cracking from the battering to gain entry and access to me, and after my daughter's phone call how we hid behind bushes dressed in our pyjamas in the paddock while he spotlighted the area with his gun hanging out the window. As I packed the car with basic necessities for my four and two-year-old daughters and myself- I looked up at that night sky again as I had earlier in the night and was grateful for the help I had had that night. All through my life, I have had the most incredible synchronicities, and I often smiled at the night sky with relief and often joy. It's as though we shared this life I was having.

After leaving my first husband, what I could only describe as Divine intervention ensued. Within the fortnight, I had met the man that I had loved as an eighteen-year-old. He had told me at eighteen that if he was ever going to marry anyone that it would be me as he loved me, and he couldn't be with me at this time. I had spoken with him twice in fifteen years. On finding out my circumstances, he immediately and unequivocally offered the girls and I protection and a home with no expectations other than our safety. It was instant love for both of us again. I had loved this man from the moment I met him at seventeen. It was an unexplainable recognition. He was to be my second husband and the reason that I asked the stars and beyond for Divine support to heal this deep pain in my soul. It was delivered and started immediately on my asking. Divine guidance is just that. This inexplicable flow of circumstances and situations that just propel you down a path. These people started to enter my life with knowledge and awakenings for my future.

On the 15th of May 2015, my estranged second husband had purposely taken life from a gentle young man while he slept and then intentionally took his own life. My daughters and I knew this young man as he had been part of our family circle of friends in our often-idyllic life on our farm near the Snowy Mountains region of Australia until that all changed. In 2009 we had lost our first biological child as an unviable pregnancy with complications at 18 weeks during this time of drought, financial hardship and worry. It was too big and too much, and both of us had unhealed pasts that had surfaced with the trauma and loss. The girls and I moved away from my teenage love and the man that they now had loved as their dad for more than ten years. My husband deteriorated to the point where we were scared and so, so sad at the abuse and what we had witnessed as he succumbed to mental health issues and refused help and support from Dr's and mental health clinicians. We moved to Cooma initially and found that the supportive friends that we'd once had were no longer in contact. I left behind the household items that were replaceable and refurnished the girls and I from the Salvation Army. It was during this time that I began further studies in Community Services as my life path had offered insights into mental health issues and the toll on those that love them. We still saw each other occasionally and involved the girls. I wanted to be with the man I loved but not by sacrificing my daughters or my own safety. I sensed massive darkness and could see him change in and out of it whilst he was talking to me, which was often abusive and threatening. One night I suddenly felt like checking employment in my hometown of Gundagai as I had been working in Corrective Services NSW and Canberra Gaol. I distinctly heard a voice tell me to move to Gundagai as soon as I could. I had this feeling of warmth and glowing with the words which I knew over my lifetime I had trusted before. The girls and I moved to Gundagai in 2012 and never heard from him after our last meeting in Cooma. The girls called by phone and there was no answer, they left messages on his birthday, Christmas, Easter and in between.

On the 31st of December 2015, I found myself in a place I had never been before. The weight of the previous seven months, combined with what I knew lay ahead for me was heavy, and I was tired. Tired of this heaviness of the weight that other people had inflicted, which then put me in a space of recovering from the damage that they had done. My solace has always been nature and the night sky, and I often spent time just connecting in the peace of the night. Here I was with my feet firmly planted in a strong, trusting and composed state upon the earth- with my eyes, and my breath being surrounded by the feelings and sounds of nature at night and communing with those beautiful energies that had supported me all through my life.

I asked that I please be sent some help to get me through this massive grief and pain, this massive clean-up of someone else's choices. That my daughters are strong enough to live through this situation and that I am strong enough to get us all through to the end of it. That I am going to need something else to help as I had accessed the counsellors, the Doctor's, the Social Workers, and they had all helped a little and from my academic studies in Social Work and employment experience with people in crisis- I knew they had done all they could. I had this pain so deep that nothing had relieved it, and I was really worried that this deep, deep pain was going to overwhelm me and I wouldn't be able to be strong enough to get my daughters through this and attend to everything I needed to do. It had already been a little over six months, and I thought it would have subsided just a bit by now. I remember looking up to the sky in all its twinkling glory and adding – there is more to me than my grief, and I need something more, but I don't know where to find it or how to get it. With tears gently trickling down my face I felt this familiar, peaceful presence, this truly comforting glow all around me and also within me - the same feeling of that particular energy that had always just been part of my life when I took the time to connect. From that precise day forward things began to happen and when I was finally brave enough to confide in my sister about what I was feeling, seeing, hearing, dreaming and writing about she told me that I was having what's termed as a further Spiritual Awakening.

In recent years I have had the opportunity to delve a lot deeper into many things that I suspected were part of me and that I have always had a profound knowing of being part of and connected to. I always felt that there was more to know or find out, that sometimes I knew things and felt things that no one that I knew talked openly about. My joy is being able to offer services that support others on their journey of healing, discovery to heal, to see the goodness in themselves and to confirm their innate knowing of something much bigger than us that offers only love from a loving place. The personal perspective is often obscured by peer pressure or conclusions that are formed after the mistreatment by others or from traumas and fears that shutdown the exploratory and joyful nature of who we really are. These are handed down through our DNA, also often unknowingly from our family's interactions with us from pre-birth and from our society's expectations and our unique personal essence and innate survival instincts. I know this because my journey has included the identification, acknowledgement, acceptance and releasing of so much clutter that at fifty-one years of age, I feel that best I have felt in all my years of life.

My journey into the metaphysical began many years ago as a young child raised in rural Australia whose favourite place was on the edge of the river. It was more than the sound of the water flowing in between rocks and over half-submerged trees. It was more than the shaded, peaceful places under the willow trees that even on the hottest days offered significant reprieve for myself and other life from the sweltering summer sun. It was the feeling of pureness and peace that often inspired me to smile and gently close my eyes to experience the world around me on a much deeper level. With my eyes open or closed in complete safety and serenity, I often thought of absolutely nothing, nothing at all, but I was so present and alive in those moments and never did I feel as though I was alone. It was the experiencing and the knowing that this level of inner peace was Divine in nature and I was part of it all as I sat there absolutely glowing with pure happiness and contentment of being exactly as I was and where I was. Blissful. Just being able to breathe in the cooler air and watch as tiny birds came closer and fleetingly sipped from the stiller waters edge or a sudden splash as a magnificent rainbow trout jumped from the water's depth to snatch a flying insect from the air. They all allowed me to watch their life and it often occurred to me just how everything around me is dependent on everything else, and it was a magnificent design that as a human, I was also designed to fit into.

I have always been a free spirit, completely and utterly so peaceful when in nature near a river, and especially at night as the air was so still and everyone else seemed to be shutting down their clatter of the day. Many nights I spent at my window above my bed just watching and listening as the river kept flowing not far from the house and the night sky just offered such an incredible view that even then, I realised was vast and immeasurable. I had this knowing. This delight in the colours, the sounds, the feelings of glowing from the inside and this feeling of being part of everything around me. This sense of harmony, as though everything from the sky to earth and in between was just waiting for everyone to rest and settle so that nature could truly breathe and release the discordance of the human's day. It was so much bigger than me that I felt quite protected and comforted. I often received interesting thoughts and concepts during this time with answers to my questions or solutions to problems just gently arriving as I noticed them and acknowledged the messages I received. Sometimes I felt as though I was having a conversation with my grandfather who I never got to meet, and other older women that comforted me in times of need. Sometimes it felt sparkly and bright around me, and I could literally feel happiness just light me up. Other times I would hear wise words of wisdom, and I had particular reverence when these messages came as they were always accompanied by a feeling of trust and love. I never questioned any of this as I thought everyone felt this way and did the same when they were alone in peaceful places.

I always achieved good grades at school and enjoyed the stimulation of learning. It was like an exploratory adventure to see what else there was to learn. As a child, I was confident in my ability to manage myself and had a few close friends in town that lived a different life to my family and I. My capabilities as a young woman were empowered and diverse, and this was in part a reflection of a non-gender specific rural upbringing where I was able to do what I was capable of and had ample opportunity to learn and discern limitations that often had no foundations other than what was expected by others. I enjoyed my femininity and relished in my capabilities. The town was fun, and we often visited my nan after school where we would be treated to lashings of cakes, pikelets and biscuits for afternoon tea served with laughter, love and many teaspoons of sugar in our tea. My mother's mum was Nan, and she had many stories and conversations to share as she sat for hours on the front verandah of her house in the main street and said hello to nearly everyone that passed. We often asked her questions about our family's origins as it was suspected that our olive skin and dark hair might have meant relatives of Aboriginal descent as was often referred to offhandedly. This particular question was often asked as we all wanted confirmation of what we already sort of knew. She would just laugh, cover her mouth, look away and never answered the question. I remember dark Irish being laughingly referred to, which I later found was a common term offered to in many families by their grandparents to disguise Australian Indigenous heritage. Nan mentioned how her mother in law used to cross the street when she saw her coming and how she started working as a home help for families when she was in her early teens. There were a few stories that she shared many years later that could only be described now as resilience building for her and unfortunately, many other young women throughout the ages. It ended one day as she packed her things and waited on her suitcase on the side of the road for my not yet grandfather to pick her up. Nan's sister worked for another family close by, and my great Aunt told me they had a certain meeting place where they would each walk to on certain evenings just to hug and smile and share their stories with each other.

My father's mother was Gran, and she was a woman of grace and poise. She eloquently and sufficiently managed herself on the family farm which was granted to my grandfather on his return from Gallipoli with the Australian Light Horse Brigade of the Australian Army. Gran role modelled a deep faith in her church, her family and herself and was a loving, strong, capable lady of substance. Both of my grandmothers were women living in times of war on foreign soil and societal division in Australia and were remarkable mothers and grandmothers that always offered love. I come from a long line of proud, loving, strong, capable women who have lived through the many changes in history. My two daughters are the next generation of women seeing many changes that one day their children and grandchildren may also write of.

On Good Friday 2016, I accepted an invitation to attend local markets with a friend. We walked around the stalls, and outside I started walking toward a particular stall that had the most beautiful display of different coloured small stones that just made my heart sing- literally. I could feel like little whirls inside my body. I purchased ten of these stones of different colours and shapes as the man talked to me of geology and crystals. I took my parcel home and unwrapped them and started reading the small notes on each one he had included with the stones. As I held each one, I felt tingles in my hands, and this glow just lights up in my heart and head. I resonated so strongly and felt a sense of happiness and emotions changing as I held them. Crystals came with me to bed that night and have done ever since. My affinity with crystals is now shared with others through my crystal sales and workshops as many more people are awakening to what many people all over the world have known for centuries. What I experienced then and since changed my view of what was possible, and it all was so very welcome and perfectly timed.

The deceased Estate finalisation took three years, and I could no longer continue my Bachelor of Social Work studies and could not possibly spread myself any thinner any longer. In the following years, I was able to attend a number of Theta Healing® courses that healed my many wounds, deepened my connections to myself, my intuition and provided so many answers to questions that had alluded me since childhood. Theta Healing® offered the most transformational changes to all parts of my life and healed so much of the pain that I was carrying. I chose my health, my healing and my future as I realised what profound shifts I was experiencing emotionally, mentally and physically. I do not get sick or ill and have not needed to visit my medical doctor for nearly four years, and I take no medications. I used to wear reading glasses, and I haven't needed them for over two years. If Theta Healing® could do this much for me, then there were many people out there that would love to experience this for themselves; and so, I kept learning and practising and working on myself to improve my skills and insight. During this time of healing, I was guided to learn Usui Reiki to Master level, which caused new doors to open that offered further healing for myself and new experiences in energy healing modalities for others. A whole new world of insights and skills had opened up for me, and I now have opportunities to work with clients in ways that I hadn't known were possible, and that benefited them, their families and communities. Spiritual or energy healing and connection with metaphysical aspects has been part of the faith and Divine connection in many cultures of the world, and for me personally, it was the most natural and welcome addition to my life.

I work with mainly women and children, and in mid-2019, I was successful in my submission for government funding to facilitate wellbeing programmes and healing sessions in Indigenous communities in Wagga Wagga. My programmes incorporated connections to nature, to Spiritual concepts and nurturing of the mind, body and spirit with good nutrition, hydration, optimism, and self-love and were so gratefully and gracefully received. What I found were many women that had never spoken of the pain they carried, and the stories and healings were so insightful into what incredible resilience women have. The results for each were unique and significant with collated results showing resounding success for Spiritual healing to promote positive emotions, identify and release impacts of trauma and lighten the weight they had been carrying on a number of levels. A positive sense of identity and belonging, being loved and knowing you are loveable is a foundation that many people all over the world struggle with from childhood and just how does one build anything on unstable and uncertain beginnings?

Theta Healing® and Reiki lifted me above the waterline when I was gasping and gurgling in a struggle to overcome the emotional, mental and physical toll that my life had incurred, and it was the spiritual soul aspect of me that required the healing. Now my mission is to offer healing to lift others above that waterline into a new consciousness so they too can make informed choices into how they heal, and the life they want for themselves. It is soul nourishment and connection that for too long has been overlooked as a vital component of our overall wellbeing maintenance and healing. Our natural way of being includes our intuition and enjoying all of our innate gifts and capabilities which offer new ways forward that encompasses much more love, connection and include ethical and moral standards towards ourselves and each other. Spiritual people have known this for centuries.

My life has been truly enhanced by the many healing practitioners, and gorgeous souls that entered my life throughout this healing journey and Tina Pavlou of The Goddess Rooms in the United Kingdom is one. I first knew of her through mutual friends and online, she piqued my curiosity with her openness and expressive love and passion for women's wellbeing and Divine connections. Her big heart and incredible intuitive healing abilities have offered online support to many more women than just me and her regular doses of soul food to her groups are inspiring in her commitment in creating positive change in our world.

As women, we are known as the nurturers of others, and so often I remind women of the need to fill their own cup of nurturing. Seek joy and healing for yourself and others will benefit from the wellbeing you radiate. Forgive yourself for what you didn't know before you knew it and seek healing to enhance your path forward. Light up your own life with the beauty and love that is within you- find your treasure within yourself and connect to which you hold most Divine. Grief is your reaction to your loss of someone's presence. Others and I will tell you that it is indeed a lovely space where they are, and we haven't lost them. There are many healers to hold your hand to begin the path and many more way showers to choose from as you move forward on your awakening to what is available and possible.

My journey has led me to this amazing opportunity to share my story of overcoming obstacles, of Divine healing energies that enhance life experience, intuitive insights and connections that solidified an inner knowing for me and are available to us all. My healing story is here to inspire the women that are living in situations far less than they deserve to find their power and trust that you are indeed loved and have always been loveable- you just need to see it and feel it for yourself.

ABOUT THE AUTHOR

AMANDA ELLIOTT

Amanda is an Intuitive Healer and facilitator that combines her certifications, skills and abilities in Theta Healing®, Usui Reiki Master ship, Access Bars and other Intuitive energetic healing and meditation techniques to offer unique healing appointments, workshops and programmes for those that are choosing to improve the way they feel and discover new possibilities for themselves now and into the future.

Amanda's academic qualifications include Community Services and Social Work studies, Trauma Training for High Needs Children, Suicide Intervention Training and Training and Assessment group work which have supported her previous employment experience in Canberra Gaol as an Alcohol and Drug Caseworker, Corrective Services NSW supporting parolees into community settings, Women's Crisis Accommodation services and Out of Home Care/Foster Care as a crisis youth mentor.

Amanda is having an incredible journey that has led to the development of her Intuitive Healing business that offers personal appointments, workshops and programmes to a wide niche of adults, youths and children. Amanda's online and in-person sessions have helped others reduce anxiety, release feelings of hopelessness, move forward from the pain of old relationships, overcome the trauma of sexual abuse and domestic violence, restore confidence in themselves and their ability to cope, have insights into their own Spiritual abilities and capacities, have significantly less to no body pain, improve sleep patterns, release old fears and triggers from the past, release addictions and much more. All clients have improved results immediately and are able to compare before and after emotions, body pain and patterns of thinking. Testimonials and reviews are available on Amanda's Facebook pages, and further documentation can be emailed on request.

In 2019, Amanda delighted in providing Australian state government health funded healing sessions and programmes in the Indigenous community in rural NSW where client's unique and significant results showed resounding success for Intuitive and Spiritual healing to promote positive emotions, identify and release impacts of trauma and lighten the weight of the past that many people carry on a number of levels. Collated and documented results are available.

Amanda produces unique, energetically enhanced crystal and essential oil products which are available through her online

Etsy Shop and uses these enhancements for herself and her clients. Individual appointments are available in person and online, and support people of all ages to be reconnected with their happiness, manage emotional triggers, heal and recover from their past and build on strengths and positive beliefs to enjoy an improved quality of life and optimistic outlook. Her clients have been consistently delighted with their results from these sessions and techniques which are exciting and offer optimism for the future for individuals, families and communities. Our world is changing, and so is the way we heal.

Amanda is happy to answer any questions or inquiries about her services via email or through her Facebook pages messenger.

Amanda Elliott Contact details:

Email: amandaelliott2722@outlook.com

Facebook:

• Amanda Elliott Healing and Training for Healing appointments, workshop and programme information.

facebook.com/amandaelliotthealingandtraining

• Soul Spirit Connections for Healing appointments, crystal and oil sales and information, Intuitive insights and interactive groups.

https://www.facebook.com/soulspiritcrystalconnections

Etsy Shop : https://www.etsy.com/shop/divinesoulspirit

5

ANNA GERBER

$\mathcal{I}$ was born in East Russia close to China, my mum worked as a waitress in a restaurant, and my dad was in the army. My Mum has been married three times, she had one daughter from her first marriage and a second daughter from her second marriage. I was from her third marriage. My parents were so excited to find out they were pregnant with me, but there was only one problem… they wanted a boy! My dad was living in a house with three women, and he wanted a son so much it affected me for my whole life. I am 36 years old, and only now I know what it feels like to be a woman. To love being a woman and not to feel a disappointment for being a daughter instead of a son. When I was little, I remember my parents used to joke about me being an 'it' who arrived. It is one of my first memories. In those days they did not have any scans so when I cried my first breaths, they said to my dad, "it's a girl!" and he slammed his fist and shouted: "Damn it," but I know he fell in love with me as a baby. I certainly loved him. I remember being a little girl and being absolutely obsessed with my dad and crying my eyes out as he went off to the Army. I remember him with his uniform on coming back home; I absolutely adored my dad.

At three years old, I started to feel really strongly about wanting to be an actress. I always told everyone that I would be an actress and I would be famous. My dad didn't like this, and he always said that you need a decent job and being an actress was not really a proper job.

By age 11, my parents decided to move to Siberia as my dad was originally from Siberia. They were doing their best for us, and there was more opportunity for my future as an actress; more opportunity in every way really as we were moving to a capital city - a far cry from our small town previously. I didn't know what it really meant for us to move somewhere else, but when we moved, I went to a new school and realised my life had changed. It was so different, the people, the culture everything was different from where we lived previously. Years after, I realised I was depressed for about a year. I had dreams about my birthplace, and at school, I had to fight to assert my real personality and prove who I was. At first, people really tried to bully me. I was quite a small child, and it was hell being bullied, and I can see it's easy to sink lower and lower, to hide and run away, but I fought back. I fought back hard physically at first, and I would stand my ground and not give up even when the bullies were bigger than me. Sometimes I just wanted to cry, but I never cried in front of them, I just fought harder, so the bullies didn't have a chance and eventually I earned their respect even if they didn't deserve it. To this day, I have always been strong enough to protect myself and protect others who were being bullied as well. I started acting at nursery, and I proved to everyone I was a really good actress. I loved being on the stage, and people would applaud and compliment me for my acting skills. I loved pretending to be other people, even acting like boys. My first-ever part in a play was as a man disguised as a wolf. Playing parts for men and dominating the stage was fun, and I wasn't sure if my dad would be proud of me, pretending to be the son he didn't have. In the end, I became a real celebrity at my school.

By age 13, I strongly felt I wanted to be an actress as my adult career. I took every opportunity that came my way to become an actress on the stage. For a teenage girl, I had about 15 different classes, including music school, cross-stitch, knitting, crochet, rowing, wood-burning, cooking lessons and making jewellery. I was a very busy teenager, and I was a really good girl; if mum said to be home at 9 pm, I would be home at 9 pm. I got used to school, friends, our new home, but in my dreams, my birthplace was calling me every day. I had never felt so down or uncomfortable within myself as I did whilst I was living in Novosibirsk.

My dad's parents lived in a little village about 400km (about 7 hours' drive) from us, and every school holiday we always spent it there. When I look back now, I realise that was the best time for me; but at the same time lots of people were starting to go abroad and we, as a family, were jealous as people were coming back from places like Egypt and Turkey and we always felt like we would be working from morning to evening and helping our grandparents with the chickens, growing fruits and vegetables, and preparing the logs for Winter. To be honest, I would never change that time for anything else in the world.

I always felt there was something special about this village that my grandparents lived in and I always wanted to be there. I asked my parents if I could stay and go to school there and live with my grandparents, but the answer was always NO! They felt there was a better future for me where we lived, and they knew it would be impossible for me to succeed as an actress if I lived in that small village.

I was so at home without shoes on, walking on the ground and being surrounded by beautiful pine forests. It's a very sacred place for me, but I didn't know what sacred was at that time. I just felt it was so right to be there; to just breathe the air, to walk and just to be present. This place still and will be for the rest of my life my sacred place, the place that gives me limitless strength and the most beautiful place on earth. No matter how many places I would love to visit (I have a big list), this place is where my soul belongs. I still like to wander in forests and hug trees as it reminds me of home and brings me enormous comfort.

At the age of 14, I had the chance to go to drama college which was one of the most famous colleges in Russia – everyone knew that I would get there, everyone believed in me, everyone knew how talented I was, and I myself was 100% sure that I would get there. I was one of 1500 applicants maybe more, and when I completed day one, I was so pleased to find that I was accepted to go onto the second stage of the process. After the second day, in the morning my mum woke me up and she said that I wasn't on the list. I started laughing saying 'you're such a joker mum, I am on the list, I don't believe you' – the way she looked at me, I then understood she was telling the truth. I still didn't quite believe it even after I made the phone call myself, but my surname was not on the list, so I asked my dad to take me there and check for myself as I was sure it was a mistake. I couldn't find my surname on the list, and my brain could not understand what was going on, 'it can't be true,' I thought to myself. All that I remember from that time was I didn't want to eat, I didn't want to go to the toilet; I just lay on my bed, and I didn't know how I was supposed to go back to school and face the fact I hadn't been accepted into the college. It's funny how our greatest failures can actually be successes as years after this happened to me, I discovered that no one who had made it onto the course was happy about it in the end. They told me in their words that this was the worse course ever in the whole history of this college, and I wondered if this could be God protecting me?! I began to think that everything may happen for a reason, and I carried on.

Another two years of school gave me a chance to prepare myself for something bigger. My dad, who never believed in acting said to me that he could see my passion, and if that was what I really wanted to do then he would do everything to help me reach my goals. At age 17, I was 100% ready to come back to college and prove to those who didn't want me before that I am deserving, I am worth it, and I am talented. I completed a few months of the pre-studying course before the exams, and these few months were one of the greatest times in my life. I met people who I keep in touch with now, even to this day. The owner of the college used to point at me and say, 'she is the star, she is the talent', and I was happy and so pleased someone could say that about me, I was really inspired and started to believe in myself even more. Closer to the exams, my parents heard how highly this teacher had spoken of me and suggested I should try to get into the university in Moscow. I didn't think I was ready. I still didn't think I was good enough. But my dad was insistent there would be more opportunities, especially for what I was hoping to do. But for me, it was still just dreams. I was still really a child, and I told my parents that I didn't think I was ready for Moscow and told them I wanted to complete college first. My dad said to at least try, and I agreed with them, so I passed the exams for university and my Mum and I set off to Moscow. It felt like I had arrived in a completely different world.

Everyone in college was shocked, I had made it so young. Some were happy, and some were jealous that I had got into an acting school in the capital city of Russia and was following my dreams. When I moved to Moscow, I remember feeling the same as I had when we first moved to Siberia however, on the flip side I was overwhelmed and overexcited, but then something happened...my mum left me... I realised the next time I would see my parents would be in 6 months' time and that was a big shock for me as we were always so close, and I had never lived apart from them. I was now in Moscow by myself, I didn't have any friends or family here to help me. We didn't have mobile phones; it was only house phones and every day at 9 pm

Moscow time, and midnight Siberia time, I had a chance to speak to my parents. At this time, it was so expensive to call across the country. I reckon the phone company boss must have become a millionaire just through me. We spent so many hours on the phone together. At one point I was crying and saying I wanted to come back home and didn't want to be there it was so tough. Some people at 17 are pretty wise and mature but not me, I was still a little girl in my mind. One friend of my Mums said to her, 'how could you let your 17-year-old daughter go thousands of miles away, without any friends or family,' and at that moment my mum realised what she had done.

But just as she realised that, I was realising something else. I was beginning to enjoy my freedom, and I was starting to get used to my university friends and Moscow. It's like another country within a country, Moscow is so diverse and fantastic it changed my life, and it changed me. I fell in love...I fell in love with Moscow, and from that point, I couldn't imagine my life without Moscow. My Mum was now asking me to come back home, and I said, 'no, my life is here now.' I felt like 'a fish in water' I absolutely adored and honoured Moscow with everything 'She' is, as we say in Russia! However, every time I had a break, the one place I was dreaming of was my village in Siberia.

My four years at University were full of ups and downs, and most weeks there would be at least a day when I didn't have enough money to eat, anything at all. I lived on buckwheat, which is what they give soldiers in the army. It's not great, but it's super cheap and fills you up. I was relieved and overjoyed to be successfully accepted in one of the drama theatres in Moscow immediately after graduating. I didn't realise how lucky I was to go straight to theatre after uni. I was actually, for the first time in my life going to get paid for doing something I loved. It was amazing. I had earned a little mopping floors but to get paid as an actress was something else, I was walking on air skipping home I was so happy. Okay, in reality, it was a tiny amount of money, but the acting world is a completely different world to any other occupation out there. You can't imagine how many drama students were selling burgers in McDonald's after university just because it is not easy to get a job in that world. It was something unbelievable to walk inside that building and start the journey as a drama actress in the theatre. I remember I texted my dad and said, 'be proud of me because officially from today I am an actress'!

Another chapter of my life had started, my dream was finally a reality, but how quickly did that dream turn sour? I had dreamed of something my entire life, and suddenly I had an adult job that I had strived for and worked so hard for, and the job was truly horrible. Being on stage was fantastic, but everything else was soul-destroying. I couldn't believe it. I was in a state of shock. I had graduated successfully, but then I faced the truth. My new colleagues were a mixture of different men and women from all different age groups and different success stories, but I started to feel something I had never felt before, something was not alright in this world. It wasn't the dream world, the fantasy world of fairy princesses and handsome princes I had dreamed of as a little girl. It was a world of lies, jealousy, betrayal, gossip and all the negativity you can possibly imagine being gift wrapped and trying to present themselves as a beautiful industry. After four years as an actress I was to be truly heartbroken and defeated, but right at the start, I was so optimistic I ignored these things, I thought things would get better, and I tried so hard to find the best in these people. I was 21, full of ambition, I had made it to the stage, and I walked around like a rainbow was coming out of my arse! I believed everything was possible, and I believed that everyone around me was lovely and that we worked as a team; I truly believed everything we did was for the greater good.

Then another thing happened which changed my life - my Mum called me, and she said that 'a psychic woman' had moved to our village. In communist Russia, we were taught to ignore religion and spirituality, so everyone in the village now felt free to embrace these feelings which had been denied to them. My Auntie went to visit her, and she showed her my picture. The woman was really concerned, and she kept saying, 'bring this girl to me immediately,' without any explanation. So, when my mum phoned me up, I laughed and said 'why, what for, what's going on, what' ss so important" She said the psychic had told her that I didn't have much time to live and that' ss why I needed to go to her. I must admit at that point my life was pretty good I was successfully working on the stage, I was in a beautiful relationship, my dad had brought me home, every-thing was going really smoothly, and for the first time probably in my whole life, I felt very harmonious within myself in every single way.

However, you know that feeling that you can't quite explain, but you just know there is something not right. It's nothing to do with being negative or the idea of self-sabotage, which I am often accused of, it is just a pure feeling of something inside of you, really deep inside of you that something is not right. At the time, I didn't have the time to go and see the psychic because I was so busy with the show and my performances, but then out of the blue, I received ten days off. I wonder now once again if this was God leading me, but then I just said to myself, 'why not?' and flew to Siberia straight away. My dad did not and still does not believe in these sorts of things, and when I told him, you need to take me to the village to see this woman, it caused a massive argument. 'What a lot of nonsense,' he would say but he knew me very well, and he knew that I wouldn't give up, so he drove me to the village. There we were in a car listening to our favourite songs along the way. I was on my way to see a psychic for the first time in my life, and I was quite nervous. I mean, apparently this woman had told me I might die soon; it was really quite troubling.

I was super anxious on my first visit to this woman, but something told me that I was doing the right thing. The things she told me without knowing me were so accurate; I was surprised and impressed. She explained everything to me about what would happen if I was not to be cleared or cleansed by her. I have to say it wasn't the death sentence I feared, so I agreed and decided to go and have this spiritual cleanse that she spoke of for seven days, twice a day. I didn't really have a clue what she was doing I just remember her saying some kind of prayers and she had a knife in her hand, and the final day she warned me that I would not feel very well and to be honest when I left her I thought that day that I was going to die. I had never felt anything like how I felt on that day, I couldn't get up off the bed, I felt very weak, my temperature was very high, and I slept almost all day, but the next day I was fine. When this all finished, I felt completely different in myself, and I knew that she had done something that 100% made me feel better. According to this medium, I later found that I had been cursed in my mum's womb, which would be activated when I was 21. This type of curse is common in Russia; witchcraft is very common in my country. I still didn't really know what this was all about. Was it true? Was it not? I didn't know, but I thought it was worth being open to it because there was something that I couldn't explain.

My time came to go back to Moscow, life was ticking along as normal nothing really special, but there was always a feeling of something missing. What the psychic had told me played on my mind. I was increasingly disillusioned by the theatre life and was looking for a way out. My dream was in tatters, what was I going to do? I even thought I might just go home to my parents, but it would have felt like such a failure to have returned home so when my sister suggested for me to try something new like go to another country, I thought yes, that's it. At first, I was a little nervous and didn't know whether I could do something quite as adventurous as Russians' really don't travel as tourists. In communist times we were only allowed to go on two holidays a year and always within our own country, we were not allowed out at all. It appeared almost impossible for someone like me to imagine. I didn't speak any English, and as Russians, we are really limited by our problems getting visas to travel. At the time, there were not many places where we could go, but Egypt was one of them. Since a little girl, I have been drawn to Egypt, I have many books about Egypt and always dreamed of seeing the pyramids. I honestly thought my dream would never come true. But just a few days later, I found myself on a plane to Egypt, and there was something very magical about it. It made my heart beat faster just thinking about it, and here I was actually going. It was almost unbelievably exciting. I couldn't stop looking out of the aeroplane window, thinking wow I am actually going on the biggest adventure of my life. As soon as I walked down the steps onto the airport tarmac, I knew my life was never going to be the same again. For a start, I didn't need my thick Russian winter coat and hat. I had left behind temperatures of -25 degrees and heavy snow, and suddenly I was able to stand on the ground with 20-degree heat and palm trees feeling the warm breeze on my face. It was something truly unreal to sit in the restaurants with a sea view, have watermelon for breakfast and go swimming in the sea in January. It was more of a dream come true than my theatre career, and of course, the pyramids and the aura of spirituality that surrounds them was an experience that was truly to change me.

If anyone at that time would have told me that I was going to work in Egypt I would have laughed, however, literally a few months later I came back for work which ended up being a beautiful three-year chapter of my life.

I absolutely adored working in the resort. I would tell any young person to work abroad; it's an amazing experience in every way. I started to learn English and met people from all over the world. A year later, I could say 'enjoy your meal' in seven different languages. I started to discover nightclubs and drinking. I had never done that in my life before, and it was fun, but I also started to question myself. Suddenly questions came into my head from nowhere, 'what is the purpose of my life? Just to work, eat, go on holiday, earn money, spend money, there had to be something greater or more important. Through talking to my mother back in Russia, I found out that my great grandmother was a healer and that my mum and her cousins had visions. They would see warnings in dreams, and they would have feelings about what people should do or shouldn't, and their feelings were always true. Was it just human intuition and empathy or something else, something deeper, more spiritual? I was eager to find out.

I ended up in Dover in Britain by meeting a man who asked me to be his wife. At the time this seemed to be the answer, maybe this was the something else I was looking for. Okay, I thought I am married, I am a wife so I must be complete. For the first time in my life, I got pregnant, but ironically, I lost the baby on our honeymoon in Egypt. I thought my life was over, and I was a failure, but it led me to something, something I would never have discovered otherwise. My mother said, 'never have doubts about God's plans for you,' but I wondered how this could be part of a plan, and then I had my first vision. I was terrified, but I saw my husband's mother. It wasn't in a dream. I was awake, and she was in the room, her face was in front of mine, and she wanted to talk to me. She had died many years earlier, and we had never met. She kept repeating: 'I need to tell you something, don't be afraid." But I was afraid, and I wouldn't listen, and the vision began to fade.

I started to drink to shut everything out, and after I suffered another miscarriage, it got as much as a litre of vodka a day. Everyone around me thought I was the life and soul of the party, but my soul was empty. I ended up living on my own in a tiny room, but I began to think that maybe my life did have a purpose. I didn't know where to find that purpose, so I tried belly dancing, I laugh now, but it was the start of my search. I tried yoga, and then I went to Ramsgate to a place called the Goddess Rooms. I found myself surrounded by people who don't judge you, support you in every way and just listen when you want to talk about angels and visions. There I learned to be unsure and vulnerable is really a strength as it can inspire others just like you. It was there I tried Angelic Reiki, and suddenly I had another vision of my former mother-in-law and this time when her face came in front of mine, I was not afraid, and I let her talk. I had found my purpose. The drink didn't serve me anymore. I had made a discovery that was amazing and wonderful, and perhaps so obvious it had to be true. I wanted to heal others, but I had to heal myself first. And this new drive to heal people would heal me. I started an online course in Theta Healing, and I discovered a new mission in life. My life began to make sense, and I knew for sure everything had happened for a reason. The things that had happened to me other people might see as bad, but I saw them as vital lessons in life. Without my experiences, I would not be who I am - an Angelic Reiki practitioner, a Theta Healer, an actress, a Russian Goddess. I had found my path, and if life can get any better than that, I am asking God to show me.

Looking back now, I am starting to see, without any obstacles in my way, what a beautiful transformation has happened to me in just a few short months in the midst of 2020. I am living my life alcohol-free, and I am healthy physically and mentally. I have the opportunity to learn from the best teachers. Just to have the chance to listen and to add to my knowledge is a gift. Someday I will impart that gift to others with love from me, the Russian Goddess. I am looking forward to it. So now I have a goal, a target for which my aim is straight and true, to light the path for people without goals, to bathe their path in brightness so they can follow and not get lost as I did.

ABOUT THE AUTHOR

ANNA GERBER

Anna is a 36-year-old Russian Goddess who found fame on the Moscow stage but discovered life as an actress was soul-destroying and a depressing destruction of a childhood dream.

She laughed off a disturbing discovery that the ancient practice of witchcraft had haunted her life with a curse issued to her mother when she was just a baby in her womb. Intrigued, she left Moscow to travel to a remote village in Siberia to learn the truth and put her mind at rest only to find an old woman who said she was to die young unless she changed everything she believed in.

This is the story of a 21st-century sophisticated woman living in one of the biggest cities in the world coming to terms that there is something other to life than chasing fame and material wealth. Communism had banned religion and spirituality from her life as a child, and now as a woman, she has discovered it is not only real but is something no one can afford to ignore.

6

CHARLOTTE NEWHAM

ith this cup of cacao, I surrender to the flow. I welcome all that needs to be shared. I let my creativity flow out on to these pages. I now invite you dear one, to share with me all that comes from the heart and I imagine as you read this, some things may be different in your world.

There is much change in consciousness evolution going on in the world right now.

It is 2020, and I am 44 years old, and I am currently within what feels like a free-range prison. We are in stage 4 lockdown of a global pandemic, which means we are only allowed to leave our home for essentials, and/or exercise for no more than 1 hour and all within a 5km radius of our home. With also a cat, a puppy & 3 young children home, I am stumbling along with this home-schooling attempt. Our days can be a little messy and turned upside down in a moment. I feel like some days I'm going a little bit crazy, but also loving this time all the same (if you are curious to know what happened in 2020, take a moment now to look it up).

This time has provided much space for reflection. I had hoped by now to have shared more of what lights me up to the world. You see, earlier this year, I completed angelic reiki level 3 & 4 and my master's with Tina Pavlou. I am excited to step into the space of sharing this powerful, yet beautiful, loving healing modality with others and starting them on their own healing journey as I have done so.

If I may, I would like to share with you more about my life and my journey prior to this and what brought me here to this moment now.

My life began on a farm in the English countryside, the youngest of 4 children. I do not remember much of my childhood, other than it being hard work and tiring for my parents. There was not much room for fun and play, always work to be done. There was a big age gap between us kids, so I spent much of my time alone, making my own fun, being creative, and letting my imagination run wild. Fairies and magic were often a big part of my play.

At 11 years old, I went off to boarding school. I had quite mixed feelings about going; part of me was terrified to leave my mum and dad, and all that was familiar. I was afraid of the unknown, but then there was another part of me that was super excited. I had always loved listening to Enid Blyton stories of Malory Towers. Stories of adventures of girls at boarding school. It was here at Burford Boarding school that I discovered so much of what I now believe, sparked a lot of who I am today. Boarding school is much of what you would imagine it to be, we slept in dormitories with a dozen or so girls, we all slept in bunk beds, and each had a wardrobe. I slept in the bottom bunk, and I had posters and pictures that I stuck on the bed above me. There was a common room where we could watch tv and do home-work, a dining room, a games room, and a paved outdoor area. It was up to us to make our own fun, which we became pretty good at. I was not one of the cool kids; I was the girl with the long hair dyed orange, a tassel skirt with bells and the doc martin boots. So, with this ready-made sisterhood, you couldn't help but learn and support each other in trying new things. I think I had my first cigarette at 13, and my first spliff not long after. At night we would tell stories, some stories would scare us, and many were ghost stories of the haunted boarding house of which we slept, or the churchyard next door and the priory across the road. Sometimes we would sneak out after dark to explore and see what ghosts or spirits we could find, this also led us onto Ouija boards and calling in our spirits and guides. Seems crazy now when I think back as I am quite sure none of us really knew what we were doing.

One of my great and dear friends while at school, came from a more free and alternative family than I did, I was always so fascinated when she told me about learning how to give light and practicing Reiki during her summer school holidays. I was so intrigued but shut this interest away as it wasn't anything that at the time, would've been encouraged by my family. So, I then moved on to discovering boys and what fun I had. I discovered my sexuality and feelings of lust and to be desired by the opposite sex. It was at this time also that I had my first acid trip. I got lost in the feeling of disassociation of reality like I was stepping into another dimension. I liked it, and I guess a bit too much.

After not doing so well at school, due to a few distractions, I moved on once again and went to live with my sister and her husband, whilst resitting my GCSE's. I was a bit of a lost cause really; I had not done well at school and had no idea what I wanted to do with myself. I feel like I had almost numbed all feeling and identity by giving myself away. It was strongly suggested by my family, that I became a nanny, so off I went to one of the top colleges in the country, Chiltern Nursery Training College. It was so posh. Perhaps the family thought that this place would sort me out, it was pretty much a "finishing school" but with a purpose. If you want to get an idea of what it was like think of Mary Poppins and you are halfway there.

My life was such a contradiction, on the weekends I would return to my hometown, meet up with my friends and my boyfriend. We would drink and go clubbing all weekend. My curiosity for party drugs exploded during this time. We partied hard, then come Monday morning, I would return to college, put on my uniform, starched my apron and hat, and be the good girl that I was. This continued for the next two years as I balanced the dark and the light precariously.

For 5 years, I thought I knew it all. I was invincible until it all came crumbling down around me as I was celebrating my 23rd birthday. On the third day of a bank holiday weekend in May, too much booze, too many late nights and the biggest cocktail of party drugs you could imagine, my body said: "that's enough". Yes, I was that girl, the one who had the drug-induced seizure in the middle of the dance floor, but it was not a Saturday night, it was a Sunday afternoon. I was so ashamed. It was the reality check I needed. I would not have listened to anyone else. It was the universe that had to intervene.

This was not my story. I was destined for another path.

It was my beloved's late mother who so kindly reminded me that we are all worthy of love and that the only way to find it is to follow your heart. Her words have stuck with me and guided my life since that moment. At the time, I was falling ever so deeply in love with her son. Luke and I took her words of ever-lasting love and ran with them. We allowed our connection to blossom and grow, but sadly the freedom to love like this was snatched away from us in the blink of an eye. I was deported from Australia. I had to return to England. I was given 30 days to tie up my affairs and end the life I had begun in Australia. I cried so much during that 22-hour long haul flight back to Heathrow. My heart was shattered and fragile.

I had been married to a man whom I thought I loved. We had had the fairy tale white wedding in the village church. The celebration was huge. I had been excited to start this adventure of a new life in a new land, thousands of kilometres from everything and everyone that I knew. It very quickly went from a dream wedding and romantic fairy-tale to a sad and lonely existence. I was not happy in the relationship, and very quickly fell back into the arms of alcohol to numb the pain of my heart. This was not what I wanted. I knew there was more for me but did not know how to find it. This is when Luke and I found each other. Our connection was immediate. I think we both knew from the moment our eyes met that we were meant to be together always. Within days of meeting, I had that feeling in my heart of deep and infinite love for this man. It was immense. So, leaving him so soon, made my heartache. I was in England, and he was in Australia, I felt the separation and distance between us greatly, but he vowed that he would follow me to England. We were apart for 6 months, we grew and nurtured our long-distance relationship, and once we were together again, it was electric. There were times whilst apart that I thought perhaps he would not come. How do I know that he is for real? I had to trust that I am worthy of loving and that he would be true. This is a little sentiment to my husband: My husband is the most loyal and genuine person I know. He loves me so passionately and deeply. Our souls are intertwined for eternity.

I have Sue (Luke's mum) to thank for guiding us to the truth of our hearts. She could see our love was true. We returned to Australia together, after a year or so in Europe. In 2009 we got married, on a beach in Fiji. It was so wonderfully perfect and simple. It was all about us, and our commitment and love for one another. It was around this time that I began to have an awareness of myself and my body, in different ways. I was taking care of myself physically, and I began to notice how I felt.

Our first baby was born in 2010. It was during my pregnancy that I felt more in my body than I ever had. I was connected to my body. I also experienced what it was like to have intuition. This was exciting and new to me. I had the strongest feeling and sense that I was pregnant with a baby boy. I was so intrigued by this new superpower that I had unlocked. My intuition grew stronger with each pregnancy, even more so with our middle child, our daughter. It was clear as day in a dream when she came to me as a baby earth star - looking exactly as she did when she was first born. In my dream she presented herself, saying "this is me, I am yours, I will see you at my birth". The day she was born, I was totally floored by how she was precisely as how she was in the dream. This beautiful, chunky, chubby baby, with the thickest, darkest hair and a little frown, it was magic. I was mesmerised. I knew now that there is more to life than meets the eye, but I guess I already knew that, didn't I?

After having our third baby, I was determined to regain my body. To get fit and to get strong. Along this path to health and wellness, I became quite involved with a company that along with nutritional products and food, they also empowered their tribe with coaching and personal development. I fell in love with it all. A light was switched on in me, and so I began to focus more on living a holistic life. I dusted off my aromatherapy bible that I had been given when I was 14 years old and bought my first quality essential oils. This is where my love for these high vibrational gifts from the earth began.

I was visiting a naturopath rather than a GP. I was learning so much, way more than I thought I knew. I was so taken with the holistic way of being. It honours every aspect of being and living, so much more than mainstream medicine. Not only was a light switched on, but my eyes were opening, and I could see the world differently to what I had previously. I had a desire and a hunger to evolve and expand some more. It is as though I was waking from a deep sleep. As I awoke, I could sense gentle nudges of instinct to follow. I am ready, and I am listening. It was through one of these personal development seminars that I heard about this chocolate drink, ceremonial grade cacao, and that when you drink it, it brings about feelings of bliss. It opens your heart to give and receive love. Of course, I was intrigued, but I actually left it there.

I had also learnt now that meditation was also good for me, so I was exploring that and finding a way that fit me best. Remembering I am mum of 3 kids. 'Me time' can be hard to find among nappies, sleep, food, and boobs. However, I made it work. I found my flow within the crazy. It was within a moment of meditation goodness that I got a very clear message, to go order myself some of that cacao that I had heard about. I had a strong and certain feeling that this cacao was necessary in my life (I understand why that is now). I'm not sure what I thought or felt with my first cup, but I followed the guidance on the website of KAKAO with a K. This drink tastes like nothing else I have ever tried. It is smooth, creamy, and so delicious. I was totally love struck. In March 2018, after a handful of personal ceremonies with cacao, I attended a group cacao ceremony with maybe 15 others. I had no idea what to expect, but I knew I had to attend. I knew that the energy of sharing this sacred chocolate drink would be something so very special. The cacao ceremony was hosted by Michael & Makenzie, the founders of KAKAO. As we entered the room, we each were smudged with sage and palo santo to ensure that the energy of the space was clear and pure. I knew no one. To say I was a little nervous was an understatement. But still, I knew there was a reason that I was there. So, I followed the call. Once in the room, I was handed a cup of cacao and found my seat. The ceremony was opened with a blessing and giving thanks to ancestors and elders. We each acknowledged the land and invited the spirit of cacao into our hearts. We were led through a guided meditation and then journeyed on our own while listening to music. This is something I had never done before. So many thoughts and questions began flying around in my head. I felt frustrated with myself that I wasn't feeling anything amazing and transformative, then the noise stopped, and all was still in my mind. I began to fly like a bird, in my mind's eye, I was up there, high above the clouds, soaring like an eagle. This then evolved, and I could feel the energy of the room. It was so joyous and happy and free. The collective feeling was immense. Next, I could see myself dancing in a circle with many others - all enjoying the vibe. From here, my hands moved out in front of me, ready to receive something. A sphere of golden white light appeared in my hands; its energy was electric. It was a gift of love and light. Curious, I asked "what is this for? What do I do with it?" The answer was clear, take some for yourself, and share the rest with the world.

At the end of the ceremony, we shared our experiences with the others in the circle. I found it comforting and fascinating sharing like this. I came away from this group ceremony so lit up and knowing that I wanted to share and replicate what I had experienced. For the next 12months, I kept this vision close in my heart, sharing with those who are close to me. I continued sitting in the ceremony by myself, sharing passionately with friends how incredible this cacao is. I felt it transform me each and every time I drank it. Creating a connection and establishing a relationship with the spirit of this beautiful plant medicine. I felt it heal me, connect me, and calm me.

One day, sitting in ceremony with cacao, and deep in meditation, I felt another clear nudge to look into Reiki. I was not sure why this came up for me at this time. But again, it was a firm knowing, so I trusted and followed this guidance. I did some research and found my reiki master teacher Loretta. I liked her vibe and felt aligned with her. I booked in, and within a few months, I had completed level 1,2 & 3 Usui Reiki. I was in love with this healing energy; it came so naturally and made so much sense to me. I loved it. I practiced on my children and my friends and was blown away with the power of this healing, and the love. It was magic. It was around the time of receiving my last attunement that I met Tina Pavlou through social media. A mutual friend introduced us. I met with Tina online for a reading, and we stayed in touch after that. In conversation, she mentioned that she would soon be travelling to Australia to teach Angelic Reiki. I had not heard of this before and having newly attuned to Usui Reiki and loving that, but again, I was curious. I wanted more. I booked in to discover what Angelic Reiki was all about. One thing I have noticed when I have received an attunement with Usui Reiki was the level of awareness and feeling of oneness elevate. I was excited to see what angelic Reiki would bring. It was an intensive three days of learning with attunements daily and giving and receiving healings. It was pure magic. So beautiful, loving, and gentle, yet so powerful at the same time. My intuition was in tune and alive. I began to feel, hear, and see so much during healings.

Soon after this, I attended a sound healing session. It was the first time I had ever done this too. It was amazing. At the end of the class, I got chatting with Angelique, who facilitated the sound bath. We discovered a mutual appreciation and love for ceremonial cacao. My friend who I had gone with, shared how I would like to start holding ceremonies. In jest, she said "you guys should get together", jokes aside, I had actually been dreaming of how amazing it would be to bring together a cacao ceremony and sound healing as one amazing experience. It would be magic. Ang and I got together and created this dream. Our first cacao ceremony and sound healing gathering was a month later, in line with the full moon. It was amazing and terrifying all at once; I had never imagined that I would be doing something like this, holding space, leading a cacao ceremony and meditation. It scared me so much but also gave me so much joy. We went on to host these magical circles each month over the next year. With each one, I grew a little more; our events were incredible. Ang and I worked so well together, Yin and Yang. We balanced each other's energies. I adored sharing the magic and bliss that cacao has to offer those open to receive. To be witness to their unique experience was such an honour.

Keen to grow some more, I was super excited to learn that Tina was coming back to Australia to teach again. This would give me the ability to be attuned to level 3 and 4 and become a Master in Angelic Reiki. I was so ready and open to receive this next level of pure light and love from the Angelic Kingdom.

Again, it was an intensive course of healing; this one knocked me around a lot. I shed so many layers. I cried so many tears, and I welcomed the healing. It was truly incredible to feel so held, so loved and supported, not just by the Angels, but also the other beautiful souls who were also there. A sisterhood, just like when I was at boarding school. It is as though I have come full circle and reclaimed myself.

A poem by Maria Sabina – Mexican Curandera (Medicine women and poet)

> Cure yourself, with the light of the sun and the
>   rays of the moon. With the sound of the river
>   and the waterfall.
> With the swaying of the sea and the fluttering of
>   birds.
> Heal yourself, with the mint and the mint leaves,
>   with neem and eucalyptus.
> Sweeten yourself with lavender, rosemary and
>   chamomile.
> Hug yourself with a cocoa bean and a touch of
>   cinnamon.
> Put love in tea instead of sugar, and take it looking
>   at the stars.
> Heal Yourself with the kisses that the wind gives
>   and the hugs of the rain.
> Get strong with bare feet on the ground and with
>   everything that is born from it.
> Get smarter every day by listening to your

intuition, looking at the world with the eye of
your forehead.

Jump, dance, sing, so that you live happier.

Heal yourself with beautiful love, and always
remember you are the medicine.

ABOUT THE AUTHOR

CHARLOTTE NEWHAM

Starseed what lights you up?

Charlotte is a Mother, a Lover, and an Earth Angel.

Charlotte's love is to guide people back to their hearts and bring about a reconnection within themselves and those around them.

Charlotte is an Angelic Reiki Master and Teacher, ambassador and guardian ceremony facilitator for KAKAO. She is a space holder of sacred women's circles who loves to bring people together, finding so much joy in connecting hearts and souls.

She uses Angelic Reiki to channel love and light from the Angelic Kingdom and also draws on the power of plant medicine ceremonial grade cacao also known as the gift from the Gods which assists in opening hearts and bringing about feelings of bliss and unconditional love.

She is also a passionate lover of essential oils; her home always smells incredible and has the most wonderful energy.

Through the discovery of these gifts of self-devotion, she has learnt the true value of loving oneself so deeply.

> "When I surrender into these gifts, my heart and my soul sing. With a deep knowing and passion of purpose that I am to share with as many as I can, with who are willing and open".

— *CHARLOTTE NEWHAM*

If you'd like to follow me my details are below;

Email: soulfulenergyconnection@gmail.com

instagram.com/nurtured_heart_living

7

DEE O'CONNOR

*A*ll my life, I have felt different. Never really feeling, until late into adulthood, that I could be my true authentic self. Always feeling that I had to hide parts of myself in order to fit in. Never fully allowing myself to express my true nature.

Now I realise that I am not alone. There are so many children in this world that are seeking others they feel they can connect to; people that will understand their intuitive gifts. But, when we are young, we think we are alone - especially if you grew up in a Catholic Irish family. We think we are strange. We think we are different. Never truly realising that there are so many out there feeling exactly the same way.

When did society become so frightened of those who were spiritually in touch with every aspect of themselves? So many children feel powerless and spend their entire childhoods dimming their light, feeling that if they really and truly show their true nature, they will not be accepted. I was one of those children.

When I was a young child, I could never understand why people wanted to hurt each other. I could never understand why there was always so much anger or unkindness. I see so many children of friends and family that are the kindest children, going through exactly the same situation, being wonderfully sensitive souls and struggling to cope in the school environment. They are told to not be so sensitive when their sensitivity and kindness is their absolute strength. They are left feeling weak because they struggle to deal with the harshness of others. Children also struggle with the school system, as many of them have different ways of learning, and they don't always fit into the box, leading to frustration, low self-esteem and anxiety. As the saying goes, they are "a square peg in a round hole".

I spent the early part of my school life crying, wishing I was at home with my mum and my new baby sister. I found the school environment difficult and struggled to fit in. I think I wasn't quite prepared, having been an only child right up until I started school. I certainly wasn't prepared for the strict nuns at the Catholic primary school trying to force me to write with my right hand when I was left-handed!

Nonetheless, I found one real true friend who was so incredibly kind. Then we were suddenly moving home, and I had to change schools! I was utterly devastated leaving her as we had become really close. My mother didn't drive so we went to visit her once after that, but as we were so young, and my mother was busy working, I never saw her again. It's strange, I never forgot her, and it took me years to meet someone I connected with like that again on such a deep level. I was back to feeling alienated again. Feeling that I had to search again for someone I could really truly connect to.

I wasn't one of the cool kids, I wasn't one of the best dressed, but I had everything I needed. I was just me, but after some years in school, suddenly I didn't feel as if I was enough - until I found dancing! My goodness, how I loved to dance. Being able to let go, fully embrace the dance, and glide through the air as if I were limitless, weightless even! I danced when I was happy. I danced when I was sad. I danced all the way to school. I danced all the way home. Nothing could stop me; it was all I wanted to do. It brought me such joy. Even the day I lost my beloved nan, who was a truly special person and had an enormously kind heart. Even then when I heard the sad news of her passing away, the only thing I wanted to do to feel better was dance, as I felt it was the only true way I was able to express myself.

I am glad to say, by the time I had left secondary school and dancing at 16, I had made some of my closest friends that have been with me through the rest of my life, and I truly cherish each and every one of them.

Going back to when I was very young, I had what seemed to others to be a very vivid imagination. Many things I could not share with my parents! I would dream I was out of my body, flying around the earth. I would dream that I was walking upside down on the ceiling. I would even stand at the top of the stairs and, only for the big radiator at the bottom, I was convinced I could fly! I almost took a step many times to see if it was true, as my dreams felt so incredibly real! I really truly believed that I could fly. It felt that I was always leaving my body. I dread to think what would have happened if I had tried it out. There was always a little voice right at the last minute saying 'no don't do it!' I could never shake off my dreams, as they felt so incredibly real. It felt like I could go anywhere I wanted when I was put to bed at night.

I even pulled the bedside lamp out of the wall as a child, trying to use the light with a white sheet over my head and carrying my baby sister from her cot, into my parents' bedroom. I was sleepwalking, but emanating an angelic being of light because I had obviously had many experiences of it as a young child.

But now of course, there is so much I understand. There is so much I wish I had known as a young child. It took me 44 years to have a conversation with my father, to ask had anyone else ever had any psychic abilities in the family and has anyone seen spirits. I was so frightened of being treated like I was crazy. So frightened he would look at me and say "what on earth are you talking about". But instead, he said "Of course! Your nan saw spirits all the time. She would just say calmly "they are just going about their business; they are not doing any harm!" I nearly fell over! I could not believe it! All those years feeling strange, feeling like there was something wrong with me. I tried to numb my abilities as I got into later childhood, as I did not want to feel different. I spent the next 40 years saying in my head "I know you are there, but don't scare me, don't show yourself to me. I don't want to see you.

This really kicked in when I was in my younger years at school (only about 5 or 6) when there were boys telling frightening ghost stories at school, and telling me that there were evil spirits under my bed and if I had my arms or legs out of the covers they would get me. So then spirits just became something to fear. It is common that once psychic abilities are not acknowledged by the time you get to about 10, that they can shut down.

And so it began! The years of denial and refusing to acknowledge spirit, thinking I could not possibly talk to someone about what I felt or saw, so I spent every day making sure the light was on enough in my room, that I was never in the dark, that I would never have shadows in my room and there would always be enough light that I would never be caught out by these evil spirits in the dark that could harm me, just like those children had warned me of previously. Of course, they were just trying to scare me, but it worked!

I often had dreams, not always pleasant, things I could not understand or explain, but now as I have grown older and now I have opened up to my abilities again, I understand so much of what they were all about.

So I felt I carried this secret for years; Hiding a part of myself trying to fit in, keeping in line with the other kids. I went through my teens like any normal teenager. After school, I went to college and then got a job in the City as a legal PA but did not feel fulfilled, and promised myself that when I had children, I would try to do something that lit me up and made my soul happy! I got married at 27 and moved into our new house.

It really wasn't until I had issues in my thirties with fertility that I sought out a reflexologist, I was desperate to have children, and after five years of not falling pregnant, this was my first introduction to energy work. I had been on contraception for 11 years to help painful periods, and when I finally came off them, they diagnosed me with endometriosis, polycystic ovaries and fibroids. I went through treatment and minor procedures to help resolve those issues.

Even though I had dumbed down some of my abilities, I always remained claircognisance though. Just knowing things. Not understanding how I knew, I just did, and I always felt I could read people so well, but there were times I did not follow my intuition and what my gut was telling me, and unfortunately, I learned the hard way. But they were always valuable lessons, even though they were painful ones. They taught me to truly trust myself and to stay away from those that do not want the best for me. I learned you couldn't make people like you no matter how kind you are, and no matter how hard you try, so you are best to focus your energy on those that will love you fearlessly. What I am grateful for though, is these situations taught me I had to listen to that gut feeling and to not ignore my intuition. I had to listen to that knowing and trust it. I also at a later age, now understand that I would predict some things in the future. I would get flashes of circumstances, and then they would play out in future years down the line.

I became fascinated when my body responded amazingly well to this new energy work I was having, it regulated my cycles, and it really de-stressed my body. After five years of stress, trial and tribulation and with the help of a low dose of Clomiphene, I finally became pregnant. This was my proudest achievement becoming a mother, and I saw my baby boy as a miracle as he was much longed for after five years. I enjoyed my beautiful boy for a year or two, and then we decided to try to conceive again.

After miscarrying in early stages three times and with Clomiphene not being as effective this time, I experimented with reflexology, acupuncture and reiki. And then I had my second beautiful baby boy. I had never wanted a career as a child or a teenager (perhaps a nurse as I always found myself being a nurturer and wanting to help people), but more than anything all I wanted to be was a mother. Always! But I never wanted to work nights as a nurse, as my mum worked in a nursing home, and I hated her not being there when she went to work on the night shift.

So, after a few years of enjoying my two gorgeous boys, I had this deep, deep longing and desire, feeling like there was supposed to be three children at the table, so we tried for a third child. We tried naturally and had another three miscarriages, one natural, then I went down the route of IVF and then lost again naturally afterwards.

I was very in tune with my body and always knew very quickly when something was wrong, but I had truly believed that the last pregnancy was going to make it. But unfortunately, we had moved into a new house with an old boiler, and I could not light the ignition one morning, so I got a match, and there was a loud bang, and I got a dreadful fright. I had sizzled my hair and my eyelashes, but most of all, I had experienced quite a shock.

Unfortunately, only an hour had passed, and I started to bleed. Knowing that something was wrong with my pregnancy, I rushed to my gynaecologist but sadly he could no longer find a heartbeat. I was numb. I'll always remember that day. I opened the front door, and the garden was covered in white feathers, I also had had my first visual angelic sighting out of the periphery of my eye since childhood, and even for no logical reason, my kitchen lights made the shape of angel wings on the ceiling, but disappeared after a while, and it never happened again.

My husband wanted to stop trying for another baby, but I could not emotionally let the idea go. I was convinced that child was meant to be here, and I felt so strongly that there were meant to be three so I really struggled with that decision. I was also utterly convinced it was a girl, and I had dreamt about her. I will always remember, for ages afterwards my boys would say to me, "are we going to have a baby sister yet". They had never known of the pregnancy or the miscarriage or anything about a little girl. It's like they also picked up on that someone else was supposed to be part of our family too, and she was witnessed in our home some years ago, and I know she is always watching over our boys.

Through the struggles of all those miscarriages, my self-esteem had taken quite a knocking and knowing I had to move forward without another child, I for some reason could not get this third child out of my head. It wasn't me being greedy or ungrateful; it just genuinely felt that someone was missing. That it wasn't how it was meant to be.

I had thought about how I lucky I was to have my boys, so I really wanted to be able to help other women. Once I had gone through the 'who am I to think I could do that' stage, I eventually trained as a Reflexologist. But whenever I was doing Reflexology sessions on others, they would feel Reiki in my hands, and when I started to move my hands over their body and held them in certain areas, they could feel it without me touching them, and I had never been attuned. So, I realised this was a natural ability that I needed to explore further and learn to work with the energy as I had clearly been blessed with it.

The longing for this child I had never brought into this world became too much, and I remember ringing a gifted healer I had come to know and asked her for her help because I could not let go of this obsession with this child. I had a really profound experience during the session, and I was utterly overjoyed and said to her after the session, "I saw her! Mother Mary held out a baby and gifted her to me, so I'm going to have another baby" I was utterly overjoyed! This wonderfully amazing intuitive healer was quick to stop me in my tracks and said: "be patient, let's wait, as maybe your interpretation was incorrect and let's see what happens". I had jumped to conclusions as I was aching for this child, but she was so right.

Months went by, and I suddenly realised looking back over the previous months that all the longing, all the desire of being desperate for this baby had disappeared. THAT was the healing. It had just all melted away, which I was truly surprised about as I had been so utterly desperate for this child.

So then I found myself being really drawn to learn Rahanni Angelic reiki after my experiences with the energy in my hands, but it wasn't until I attuned to Rahanni Angelic reiki that I had the rawest but beautiful experience I will always remember as if it was today.

I lay on the massage table for one of the students to practice on me, and she was obviously an amazingly powerful healer. I started to see intuitively my womb being cleared of the trauma of all the miscarriages, and tears started to stream down my face. It was very emotional, but then I heard as clear as day with my eyes closed as she was standing right next to me, but no one knew I heard the words "it's ok mama I'm here. I'm with you". The next minute one of the other students who sees spirits said: "look, look there's a little girl beside the bed. Look"! I had heard her, and he had seen her, her beaming angelic presence beside my bed, helping me let go of the pain of losing her and the other losses I had experienced. They knew nothing of her, or my miscarriage, but she was the right age of what she would have been since I had had my miscarriage.

After that experience I found myself at a spiritual group and twice without anyone knowing of what had happened previously, a little girl came through them with the message that she wanted me to be happy and to dance again. (Unfortunately, I had stopped dancing at 16 as I had come down with glandular fever and was so ill for a few months, that I was too exhausted to dance and felt weak and drained when I would attempt it, so I never went back). They also told me that when I would do my healing, she would be there to help me.

I understood that day what my experience in that previous healing had meant when I had thought she was going to come to me. The longing went away because she WAS coming to me. Just in a different form to what I had previously believed.

My longing for her had sought me to look for healing to seek to open up and connect with the angelic realm again just as I had as that little girl. I understood she was never meant to stay; she was just meant to lead me back to connect again and open up spiritually to the angels by healing myself.

I have had beautiful experiences with spirits with a friend's grandmother who I connected to, and I sat at my desk, and I could feel this gentle stroking feeling over the top of both my hands. Just a gentle brushstroke down both of my hands and then across my face. When I told my friend what had happened, she said 'yes that's what she does'. That's her sign. I was not scared as she was a kind and gentle lady, and I am grateful that she gifted me that experience to learn in a way that I was not frightened. I am grateful to have many incredible friends and family who I have known since school that only as we have gotten older have opened up and shared their spiritual experiences privately. But some will only be learning of my experiences in this book for the first time, as I hid so much over the years.

I have been on quite a journey since then. I have learnt Angelic Reiki, I became a meditation teacher, I took every Theta practitioner and teacher class that I could at the time, opening up my world to finding out about amazing and inspiring spiritual gurus such as Wayne Dyer, Deepak Chopra etc. and so many more. I have become an Access Bars and EFT Practitioner and Emotional release Facilitator. I met Tina Pavlou (the Angel Lady) when we took some of the Theta courses together. It has been amazing to watch her grow into the truly amazing teacher that she is and I love to visit the Goddess Rooms for reiki swaps with the phenomenal community she has built there of amazing healers and intuitives.

I get such incredible joy, and my soul is happy when I channel Angelic Reiki or connect into a Theta state for healing. You feel such compassion and love. It can only be described as being engulfed in a warm protective blanket of love and protection. I feel incredibly blessed to have awakened to such beautiful healing modalities that can take us instantaneously out of a state of fear or emotional pain. The most important lesson is you have to heal yourself before you can heal others. It's a journey of transformation but a very beautiful one.

I want to help anyone I can to truly connect to who they are. To empower women and to help children embrace their true authenticity so that they can accept their unique gifts and talents and accept themselves for who they truly are. There are so many incredible sensitive children in this world with God-given gifts and talents, who would not be bullied if they truly accepted themselves for who they were.

I look forward to this journey I am on, and I look forward to empowering children so that they do not have to hide their true selves, so they can fully accept themselves in their full authenticity.

There's been great resistance along the way as that little girl had decided that she was not going to ever be accepted for who she was, until she realised there are so many here that have exactly the same abilities that are hiding away, afraid of not being accepted.

So I say to you. If you are hiding who you truly are in all your magnificence. The fear is just an illusion. When you open up to this path, you will find there are hundreds of thousands all over the world just in Theta alone that have the same abilities that you have. It actually became more painful for me to hide who I was, as I was bursting to accept myself wholly and completely and to live without the fear of being judged or treated as strange.

So be brave because there is nothing more beautiful than the feeling of being who you truly are. What lies on the other side of fear is truly magical. I wasn't blessed with my experiences or my abilities for them to be ignored, for them to be wasted. I was here to use them, to help others become empowered for what is their God-given gifts. I actually am now at the stage in my life that it would be more painful for me to leave this world having never had the bravery to be who I was meant to be and help who I am meant to help.

So be brave, be bold, be strong. Be ready to be who you are. The fear is just an old story, and it's time to let it go. Shine bright and be the light that you are. Always be the light in another's darkness and always be the rainbow in someone else's cloud. Always lead from your heart. Master and nurture that incredible mind of yours and nourish and cherish your body.

Lockdown in the Spring of 2020, with all its challenges, has also produced so many blessings for which I am grateful for. It has allowed me to develop a much deeper spiritual practise daily through meditation, bringing about profound changes which helped me to transform any stress or worry I may have had into inspired ways of supporting others from a place of calm and balance - learning the full benefits of starting every day with meditation in order to bring about a positive mindset, to hold space and fully support others. This daily practice also has trained my lungs to take full breaths, breathing deeply instead of the bad habit I had formed of shallow breathing, enabling my lung capacity to be stronger than ever.

I also finally embraced a vegan lifestyle during this period and started keeping a gratitude journal, training your mind into a positive state to where your attention goes, energy flows. I also promoted a healthy mindset through watching uplifting films, empowering books and not engaging in negative media unless absolutely necessary.

The other positive experiences I have had is entering into the magical world of learning everything there is about Essential Oils as I have been on a mission to live as natural a lifestyle I possible can. This time gave me the time required to benefit from so much knowledge and wisdom from homeopaths, naturopaths and healers who have worked with essential oils for years. Nature has everything we need in order to support our bodies emotionally and physically that we just needed to remember. They have been used in ancient times, including Egyptian and biblical times.

Lockdown also allowed me to slow down, reconnect with nature and enjoy the simple things in life appreciating the garden and the countryside.

It allowed us to become more present, it allowed me to give so much support to those who are looking to find a different way of living life whether it be chemical-free or learning how to meditate. It has given me time to meditate and journal so easily, allowing me to start bringing together (coming soon) programmes which I hope will benefit many children and their families.

It has enabled others to look for natural ways for managing stress and anxiety through the loss of their jobs, or the illness of a loved one and more people are meditating and opening their minds than ever before, and for that I am grateful. The difference from beginning to the end of a group of people meditating is amazing, and seeing the transformation in others on their journey is incredibly beautiful to watch. One friend of mine who was new to meditation while she was in hospital saw her blood pressure drop while being monitored which led to her not being prescribed blood pressure tablets, by simply meditating and de-stressing her body.

It also allowed the earth to recover from the lack of respect that man had previously shown it hopefully allowing more individuals to become conscious, mindful and to stop and think about what changes they could personally make to make a difference to help us live in a greener, cleaner more empowered world instead of coral reefs being damaged and plastics overtaking our oceans. It has also allowed people to slow down and to reconnect and focus more on relationships with their families instead of always chasing things that are not important. So many have re-evaluated their lives and how they were previously living. It truly has been a big wake-up call in so many ways for those that are willing to change. More people have become more conscious and more mindful in their way of living.

I am a very different person now to when I started my spiritual journey, and I am proud of who I am, the heart that I have and the kindness within me. Everything I have gone through in my life; I am grateful for the lessons. And anyone that hurt me, well I thank them as they were my greatest teachers. I learnt so much from them. I had to heal myself until I felt nothing but compassion and forgiveness. That doesn't mean it would be right for me to continue to be around their negative energy - that is not necessarily what is right and best for me, but I can choose to let go of that pain or anger in my body that will only hurt ME and lead to dis-ease in the body. Forgiveness is our greatest protection. Unresolved emotions can lead to dis-ease in the body if left unhealed, so let go of resentments and keep your vibration high. Low vibrational thoughts only weaken your immunity and lead to unhappiness and pain. Never be defined by anything that happened to you in your life. You are stronger than you think and braver than you know. Leave an impact in the world and make it a better place. Pay kindness forward. Be love. Always. I look forward to connecting with you. xxx

ABOUT THE AUTHOR

DEE O'CONNOR

Dee is a wife and mother of two teenage boys and lives in Hertfordshire. She loves to travel and explore the world. She loves the sun, sea, nature and animals.

She absolutely adores children, and if she had not had fertility issues, she would have had many more children.

She describes children as filling her heart with joy and lighting up her world. She strongly believes every child deserves happiness.

Dee is a gifted and talented healer who is passionate about empowering those who have spent their lives hiding their true authenticity, gifts and talents. What she wishes most is for children of today to see mindfulness, meditation, affirmations and yoga taught in schools. She strongly believes that these should be taught to promote a balanced and positive mindset after personally witnessing increased levels of school anxiety in many friends' children and family members' children. This is mostly exacerbated by learning difficulties in young people or bullying, often leading to depression and self-harm. She wishes to help support them to become happy, balanced and confident individuals. She is in the midst of writing a programme to help support children completely love and accept themselves.

Dee is an Angelic Reiki Master and a ThetaHealing® Practitioner and Teacher, as well as a teacher in meditation, a master in Usui and Rahanni Angel Reiki, an Access Consciousness Bars Facilitator and an Emotional Release Facilitator.

She is also a Representative for Young Living Essential Oils and Tropic Natural Skincare to help people live a chemical-free lifestyle and help balance women's hormones. She has been on a journey of self- discovery, attending many courses and learning many modalities which have helped her become the person she is today and she is here to help others reach their true potential.

ThetaHealing® is a meditation technique where limiting beliefs held in our sub-conscious are transformed and changed to empowering and positive beliefs whilst in a theta brainwave. We even hold limiting beliefs from our ancestors in our DNA, and it is now scientifically proven that trauma experienced by our ancestors is held in our DNA. Theta healing is widely accepted and used in Japan's medical field.

Dee is also a qualified Reflexologist trained in spinal, maternity, baby and toddler reflexology.

Dee is passionate about helping those who have lost their confidence and self-esteem and helping them to overcome their beliefs and programs in order to help them to step into their power. She will work intuitively and compassionately to guide you gently into the depths of those programs, in order to free you from those beliefs which are self-sabotaging and preventing you from living the life you desire, full of joy and abundance.

If you would like to speak with Dee to discover how she may be able to help you or your child, she would love to connect with you for a free discovery call.

Contact: E-mail dee@deeoconnor.com
Website: www.deemoconnor.com
Facebook Group: The Natural Path for Women
https://www.facebook.com/groups/435470070656408

facebook.com/deirdre.oconnor.332
instagram.com/thenaturalpathforwomen

8

ELIZABETH BARON

I was born feeling like I was a QUEEN. My story is about how I forgot her and how I reclaimed her.

My name is Liz Baron, and I am an intuitive business and life coach, Thetahealing® practitioner, lawyer and businesswoman. I am clairsentient (feeling), clairvoyant (seeing), clairaudient (hearing), but my strongest psychic sense is claircognisance (knowing).

My superpower is being able to see the highest potential in all things: I can view a building and immediately know how beautiful it could be aesthetically, physically and energetically, if only its owners could tap into what it was meant to be in all of its glory. I can examine a business and know how global it could be and how many lives it could touch, if only the right captains were steering the ship at the helm, carrying out certain actions at the right time. Most excitingly, I see a glimpse of how powerful a human being can be in their future, soaring like an eagle, if only they can allow themselves to reach their highest potential; their true soul's purpose.

I bring these gifts into my coaching: I help people who feel lost and trapped, and who know they are meant for more; who know deep down that they have a bigger mission on this planet, get clarity on what their purpose is.

In my experience, many people jump into starting a new business, a new life or a new goal, hoping it is going to solve all their problems. They are then frustrated that they don't get the results they want. Why? Because they're trying to create something new, but with the same mindset they have always had.

I know this because I learned things the hard way. Yes, I did mindset work, but I ignored a lot of signs that I needed to do deeper, inner work.

My clients are based across the world: UK, Australia, Dubai, USA and so on, but they all present with what I call similar 'symptoms'. It will be interesting to see if you can recognise them in yourself. They are: freezing like a rabbit in the headlights, self-sabotage, unworthiness, lack of self-love and self-worth, giving power away, procrastination, over-giving, people-pleasing, failing to finish what they started, imposter syndrome, fear of visibility, hustling to survive, burned out, low confidence, suffer from comparisonitis and so on.

I recognise these traits, and I can help clients to remove them because I too have suffered from all of them at various stages in my life.

I therefore approach things in reverse with my clients now: we start with transformational mindset and deep inner healing work. Once a client is fully in their power, and we have removed the many layers built over their lifetime of social and family conditioning, emotional trauma and wounds, past lives, soul wounds and so on, they can move forward with ease and clarity. From that place, I support them to re-envision their life and create a strategy to get them there. From here, they are learning about the Queen version of themselves and stepping into their true purpose.

I am also still a practising lawyer and help coaches, healers, therapists, online businesses, and influencers to be legally protected in their businesses. This is part of creating strong boundaries and foundations for businesses from the get-go, in the same way that we do the healing work before laying the foundations for a solid life and business.

I have other law businesses which I run with my soon-to-be husband; all of which have contributed to my knowledge of what it takes to run a successful business.

I am currently project managing and renovating a grade II listed farmhouse in Wales, which will be our country haven and family home in 2021.

Most days, I wake up when I'm ready in a morning without an alarm, and I spend each day doing what I want. Some days I work all day. Others, I work on myself all day. I sometimes take a few hours off to sit in the garden with a glass of wine, because the sun is out, and I want to enjoy it. I drive to Kent to see the wonderful goddess Tina Pavlou and the beautiful souls at the Goddess Rooms for a whole week once every month because I know it is so good for my soul. I have created this blessed lifestyle; one of more peace, joy and high vibration, and I am beyond grateful.

Have I reached the end of my journey? Hell no. Do I have more inner work and healing to do? Absolutely! But I have come a long way. Let me take you on a journey...

WHERE IT ALL BEGAN

I had this feeling when I was very young that I was 'special' in some way. I could see energy in the air and all around me. I could see angels. I was once saved by angels when I tripped on a pillow and fell from the top of a flight of stairs to the bottom of the stairs in my home. I tumbled down and then seemingly glided to the bottom, completely unharmed, landing on the bottom step sat upright.

I had this Queenly feeling about me; like I was some sort of princess that had been swapped at birth and ended up with the wrong family. I used to think: *"a mistake has been made here and I'm supposed to be in a palace"*. To be honest, I was quite disappointed about where I'd ended up (apologies to mum and dad).

I was living with my family in a little town in Lancashire in the North of England, with my parents and three siblings. Like many families, we're not perfect, but they are very loving, and I have nothing to complain about. I just didn't feel like I'd been born into the right place. I never felt like I fit in.

As the years went by, two patterns emerged:

1) I dimmed my light to fit in; and

2) I was taken advantage of and controlled.

I was bullied a lot at school, and I did everything I could to fit in with the other children – even if that meant pretending to be someone completely different. I was also taken advantage of a lot. It started with small things, like kids asking to borrow money from me with promises that they'd pay it back. They never did and laughed at me when I asked for the money back, saying I was pathetic.

School was difficult for me. I loved to learn, but I found the dynamic difficult. When I came home after school each day, I would lose myself in playing the piano and writing songs and stories. They transported me into another world that was brighter than the one I was living.

This continued throughout my teens and twenties. I never considered myself to be very academic or clever, but I figured that writing songs and stories wasn't a proper way to 'adult' and that I had to find myself a corporate career. I just kept thinking: "if I can just keep my head down and work really hard, then everything will be OK. I'll just make sure I'm successful, and then I'll prove to everyone that I'm worthy of being here (on this planet)".

DARK YEARS OF THE SOUL – PART 1

Aged 15, I ended up in a relationship with a guy a couple of years' older than me in my last year of high school. For the first time in my life, I became ever so slightly popular. "Who's *that guy you were just with outside the school gates, Liz? He's hot*" classmates would say. "He's *my college boyfriend, and he's got his own moped.*" I would say proudly, but the fairy tale turned out to be something quite different.

That relationship lasted for seven and a half years and severely impacted my life, my confidence and my self-worth. He was ever such a Prince Charming, and he was also a narcissist. I endured seven years of emotional, mental, psychological and financial abuse. I can't begin to tell you how bad this relationship was, and it is not for this book, but it broke me on a number of levels. Let's call him PC (AKA Prince Charming) for ease.

Throughout the 7.5 years, my intuition was screaming at me to get out, but I was loyal and manipulated, so I ignored my gut and my body, and I stayed. I threw myself even deeper into academic studies in order to achieve. And to survive.

I decided to go into law fundamentally so that I could help people and 'bring about change and justice'. Elle Woods in the film Legally Blonde made it seem so attractive as a career prospect, and I set about that path.

I also thought it would make me rich, successful and well-connected, and from there, I would set up my own business to change lives. I didn't know where this came from, or what business that would be, but I knew it deep down inside. I knew that being a lawyer was an important part of the picture, but it wasn't the entire picture, nor the end game. With that, I carried out my law and psychology degree and went on to train as a barrister at law school in Manchester. I borrowed £25,000 on top of my degree student loans to train, but I was convinced that it was all OK because I'd make it all back – and some.

PC's family said to me: *"you can't be a barrister Liz, because you're too nice"*. That comment fuelled a fire within me to make it happen even more.

By this point, I had moved in with PC. Over the years, he pulled me apart from my family. He would say that all the problems between us were because of my family and they were trying to separate us. So, we eventually rented a flat together. I would leave the house at 6.30am daily to be at law school for around 8am, and I would be back later at night (the whole year was intense and purposely so, to show us what the life of a barrister would actually be like) so I spent little time with him, and that suited me because I'd otherwise be too busy to listen to my raging gut.

I spent whole days drafting opinions or carrying out mock trials, trying to navigate through a world of young men and women whose parents were chief of police, barristers, judges or politicians, and whose daddy had given them a credit card to purchase the latest Christian Louboutin shoes. They were bound to get a place in a barristers' chambers with ease, because of their connections. I, on the other hand, was the only child in my family so far to go to university and dressed head to toe in Primark or Asda's George apparel, wishing desperately that I was one of 'them' so that life was easier.

By this point, I was six years into my relationship, and I was sure PC was having an affair with a close family member, but PC denied it and said it was all in my head. I felt battered and bruised by this emotional manipulation at home and all the 'competition' on my law course. I was so tired of trying hard all the time. I had anxiety and was having regular panic attacks. I had IBS (irritable bowel syndrome) and was borderline diabetic. I was ill all the time.

My life was also gripped by self-sabotage. I was set for an A grade in my Psychology A-level and then sabotaged the final exam by failing to properly read the question which resulted in a D grade, giving myself an overall grade B. I was about to pass my driving test and then failed spectacularly right at the very end by driving over the corner of the pavement as I was pulling up to the driving test centre. I was one or two percent off a 2:1 degree and one mark off a Very Competent on the Bar course. In other words, I would work really hard to be successful and then sabotage it right at the last minute, making life a lot harder for myself.

I managed to scrape through and pass the course, but now it was time to look for a job. I'd had a job at the weekends, evenings and holidays since the age of 12, so I was not afraid of hard work, but this would be my first 'proper' job.

THE CRUMBLING

The sad thing is that I didn't even apply to a barristers' chambers. I told myself "you're *simply not good enough Liz. You'll just face rejection after rejection, so what's the point in even trying.*" I should add that I'd found out that at that point in time, I was the youngest female barrister in England and Wales qualifying at the age of 21, but I still felt that I was utterly useless and worthless. It fills me with great sadness to reflect now on how I used to feel about myself and talk to myself, but it's the truth.

I struggled to get a job and was offered one in Manchester for £12,000 per year. I could earn that in my job at Asda working full time, and I calculated that I'd spend at least half of that in driving to and parking in Manchester every day, plus tax, so it wasn't worth the effort. I carried out multiple voluntary and short-term expenses paid roles and started writing legal articles at home for a small sum of money to keep going until I found a better role.

I tried working in immigration, criminal, family and mental health law (being the areas of law where I believed I could help people), but being an empath, I struggled to make it through the day with the intensity of the energy. I realised I was too sensitive for this type of work and set about finding more commercial work that would be less emotionally charged and people-focused.

PC was allegedly working a lot of shifts and was never home. I spent most days at home, trawling through job sites and trying to work out how I could earn money as bills piled through the door. I couldn't sign on the dole for benefits because I had PC living at home who was, in theory, earning enough money to support me, only he never seemed to have any money.

My parents (who didn't earn much money) started to bring me cans of baked beans, a loaf of bread and toilet rolls because I couldn't afford food. I was trying all sorts of network marketing schemes hoping one of them would pay off so I could earn some money. I was now £37K in debt after law school and in my mind, was supposed to be in a barristers' chambers earning plenty of money to pay back those loans. Instead, I was deeply depressed and in a scruffy, rented terraced house struggling to survive. I was so far from a Queen, and I felt the most unsafe I had ever felt in my life.

One night in early April 2010, something happened with PC. I stayed up all night working out what I was going to do, and it hit me that I was at rock bottom. My life had officially crumbled. I couldn't get any lower than this.

I knew in my soul that if I didn't leave now, I would die; not because he would physically kill me, but because I felt so low about myself that I wanted to die. Yet, there was a part of me that also wanted to fight on.

When PC left for work the next day, I packed a bag and left everything. I went to live with my aunty for a few months and reassessed my life. PC kept trying to get me back. I hid behind my aunty's sofa a few times so he didn't know I was home. I knew I had to leave my hometown and get away full stop if I was to fully break away and start afresh (and not go back to him like I did several times before).

THE RISING

I got a job interview for a legal consultancy four hours' drive away in Bristol, and I got the job. It was the best thing that had happened for some time and would enable me to move away and have the fresh start I was banking on. Around the same time, I also started a relationship with an old school friend who I had always secretly fancied, and as I moved to Bristol full-time, he would drive down to see me every weekend, before he eventually moved down to be with me full-time and later married (in 2012). Let's call him SF (AKA School Friend).

The legal consultancy was a small boutique firm specialising in construction law. It was a very specialist area of law, and they told me that as long as I understood contracts, I would be fine. In truth, it took me a few months to settle into the role, attempting to navigate my first proper role as a 'lawyer', living away from home for the first time, not knowing anyone and trying to move on from what I'd been through.

The managing director (the Boss) expected a lot of me as I had come into the role in a higher position than most people, because of my barrister training. I spent lunchtimes and evenings reading up on this new area of law and trying to make a good impression. Some days I would get it right. Other days, my boss would say *"a four-year-old could do a better job"*. I was homesick, struggling, and I wondered if law was for me. I thought about giving it all up and becoming an interior designer (I'm not joking).

SF eventually moved down to Bristol, and I felt happier having someone I knew around. I started to get into the role more at work and eventually achieved promotions and pay rises (even though it was touch and go, and the Boss admitted they were close to sacking me at one stage). I made some new friends and my partner and I got engaged. I was now aged 23 and feeling like things were finally happening.

At the same time, however, I was under a lot of pressure. I was working a lot of hours and trying to be someone completely different to please the Boss. He was a 'Jekyll and Hyde' character: one minute, he loved me and was giving me a £10,000 pay rise. The next, he was saying I was useless and would have to take cases away from me. I honestly don't believe that I was so competent one day and so incompetent the next, and my colleagues said to me they'd never seen a member of staff be as good as me at my role, and yet get so berated by the Boss. It was like he was the puppet master holding my strings and we would play this dance of up and down, elation then humiliation, promotion then degradation and so on.

It got to a position where the Boss would call me into his office at 9am sharp, just before a staff meeting, and shout at me for half an hour so loudly that the entire office could hear him. We would then walk together to the staff meeting at 9.30am where the whole room would be looking at me and asking if I was OK. I felt so much shame.

It would continue like that for the rest of the week, and he would shout at others too. Many new members of staff were sacked in the first week, so to that extent, I was grateful that I'd survived as long as I had. I'd then go out on a Friday evening after work with my colleagues and get absolutely off-my-face drunk. I'd drink so much that I was zig-zagging home or had to be carried, but I didn't care. I was free for two whole days!

I'd do that each week and I'd say that Friday nights were my favourite night because it meant I'd survived the week and it was the furthest point away from having to return to work. I'd then spend a Saturday nursing a hangover and eating lots of sugar and calorific foods to feel better. We'd then have a party or drinks with friends on a Saturday night, so I'd also spend Sunday nursing a hangover until Sunday night kicked in and I started to dread having to go back to work on Monday morning.

This became a new weekly cycle, and it led to bulimia. I had started on this track on and off for a few years before this point, but this is when it became a regular habit and a full-on eating disorder (note: I only accepted that I had an eating disorder at Christmas of 2019). I realised I could eat and drink copious amounts of alcohol, and then make myself sick to regain control. It really helped to numb the pain I was feeling, which in turn (I thought) helped me to be a more successful lawyer in a man's world and earn better money. I therefore started to do it more and more.

Unsurprisingly, my health suffered more and more. I had IBS on most days, migraines and headaches, and colds very regularly. My teeth and gums started to decline. I was physically sick on a Monday morning; not because of bulimia, but because I was so anxious about having to go into work and face the Boss.

I was newly married, I was a trained barrister, I was earning £50K with bonuses aged 24 (in a position that a lot of people my age would have dreamed of), yet I was miserable. At the same time, I'd come a long way from the darker days, and I recognised that. I was always very self-aware – I just ignored a lot of it when the truth got too painful.

I was seeing an acupuncturist and a healer because I knew the doctor and medicines were not the answer. I was lying on the couch of the healer one day, and it came to me like a lightning bolt: I was unhappy, and no amount of money, promotions, success in my work, being married, having friends, etc. would make me happy.

I had always been waiting for 'that next thing' in life that was going to make me happy: the degree, the qualification, the job, the salary, the promotion, the title, the pay rise, the bonus, the wedding, the new car, the house, the designer handbag and so on. I realised that each time I got the 'thing' I thought would make me happy, I felt happy for about a day or so and then felt unhappy again. I'd then be searching for the next thing or setting the next goal. I needed material things to make me happy, and even if I got a mansion and a helicopter, I still wouldn't be happy.

I felt like all the parts of my life formed a jigsaw puzzle that on the outside looked like it was complete. I should have been happy on paper, but I was miserable. There was a missing jigsaw piece, and I couldn't quite put my finger on what that was.

THE PRINCESS

I started to get to work on myself. I read self-development books, watched training videos and journaled around my life. I had always been introduced to self-growth and spiritual concepts as my mum had been 'awake' for years, but I'd ignored them because that world didn't seem to fit into my corporate/legal world reality.

I left the job for a lower paid one, having realised that the money wasn't worth risking my health or my sanity. The law firm agreed to pay for me to cross-qualify as a solicitor, so I went down that path. I was working all week and at university once more at the weekends, working really hard again to move my life forward. Meanwhile, I picked up a new 'boss' that was a difficult character. Let's call him TT. He was a recovering alcoholic and very competitive with his staff. He would say that I wasn't good enough because I hadn't trained at a more prestigious law firm. He would say that I belonged chained to the kitchen sink. He would go to clients and take the glory for the cases I won. He would be rude about me behind my back to other colleagues. He would force clients into messy, protracted and costly litigation in order to be able to raise big bills to justify his existence at the law firm, which I found repugnant. He was the complete opposite of my previous boss (the Boss), and yet he made me feel the same: controlled, persecuted and like a caged bird.

I longed to work for myself. I had always felt that there was a budding entrepreneur inside of me, and I thought very fondly of my grandpa, who was a self-made millionaire. I knew now that I was good at law, and I had an established set of clients, but I didn't seem to be good at fitting in law firms working for other people. I felt that they were very stuck in their old ways, and I could do things a different way; a lighter, more heart and soul-centred way.

I knew I had to stay with the firm for a while, at least until my solicitor cross-qualification was done. So, I 'coped' in the week and began drinking heavily again on a Friday night to celebrate another week of work completed.

My husband SF could not understand why I couldn't just work a normal 9-5 job like 'normal' people. He thought I should be really content with the job I had and work my way up the ladder over time. He pleaded with me not to start a business because, in his view, it wouldn't be successful. It hurt me that he didn't believe in me, because if I could bet on anything, it was myself.

It occurred to me that there was this pattern of men around me trying to control me, and I wasn't going to accept that anymore. We separated after three years of marriage and promptly divorced.

It was now 2015, and I was 27 years' old, living alone with my dog and trying to navigate single life again. I was very close to completing my cross-qualification. Despite having earned good money for some time, I never had any money or savings, and debts were mounting up. I still had my student debts, and I was now eating into credit cards in order to be able to pay for basics, as there was now only one wage coming into the household.

PRE-QUEEN

I started to think more about the future life I wanted to create and what life was all about. I wondered why the same patterns were occurring and why, despite earning lots more money, I never had more money available. I plunged into general and money mindset concepts, which developed into further awakening and spirituality over time. I did tonnes of work on that, and I felt brighter. I knew that I was destined for something bigger than this.

As soon as I cross-qualified in June 2016, I set up my new law practice as a limited company and handed my notice in at work (which did not go down very well). I started to have conversations with potential clients to get new work into the business, and I took action every day to get it off the ground. I engaged an accountant and a mindset coach to help support me and keep me on track. I focused on the fact I was different in my marketing; playing to my strengths of working pro-actively with clients to prevent disputes and ultimately, help them to be more successful in business.

I had started seeing my soon-to-be husband, and it was early days in our relationship. We had been best friends for five years, and he had always supported my big dreams and visions for my business and the life I wanted to create. He had more faith in me than anyone else I'd ever known, and our friendship blossomed into a relationship.

I made clear to him that nothing was going to get in the way of my business and my dreams, and I would not be controlled, manipulated or abused ever again. Despite this rather frosty welcome, he stayed and lovingly held me whilst I got to work. I called myself 'the cold-hearted b**ch', and yet he saw past it all.

He helped me in so many ways to turn the dream into a reality, and after 10 months in business, I had hit the six-figure mark. I was astounded by my own achievements, yet, at the same time, I wasn't surprised at all, because I knew deep down inside me that there was a lot more success to be had.

My husband joined the business after the first year (he is also a construction lawyer), and we continued to build the dream together. I felt that I'd healed that pattern of men trying to control me because he was and is the opposite of a controlling man. He is a constant support for me going for whatever I want and always has 100% faith in me. To this day, he believes in me more than I do.

I still had debts, and he had left a long-term relationship too, so we were, in effect, starting our lives again together. We started paying off debts and getting back on track. We had plans to buy a house, pay off the debt, and build a lifestyle that we were happy with, rather than fitting into the 9-5 grind of the corporate world.

I was healthier and happier. I wasn't getting ill all the time like I was before. I was, however, working extremely hard and hustling, because I believed that was what was required to build a business, and it couldn't be done any other way.

I was still delving even deeper into mindset and spiritual practices, realising that this was the missing jigsaw piece that I had previously been looking for. I'd begun to have visions and knowings about my future. I saw myself as a healer and coach: on stage, in books, teaching thousands and even millions of women from all over the globe. It seemed a world away from where I was at, and I didn't feel good enough to do that just yet, but I believed that I was stepping in the right direction and one day, I would step into my true purpose (whatever that looked like).

I kept getting the message from different places that I needed to work with my emotions, my divine feminine and open my heart again. I was too numb and used to working with masculine energy, but I didn't know where to begin, so I largely ignored the messages and forged on the best way I knew.

DARK NIGHT OF THE SOUL – PART 2

One Friday night in November 2017, I was at home on the couch relaxing in front of the TV, when I received a phone call from the police. In that moment, my world turned upside down. I can't go into detail in this book, but it involved my past, and it shed light as to why my intuition had been screaming at me for many years.

I started counselling because I knew that this revelation was big and I would need some support, but after the initial shock, I felt

OK, and talked myself into believing that I was now over 'it'. I realised that the reason why my past had come back to haunt me was because I ran away from it in the first place. I never healed from it. I simply moved four hours away in the hope that I could forget all about it. I only swept it under the carpet. Nothing could have prepared me for what followed.

Criminal proceedings were brought, which led to me being a witness for the prosecution and being on the witness stand during a two-week trial in 2018. Imagine being a trained barrister and solicitor, and then being on the witness stand as I was cross-examined by a defence barrister! He was tearing into me for what was probably only about 20 minutes, but what felt like 20 hours. He called into question my honesty, my integrity and my validity as a human being. He said that I had been dishonest to the police and to the jury. I have never felt so persecuted and so judged.

On top of all that, once I had given evidence, I was allowed to sit in the gallery so that I could hear the rest of the trial. For the first time, I heard details that I'd never heard before, and I had clarity over what I had actually been through in my teenage years. I cried. I prayed. I begged God for mercy. I shouted angrily at God and asked why I had been put through all this torture, now twice. It was the most traumatic experience in all of my life.

FURTHER AWAKENING

This barrister was just doing his job, and I knew that, but it felt like a punch to the gut that I had felt lifetimes before. I realised that I had been persecuted many times before, in different lifetimes, and I had a deeper spiritual awakening.

My business suffered for two years as a result. I say suffered: I didn't lose clients or money thankfully, but there was no growth. I carried on pretending everything was fine to clients. I soldiered on in front of friends and family. But deep down, I was in pain. I had lost my ambition, which was probably my most obvious characteristic. I didn't care about anything. I didn't want to get out of bed in the morning. I couldn't work out whether this was depression, or whether it was what 'normal' people feel like when they have a normal amount of ambition because they realise that life is not all about chasing big dreams. I wondered if it was part of me growing up, and I wasn't interested in my big dreams and visions any longer.

At the same time, I kept having the familiar nagging feeling I'd had a couple of years before around a bigger soul's purpose, and that I wasn't living that purpose. As my spiritual and soul connection deepened, I felt more and more that there was something important I was here to do on this planet, and that what I had experienced was part of the journey in order to help me and my mission.

Becoming a healer and coach came up time and time again. Yet, every time I tried to launch something, it just fell flat. Every time I tried to push forward, it was like attempting to walk through sticky treacle.

I asked the Universe: *"why do you show me that I'm meant to be a coach, and yet you won't let me get on with it?!"* I went round and round with this for about a year. I kept trying, getting frustrated, stopping, starting again. I eventually surrendered, realising that the vision was about the future and not for now. I'd finally got the message from the Universe.

EMOTIONS ARE THE KEY

One day, later in 2019, I was talking to my mum, and I said my energy flow felt blocked because money wasn't flowing in. She introduced me to The Emotion Code by Bradley Nelson and did a little session with me by video call. The next day, a client paid £10,000 into my bank account.

I was happy and shocked, and I realised that there was something to this work with emotions. I started to work on myself and my emotions more, using the Emotion Code and Ho'ponopono (a Hawaiian forgiveness prayer). I began to feel lighter and more content. I could feel my fire starting to come back, and I realised that the emotions I was holding in my body from years' worth of trauma were blocking me from being able to move forward.

GODDESS RISING

Turning to February 2020, I received information from my guides that it was time to GO and proceed with the coaching. I felt like myself again, and it was time to step into my purpose. I didn't really know how to achieve this, but I kept meditating and tuning into my guidance team for answers.

Magically, I kept being put in the path of people who could help me. I had an angelic tuning fork session which led to so much healing and awakening that, at one point, I felt Archangel Raphael was remoulding my body and my DNA (so much happened in that session, but it is perhaps for another book). I was gifted a free session with a lady who channels Mother Mary and her own spiritual council, and she helped me to see that I could trust my own intuition and that I was around the corner from a breakthrough. I was put into Tina Pavlou's Facebook group, When the Goddess Calls – The Temple, so that I could take part in her various online meditation events and her daily ThetaHealing® clearings and mantras. I was shown the Young Living oils and started using those daily. This helped to continually clear me and keep my vibration really high, especially during this time of fear in the world with the COVID-19 pandemic, so I kept channelling clear guidance as to what to do next.

During those courses I remembered past lives where I was a Queen. In one life, I was a good Queen who had my kingdom taken away from me by a man I trusted (here's the men controlling me pattern coming up again). In another, I was a bad Queen whose favourite saying was "OFF WITH HIS HEAD!" I had to laugh because that's been one of my favourite sayings in this lifetime. So now you know why I frequently refer to the term 'QUEEN'.

I channelled my signature program, Pauper to Queen. I was told the course name, the name of the modules, what should be included in the modules and how to run the course. I was told to run a 3-day free masterclass in May and invite people to it, and then sell the course at the end.

That's exactly what I did in May of this year (2020). It was my first time doing any online training in any format, and my first-time coaching, yet it felt so natural and like I'd been doing it for years. I was channelling guidance as I was coaching, and I felt totally connected and supported by the Universe.

It proved to me that I could do this and that now was truly the right time to step into my coaching path. It also resulted in me taking on three new clients. I was in awe at how easy this was.

At the end of May, I clearly heard *"ask Tina Pavlou about doing a ThetaHealing® course"*, so I did. Tina responded to me and said she had a course starting very soon and there was a space if I wanted to join. I leapt at the chance and changed all my plans to make it happen because I knew that my soul *had* to be there.

I completed the course, and at the end of the last day, I hired Tina to be my coach and healer on a 1:1 basis. I knew this was just the beginning of my deeper healing journey. I quickly went onto the ThetaHealing® advanced course so I could become a practitioner. I was introduced to the Goddess Rooms and the sisters who are part of it. I went back again and completed my Theta-Healing® dig deeper and manifesting & abundance courses.

I finally understood what it meant to heal and clear my own beliefs, my ancestral lineage, my past lives and soul wounds. I started to see myself differently and realise that facing the inner work head-on and stepping into my power was a huge part of stepping into my Queen. This is beyond making sales, earning lots of money and being successful; it creates peace, joy, freedom and fun. This is the REAL missing jigsaw puzzle piece I was seeking all those years ago.

Doing this work, in turn, allows me to then carry out transformational healing work with clients and empowers them with the tools to heal themselves and create the lives they deserve. This is the ripple effect I want to create in the world, and by doing the work first myself, I am leading from the front. I do the work, and I show my clients how I'm doing it (including all the messy unsexy parts of the work), and then I support them in doing the same.

I couldn't do this if I wasn't continually doing the deep, transformational inner work myself.

My Pauper to Queen course, whilst channelled, takes my clients through the journey I took to go from the 'pauper' and stepping into the Queen part of themselves (but skipping all of the procrastination and self-sabotage in between); allowing them to remember that true freedom is living a life of passion and joy, which, in turn, allows them to step into their power and find their true purpose.

Spoiler alert: your true purpose is to raise your vibration, remember the divine being that you are, and shine your light bright to help other souls remember the divine beings they are.

THE QUEEN

This is where I am now. I'm where I first started; remembering my sovereignty as a divine being.

I now know why I have been through all the things I have; the various dark nights of the soul, the pain, the crumblings, the heartache and the trauma. I am the Goddess in my family that is here to heal my ancestral line. I am here to help other women heal from their wounds and remember their divine nature. I couldn't be fully embracing my soul's purpose if I hadn't experienced the same for myself.

I ask myself daily: *"what would the Queen version of me do?"* and I make sure that my energy is calibrating to that Queen. From that place, my vibration is high, and I can be of true service to my clients.

I recognise that I have come so far in my journey, but I also know that in many ways, this is just the beginning. My awakening and healing journey will never stop. I will keep diving deeper and stepping further into the Queen that I am. And whilst that vision of stepping on stage and impacting the lives of thousands and millions of women still scares me, I know that is what I'm here to do, and I'll continue the magical journey of life until I do.

From one Queen to another, my parting word is this: if you do nothing else in this life, concentrate on doing the deep inner work, raising your vibration and shining your light as brightly as you can. You've got this, and I love you xxx

ABOUT THE AUTHOR

ELIZABETH BARON

Liz Baron is an intuitive business and life coach, and a Theta-healing® practitioner. She works with lawyers and other professional and corporate women who feel unfulfilled and know deep down that they have a much bigger purpose and mission in this world.

Liz is also a lawyer of over 10 years, having trained as a barrister in the UK before cross-qualifying as a solicitor, ultimately leading her to set up her own practice. As a lawyer, Liz now helps to coach healers, therapists, online businesses and influencers to get legally protected in their businesses.

Liz is a multi six-figure businesswoman, having set up her first business four years' ago and continuing to create new businesses in alignment with her passions. Liz loves to help women set up their own businesses; creating strong boundaries and foundations from the start, and doing the deep inner healing work to achieve peace, freedom and an amazing lifestyle.

Her mission is to give women the tools, mindset and confidence to stop self-sabotaging, take back their power and achieve their big dreams.

More personally, Liz is based in the UK between Bristol and Wales and lives with her soon-to-be husband and two dogs, Basil and Banjo. She is in the process of project managing a Grade II listed farmhouse in Wales that will become their family home.

Liz loves to travel and has been to China, USA, Mexico, Egypt, Cuba as well as touring the North of Italy by train.

Contact:

Email: team@elizabeth-baron.com
Website: www.elizabeth-baron.com
Facebook business profile: @iamelizabethbaron

facebook.com/Iamelizabethbaron111
instagram.com/Iamlizbaron

9

EMMA CLAYTON

I had it all! Or so it seemed...

The good old "job for life" in the city, earning a six-figure salary, with a brand new black Range Rover Evoque on the drive of my detached home, sporting a designer handbag and going on adventurous long-haul holidays every year. I was travelling the world business class, staying in 5-star hotels and dining at the best restaurants - all perks of the job. The bonuses were insane, and the pension was pretty damn good too.

My colleagues, friends and family admired me for my confidence and so-called "success".

But inside I was a mess. I didn't believe I deserved any of it because I didn't feel good enough. I had this completely irrational fear that someone was going to realise and take it all away from me. I wasn't academic or as intelligent as most of my peers

- I left school at 18 and was fortunate enough to get an entry-level job in the administration department. I felt I was nothing special, and as a result of that core belief, I spent most of my 20-year career feeling like I didn't fit in; like a fraud or an imposter.

As a result, I put *so* much pressure on myself to perform to such a high standard, that maintaining it was exhausting. I was working all the hours, was always available on my phone and would travel on weekends. It felt like I was never at home, I rarely had the energy to socialise or exercise when I was, and my diet was far from healthy. Yet I couldn't say no to taking on more. I had inherited my parents' solid work ethic and had convinced myself that I thrived on pushing myself outside of my comfort zone and that I could handle a certain level of stress, but the truth is I was on the brink of burnout.

Then there were the less obvious, hidden stressors.

I would overthink every email I wrote, hoping it wouldn't be taken the wrong way to the extent I lost sleep over it. I would second guess anything I wanted to say in a meeting, wondering if it was clever enough or if I would look stupid for saying it, and as a result, I would keep my mouth shut throughout and not say a word. I dreaded innovation meetings where you got to share your bright ideas - because I didn't have any, certainly none worth sharing. I would freeze, pretend to be taking notes and contribute very little as a result. Then I would worry about how that lack of contribution would be perceived by others and how my performance rating would be affected and would regularly ask for feedback in an attempt to get the validation I needed. I assumed others were judging me because of what I was wearing as I wore largely black to cover the fact I was overweight. You get the picture. I was all up in my head: overthinking, doubting myself, and worrying about what others must have been thinking about me.

Over two decades, I learnt to put on a convincing mask of fake confidence. No-one really knew that how I was showing up to the outside world was not representative of how I was feeling on the inside. I don't think I even realised the extent of the incongruence myself, not whilst I was in the thick of it. If I'm honest, it was so "normal" for me to feel like this, so I just "shut up and put up".

Don't get me wrong; I loved the company I worked for. I met some incredible people and had amazing opportunities to learn, grow and travel the world. I made life-long friends, and I was actually really bloody good at my job. But deep down I knew something was out of whack; I just couldn't put my finger on it.

From my very first day at work in 1997, I found myself like a fish out of water in a very technical environment. It was like they spoke a language of their own, that I couldn't get my head around. I never considered myself "technical". Instead, I was a "doer". I could see what needed to be done to get from A to B, and I got on with it. I never failed to deliver and was relied upon to make the impossible possible. I moved my way around different departments as I climbed the career ladder, following my nose in terms of what I fancied trying out next. I always seemed to get the jobs I went for, so I knew that despite my own self-doubt, I was highly regarded (even if I didn't believe I was worthy of it). I went from admin to claims to sales and marketing, into various project roles and always ended up in team management positions.

I was a natural people person. I could adapt and relate to most, motivating and empowering them to move forward. I would pick up on any "elephants in the room" and call it out; I was like a human barometer. I really cared too, not just how my team was performing on the job, but how happy each of them was, both in and outside of work. I felt at home helping the individuals in my teams develop and grow into their potential; it's what motivated me to be the best I could be so I could lead by example. It made me a popular manager, coach and mentor. The leadership path had chosen me, and as I would learn years later, I was very much an empath.

But with increasing responsibility, more experienced, confident team members to lead, bigger budgets and exposure to the most senior people in the organisation, the more I worried and doubted myself. Yet still, I pushed and strived to prove myself and progress.

I had been desperate to be nominated for an in-house leadership development programme because that nomination meant *someone* thought I was worthy of promotion. I got that nomination in 2014, but what I hadn't bargained for, was just how much I was about to learn about my inner demons.

We were thrown into one role play situation after another. I *hated* role play. The anticipation of this one particular scenario left me experiencing a full-blown visceral panic attack. My head was racing, my vision blurred, my stomach was churning, I needed to go to the toilet, I was aware I was holding my breath, and I was sweating and flushing from the chest up. I was aware there were people around me, depending on me to play along. I did play along. I can't recall what I said as I was too busy willing the ground to open up and swallow me whole. *Let me be anywhere else but here!*

Apparently, I was so good at covering up what was really going on inside that no-one noticed except for the facilitator. She took me to one side and asked me what was going on. The floodgates opened. I cried harder than I'd cried in a long time. She had seen through the mask, and in a strange way, I was relieved. She was so kind and held space for me to release all that pent-up worry, without any judgement whatsoever. She recommended the first book I was to ever purchase from the self-help shelf. It was called 'Taming Your Gremlin!'

I realised I had opened a box that could no longer be ignored, but I needed help and support, so I plucked up the courage to book in to see a psychotherapist which is something I never thought I'd do. After I told her my life story in our first session, she told me I had a high functioning generalised anxiety disorder, low self-esteem and a lack of trust due to childhood trauma. I was 34 and in complete denial.

I remember downplaying my so-called "trauma" because I wasn't abused, raped or abandoned. It didn't seem worthy of my story (hello imposter syndrome!). I also argued that it was "just" worry and nerves and that "I wasn't susceptible to mental health problems" (yes, those words actually came out of my mouth, oh how naive I had been).

The reality was I had struggled from a young age with worry and doubt, which I now know to mean anxiety. On reflection, not one particular person or incident is to blame. It was a series of situations, events, comments and messages from home, school, friends and family, or picked up on the TV, all of which caused the little girl in me to make those things mean something about her. None of which were necessarily true, but she went on to *believe* they were. That's called life! And as children, we're quite good at finding ways to cope - resilient even.

It all started as a slightly larger than average gymnast, parading in a leotard sure sets you up to compare your body to the next girl. I don't remember *not* having a negative body image. For me, it was always my thighs I hated.

Later on, at secondary school I was bullied, first by the girls, then the boys. They were nasty and went straight for the jugular calling me "Thunder Thighs", "Blobby Clayton" (back in the days of Mr Blobby!) and "Pan-Cracker" (referring to the toilet pan!) They were novel, I'll give them that.

I was a normal, fit and healthy young girl growing up, undeserving of their taunts, and I know that now. But at the time, I found a non-judgemental, comforting friend in food. I would spend my bus money on four bars of chocolate and eat them on the walk home. It was a way to escape; I felt better for it.

I went on my first diet aged 13, but I didn't have a clue what I was doing. I would sometimes starve myself all day, knowing that I would be able to make up for it in secret on the way home. Always in secret. I would lose myself during a sweet binge on chocolate and ice-cream. In those short moments, everything was OK. That started what I now call the binge and restrict cycle of disordered eating, which would continue into adulthood.

The week before I started my career at 18 years old, just as everything seemed to be looking up, my boyfriend of two years cheated on me with an older girl, who happened to be teeny tiny. I was not only heartbroken with my trust in tatters, but my self-loathing took on a whole new turn for the worse.

My binge eating behind closed doors got worse. It was like a punishment for not being good enough - not that it made any sense. I discovered booze and partying hard; only now I wasn't as active. I had a string of failed relationships through my 20's and gained weight year on year. Still, I tried every single diet going, would stick to it for a week or two, lose weight, and gain it back (and some).

It was turning 30 that was my first grown-up "eff this shiz" moment. I was on the Spanish Canary Island of Tenerife with my best friends, sister, and mum, getting dressed up for a party in our swanky villa. There was a lot of laughter and music coming from below my balcony. At that moment, I was aware I was surrounded by so much love and fun, yet I felt so alone and miserable on the inside. I hated what I saw staring back at me in the mirror and was disgusted at how I had let myself get so out of shape. I was fat and ugly, and I sobbed into my cocktail!

Yet at the same time, something inside me was telling me there was another way... a *better way* to think and feel about myself. That this was not my all. I made a vow with myself, there and then, to end my self-destructive ways and not let history repeat itself in my 30's. I was meant for more.

It took me a few more years of experimenting with dieting before I realised, they don't work. The restrictive nature of dieting will almost always lead you back to a binge; it's the way we're wired to keep us from starving to death. I knew it wasn't as simple as calories in - calories out, if it was then why were so many other women, myself included, struggling to lose weight and maintain it?

My first investment in seeking the answers was £1000 to go to FitFarm UK for a week. I lost 7lbs or so, but what was even more impressive was what I gained. Knowledge; of the effect of sugar in our bloodstream, and the knock-on impact on our energy and mood. Of just how much sugar is in all the processed foods we consume for convenience. Of how bad diet coke is for you. Of how to cook healthily, from scratch. Of how much I missed moving my body for the sheer fun of it vs the kind we do for punishment.

I remember clearly the moment the penny dropped... I said to the nutritionist, "so it's not that I'm greedy that I reach for these foods?!" She was so kind! It made me hungry to *learn* more. That was a decade ago, and I have never looked back on my personal development journey.

Therapy taught me to recognise and respect my symptoms of anxiety, of which binge eating was one of them. Being the high achiever I was, now I knew it was there, I wanted it gone.

Still, I had convinced myself that *when* I lost the weight, *then* I'd be happy and free of anxiety. I got into Crossfit (I'd always enjoyed lifting heavy weights) and hired my first health coach. She worked online and helped with nutrition, training and the mindset side of things which was still relatively new to me. It was another big financial investment, but in committing, I felt like I was backing myself.

I temporarily gave up booze and was loving eating a high fat, high protein diet, and with the weight training and newfound love of running, I lost a fair amount of weight. I had stuck to it for 3 months which was a new record, and I'd never felt so good in my body, not just from the new shape and size, but from the newfound energy and zest for life I felt. I was listening to podcasts and experimenting with meditation and journaling for the first time. My anxiety, all the doubt and worry was reducing, helped by the fact work was going through a quieter, more manageable spell.

Then, out of the blue, I was offered a promotion at work. It was literally handed to me on a plate. He said, "I've created this new team, it's a bit of an experiment so there are no guarantees at the end of it, but I want you to be my Head of Strategy & Operations." It was one of those jaw-dropping, "did that really happen to me?" moments. Then I started to worry! That he must have got it wrong, surely he meant to offer it to someone else?! That it was too big a risk to take if I might not have a job at the end of it.

After sleeping on it, I woke with this strong knowing that not only does everything happen for a reason, but whatever happened, everything would be alright. So I negotiated the terms I wanted and accepted the offer.

As I threw myself into this new and exciting challenge, my exercise was the first thing to go out the window. At first I kept up my new eating regime, but with more travel to Zurich and Boston, that started slipping too. Then my anxiety took a turn for the worst. There I was, hiring creative, innovative talent from outside of our industry, one of whom had not one, but three PHD's to his name. My imposter syndrome was at an all-time high. My good old friend, food, always on standby to help me through it. I regained the weight I'd lost, and some. Again.

I'll never forget the meeting that sent me into a downward spiral. I was leading a project that was a big deal. I was preparing an update to three senior leaders that wasn't particularly positive, but I felt alright about it because I wasn't going to be in the room with them, I'd be dialling in on the phone so I could effectively hide, and my boss and a peer of his were going to be there to actually deliver the bad news. Or so I thought. Ten minutes before the meeting was due to start, they both made their apologies and said that I would represent them and give the update.

That same sinking feeling of wanting the ground to open up and swallow me whole consumed me in an instant. I gave myself a little talking to "come on Emma, you can pull it off, just deliver the facts and answer their questions, it's no big deal". So I pulled up my metaphorical big girl pants and dialled in.

I don't remember much about the call as my head was in such a spin. I remember they challenged me - a lot. I remember I couldn't pretty up the story; I told it as it was. I remember the piercing silence of the three of them in a room together on one end of the phone. I imagined them exchanging eyebrow raises and silently agreeing not to waste any more of their time. The meeting was cut short, and when the initial relief passed, the embarrassment and shame sunk in about what I woulda, coulda, shoulda said, but didn't.

The feedback I got later from my boss was that I needed to put a positive spin on it and tell them what they wanted to hear. There it was, confirmation that indeed I wasn't good enough. In fact, it was worse than that. I'd failed. My reputation was compromised. I felt like sh*t and struggled to get out of bed for a few days, throwing a rare sickie. I sank into what felt like a six-month binge.

I would daydream about getting laid off, and they say be careful of what you wish for! It turns out I'm a pretty good manifestor after all.

I knew our team was in trouble before it was confirmed. It was just before I set off on a month-long trip to Asia, for both work and pleasure, but it wouldn't be made official until I returned. So I set an intention to use my time overseas to review my options and come up with a contingency plan.

I did the pros and cons of taking a severance package, on the plane to Hong Kong. It brought up my biggest fears around not having a steady income, insurance cover and pension plan. That's when I realised - they weren't my fears. They were my parents. After all, that's how they'd been brought up, to value the financial security you (used to) get from a job for life. When I looked past them, there wasn't much of an argument against it, especially when I considered what I wanted from life - to be less stressed, more me, to be free from food and anxiety, and comfy in my own skin. Hell, throw a few sunsets and sunrises and other simple things into the wish list as well, and the list looked more pro than con.

After a week working in Hong Kong and Singapore, I got on a short flight to Bali, for a week-long yoga retreat in Seminyak. I had tried yoga before but hadn't practiced as much as I'd hoped to in the lead up to the trip, but I was looking forward to it. I couldn't have anticipated how divinely timed this trip was going to be, to one of the most spiritual places on the planet.

We'd start the mornings with an early alarm. In silence, we would journal, followed by yoga practice on the veranda as the sun rose, then breakfast. It was awkward at first, but I came to really appreciate that couple of hours first thing to connect with how I was feeling, get out of my head, be in my body as it moved and stretched, and just be. My own mantra being a reminder to "turn inward and tune in".

I had my first ever experience of consciously noticing energy moving in my body after working on our hips during one morning practice. Lying in savasana, I thought I felt the instructor's hands around my pelvic area like she had placed her hands on our heads the morning before. But after it didn't disappear, I realised it couldn't be. Apparently, that was energy. I was wowed and wanted more. I started to realise how up in my head I'd been, and how disconnected I was to my body.

We had the opportunity to climb Mount Agung, the tallest active volcano on Bali. We would set off late and climb overnight so we could see the sunrise from the top. Now, I'm a bit of a sucker when it comes to a sunrise (or sunset, I'm not fussy) but in crept the worry that I'd hold everyone else up if I went along. I was my heaviest ever and far from my fittest. But with reassurance and encouragement from the others, I decided to go for it and mentally prepare myself. But I don't think any of us had quite bargained for just how challenging it would be.

It was a head torch and rain-mac on, single file, one foot in front of the other situation. I was puffed out by the time we'd climbed the initial steps to the temple before we even got on the volcano. There was no let-up; it was consistently steep uphill all the way. Each of the groups that set off after us were overtaking us. Even a group of young Chinese people in jeans and flip flops overtook us with ease.

I was very aware of how quickly I got all up in my head, kicking myself for agreeing to do it when I wasn't physically capable. Worrying that I was going to hold everyone up, ruin it for them if I was the only one that couldn't make it, worry, worry, blah blah blah. I was frustrated that I couldn't seem to stop those negative voices in my head that were physically weighing me down, and I had a complete emotional meltdown about an hour in as a result. It actually really helped me to let it all out, release it, share out loud what was taunting me in my mind. Thank god I was surrounded by the most supportive and understanding group of women who all admitted to going through their own tests of mental strength as well. It enabled me to realise I wasn't alone, take a few deep breaths, change the narrative in my head to focus on the reward of the view from the top, and continue putting one foot in front of the other.

Our local guide was amazing too, and whilst we didn't make it to the top, he found us a decent sheltered spot above the cloud line, built us a campfire to dry off and warm up, then got out the coffee and banana fritters to cheer us up as we played motivational tunes and sat together for the sun to come up.

That was such a beautiful, bonding moment for us all, one that I'll never forget. I can still feel the emotions of it now when I think about it or see photos. My roomie, Alice, remains one of my soul sisters today.

It's only when the sun rose that we realised just how far up we had climbed. Then came the descent. I found that a lot easier than others as I was the only one in proper walking boots (although they were half a size too small and I had forgotten to trim my toenails - ouchie - bye-bye big toenails). So it was my turn to support the others with a helping hand down the rocks and boulders that we'd not so long before been scrambling up. It seemed to go on and on forever until we finally got back to the minibus, with wobbly legs, sore feet and tiredness from being up all night.

But it was like the worst was yet to come. A couple of our group had made it to the top (good on them) which meant they would take longer to get back down. In the 3 hour wait we went through all the feels, cold, wet, tired and hungry - we were laughing hysterically one minute, winding each other up with our impatience and getting angry the next. Then to top it off we had a 3-hour drive back to the villa. Boy, was I dreaming of hot, salty chips and a big burger or what?! Only when we finally got back, about 17 hours after we'd left, there was a table beautifully laid out with fresh, colourful salads and boiled eggs for protein. That was it; I couldn't face it. I wanted chips! Something hot and comforting and satisfying to fill this empty hole inside me. I wanted to be transported out of here, away from people, to where I could eat what I wanted without being judged, but I felt trapped. So I sloped off, I had hoped unnoticed as I didn't want any attention - I felt stupid for having to explain I was upset because I wanted chips!

I put my bikini on and dived into the pool to hide my tears of frustration. It felt like slow motion as I moved through the water. I'm a Pisces, and I live by the sea, so I've always been drawn to water, it feels like home to me. And in those moments underwater something came over me.

You could call it a breakthrough, which is often preceded by a breakdown. The realisation that I was presented with an abundance of delicious, healthy food that would nourish my tired body and help it recover, but I didn't want that. I wanted the crappy junk food I'd relied on for decades to make me feel better in times of stress, anxiety, fear; you name it. But it wasn't available to me at this moment. And as Bob Marley had sung earlier on the volcano as the sun rose, "every little thing is gonna be alright".

It may seem dramatic to some, but it was real for me and was a pivotal moment in my journey of finding the freedom from food I'd been seeking for years. For once in my adult life, I had allowed myself to feel all the feels rather than suppress them with crap food. Instead, I could see that hugs and love from my new friends could be just as comforting, if not more so. I tucked into that plate of healthy food and sent grateful thoughts to every mouthful. A plate of chips would not have resulted in any of that - only more shame and resentment.

What also happened later on that trip around Bali, after my boyfriend Adam had flown out to join me, was a moment of clarity that was about to drastically change the course of my life.

I'd been to a meditation class whilst staying in this beautiful resort amongst the paddy fields. I was also fasting, not through choice but due to being struck down by good old Bali belly and genuinely not being able to stomach any food. Walking back to my hotel room I was struck by a sudden knowing - call it an epiphany, guidance or a download - in that moment, I knew I had gone through all the challenges I had to date, for a reason, one that was bigger than me. It was my purpose to help other successful, high performing, overachieving women who were struggling silently behind the scenes with their relationship with food and body, with anxiety and fraud like feelings of not-enoughness, to overcome these challenges and find comfort in their own skin, freedom from unwanted habits around food and a real confidence to show up fully as themselves.

I realise now that I was more of an open channel for guidance than I had been in a very long time. I was eating healthy, fresh foods, being really active as well as grounding in the slower pace of yoga, and meditation in Bali of all places. I had paused the human-doing, got out of my head and embraced the human-being. I had woken up, reconnected with my intuition. I was guided, and there was nothing to fear.

My decision about whether or not to leave the corporate world was a no-brainer. And I've *never* looked back.

In October 2017, I woke up on my first day of freedom from the corporate grind. It felt flipping amazing. I hired a business coach to show me how to set up online and started a level 4 diploma in Nutrition and Lifestyle Coaching. I was going to University after all, only at this point in my life at nearly 40; I was finally on a clear path. My own path, driven by passion and purpose.

One day, as I drove to a yoga class at 10:30am, Whitney Houston's "One moment in time..." came on the radio, I realised just how free I felt, to be "...more than I thought I could be". Happy tears fell; I was overwhelmed by a sense that the next exciting chapter of my life was just beginning.

The next instalment of which will have to wait for the next book!

In the meantime, it is fair to say that I've accepted the skin I'm in and am learning each day to love and nurture my size 18/20 (UK) body more and more - after all, it's the only one I've got in this lifetime, and fighting against, and hating on it has not got me anywhere. It's time to be a team. I turn to food for comfort less than ever before; I won't say never because that wouldn't be true. I don't diet though, I refuse to, and yet I am losing weight, and my body is shape-shifting, slowly but surely - and I'm totally cool with that. Nourishment and kindness comes first; weight loss is a pleasant side effect. My anxiety is way more subtle these days; it creeps up on me in the form of resistance to taking action and showing up in a way that I know will help me move towards my dreams of making a bigger impact in the world. But I have the awareness to recognise it, and the good intention it has to keep me playing small and safe. I have the tools I need to move through it - to walk with the fear and do it anyway. When I focus my attention on building my self-belief and simply being more me in every part of my life, every damn day, the result is peace of mind, sense of freedom and a new lease of life which allows me to go after my big dreams - worry and doubt free.

And that result right there fuels my mission to help as many other women, including you, achieve the same, because if I can do it, so can you. When you *truly believe* that you are more than enough, just the way you are, everything changes on the inside.

Real confidence is an inner game. Master your inside reality, and you get to have it all on the outside, and not because of what you did, but because of who you are *becoming*.

When more women step into and own their power, the world changes.

I am committed to always learning, growing and evolving and passing that on to my community so they can grow with me. I have found myself on a deepening spiritual path and am grateful that has led me more recently to Tina at the Goddess Rooms and ThetaHealing®. How does it get any better than this? Show me.

ABOUT THE AUTHOR

EMMA CLAYTON

As a global confidence coach, career mentor and online content creator, Emma Clayton brings high-performing women out of hiding to confidently claim their dream career and life, whilst creating freedom and success on their own terms.

Emma was once a high-achieving, corporate director earning a six-figure salary - who felt like a total fraud at risk of losing it all, despite her experience and a long list of accolades. During her 20 years with a global Fortune 500 insurance company, she was always taking on the impossible and delivering against all the odds, *and* against herself. When she manifested an attractive severance package at her job in 2017, she jumped at the chance for freedom.

Although she never looked back, what Emma didn't know was that escaping corporate wouldn't cure her insecurity and imposter syndrome overnight.

Emma dove into ways to heal and grow, to learn to love the skin she is in, and to find a more authentic level of confidence than what she'd known before. She hired her first business coach and got ready to launch her food freedom and body love coaching business. When she realised that what successful, high-performing women really need is a mentor to help them tackle stubborn blocks to self-belief that she'd had, she pivoted to include this amongst her offerings.

Once Emma started teaching her clients the tools, strategies and methods that had completely changed her own life, she began seeing them break through with dream job promotions or complete changes in career direction and feeling more seen, heard, and fulfilled than ever before. Through her signature R.E.A.L process, Emma helps her clients liberate their inner courage and confidence, to rise into their unapologetic, fully expressed selves at work and in their personal lives.

Emma offers her clients a unique and powerful blend of support from her training and certifications in Leadership, Stress Management, Neuro-Linguistic Programming, Nutrition & Lifestyle Coaching, Mind-Body Eating Psychology, Jikiden Reiki, ThetaHealing® and Beliefetics®.

When Emma isn't hanging out on Zoom with her awesome clients, she can often be found renovating her home with her partner Adam, renting out their quirky backyard AirBnB —

lovingly built from scratch and named 'The Pizza Hut' for the attached wood-fired oven, or having snuggles with her cocker spaniel, Buddy. If you're lucky, you might even catch her reminiscing about her gymnastics days and (still) pulling off the splits for fun.

Find Emma at

www.emmajclayton.com

or

https://business.facebook.com/EMMACLAYTON.XO/

10

LIZZY ADAMS

So, where do you start? I have always had a gift, especially from a young age, but instead of embracing it, I created fear towards it. To me, it was more of a curse than a gift.

I must have been about four or five when I realised I was different. I have always felt safe with animals but not with humans. Whenever there were arguments in my home, I would hide behind the sofa with my dog, and she would just sit with me. I just felt safe knowing that she was there. I just felt calm around animals, safe as though they were looking out for me.

When my parents divorced, I was about seven. I went to a catholic school where all the pupils thought that it was haunted. It was an old school; we used to muck around and say "redrum" in the mirror and wonder why nothing happened. A small part of us expected some horrible zombie to turn up in the mirror and shout murder, or the infamous horse to just appear! But it was always just our own reflections. Thank goodness! Imagine trying to explain that to a teacher or a parent. My friends and I would love to make up ghost stories and talk about the St. James Hotel that was due to be knocked down and how it was so close to our school and massively haunted. We used to wonder if the ghosts from Dover castle would wander down to the school just for a bit of excitement.

We used to think well if St. James hotel is demolished, then the ghosts must need to go somewhere so that they aren't homeless. So, in our minds, we thought they haunted our school. I look back at the stories we told as children and find them quite funny. But at the time we scared each other witless.

Nothing paranormal or spiritual actually showed at first. My childhood was pretty rough; my mother was in a violent domestic relationship with my stepdad, and I just felt very isolated.

Then I started to notice I was a little different from the other children. I started hearing and seeing things that can only be described as 'not there'.

At first, I thought it was me being silly; I mean I was only young, so clearly my brain was being daft.

But how do you explain seeing a building clear as day that was not there? How do you explain hearing your name being called by your mother when your mother didn't call you?

Or seeing a woman in a car but there was no one there?

I just couldn't explain all these things that were happening. I remember walking to school and seeing this old mill style building; I didn't pay much attention to it. I just thought, how did I never notice that huge building before?

That day one of the children's grandfathers had come in to tell us about the history of Dover. All of a sudden, this building came up in a picture. I popped up and said I had seen that building on the way to school today. The gentleman very sternly told me off and said, in fact, it was no longer there. The children started to laugh, but I knew what I had seen. I could have described the building to you, and I have never seen a picture of the building before. I felt humiliated. I thought maybe all the stresses and trauma at home was causing me to see things?

I mean I had also seen a woman in a car and a little boy sitting on a windowsill at school looking outside up to the trees. Who do you tell and how do you not sound like your mad? So, I kept quiet.

I started to see more people, buildings and hear sounds that to everyone else was not there. I slowly used this as a barrier to stop me from getting upset from all the worry and pain that surrounded my life. It was to me like they were looking after me and keeping me safe from the harm of those that should be there for me.

I remember as clear as day at the age of seven, myself and my mother were walking home from school. She stopped outside the sports centre which at the time was in the town. She looked at me and told me she had met a nice man and that they were together. To this day, I don't know where it came from, but I shouted at her. "THIS MAN IS BAD!!! THIS MAN WILL HURT YOU!" Of course, my lovely mum smiled and tried to reassure me that she knows he is not my father, but he is a good man… No, he wasn't. My mum endured years at the hands of a narcissist that tried to kill her, repeatedly hit her, and even tried to mentally abuse me. I will never forget that day I had so much passion and felt like I needed to protect my mum. But yet I didn't even know his name, or I had never even met him. The only way I can describe it was that I had been given this warning to give to her and didn't know why. This memory is still clear in my head, and I'm now thirty-four.

To get me through the days when I wasn't at school or in after school; Instead of spending time at home because I didn't feel safe, I would often go to visit two horses and spend the day hiding away with them, talking to them and feeling that I was safe when I was with them. I didn't want to leave. I didn't want to go back to the trauma. It was the same feelings I had with my old dog. I felt a sense of protection, and nothing could hurt me.

At the age of thirteen, my mother passed away on her birthday, 1st April 1999.

My sisters and I all felt a stabbing pain in our liver areas, and although we were in separate places, we all just knew she'd passed. So, when my stepsister saw me the next morning to tell me my sisters were coming early as it was my mum's birthday, I just replied: "it's okay, I know she has passed."

I rushed to my best friend's house, and he sat and just consoled me. At thirteen, what do you say, or do, it was a tough time for my friend, but he was amazing. He went inside and came out with a crystal I still have today. It was a tigers' eye. He mentioned it was his mums, but it would keep me safe. I treasured this little crystal and still do. Little would I know there would be a little meaning it held.

Throughout being a teenager, I shut myself off from the spiritual world. I believed I was bad luck. See my birthday is on the 23rd day, the 23rd hour of the 23rd minute. Sounds awesome but I learnt that 23 was an enigma and bad things happened with the number 23. Just look throughout history.

The way my life was panning out, I strongly believed this. Not only had I endured a traumatic childhood from being mentally abused by my stepfather, but I'm also a survivor of child abuse.

The first 14 years of my life was full of abuse, upset and trauma. But I am a strong believer that what doesn't break you makes you stronger.

I would go to the woods behind where I lived and would just sit there. I would feel forces around me, but I shut them off. I began to think they weren't looking after me, how could they? They were ghosts, manifestations or visions! I would shout at them and say if you were there to protect me, why is all this happening to me. I was so angry. I was just a mix of emotions and felt destroyed. But I never once showed it. To the world, I was made of steel, but beneath I was breaking, wishing that the entities around me would just for once, show and protect me.

The place where one of my abusers lived was an old estate type building in the middle of nowhere that had been converted to flats. The sheer arrival, I knew it had spirits there. Things would happen, bumps, shuffles or footsteps even.

I remember one afternoon the tv turned off and would not turn back on. Then it turned on and turned back off again. When this happened, I knew I was in a situation that I didn't want to be in. I look back now, and it was like a force was trying to protect me, but I was so broken I had shut everything off and couldn't see it. But on that occasion, the entity saved me from an afternoon of abuse. For that, I will always be grateful to whatever or whoever it was.

Years went on, and occasionally I would feel a presence in my home. But I would just ignore it. I would be subjected to sleep paralysis or night terrors, but I never thought much of it.

My dad would always say be more afraid of the living than the dead. He never dismissed that spirits existed but always tried to reassure me.

When I was eighteen, I started to work in a pub; it was an old pub that had been many different places in its time. For the next fifteen years, I somehow created a strong fear of what I would feel, see or hear. I didn't know how to embrace it. I had been so shut off from that side; it became something frightening to me. So instead, I blocked out the voices, the movement of objects and sights. I would laugh nervously at things and try to shut away from what was going on. Even though deep down, I knew they were trying to connect with me.

Throughout the years I worked in hospitality, I became scared of the dark, frightened of everything unknown. I knew like a sixth sense there were a lot of good in the building, but also some not so good.

I'd always say good morning and good night when I left work. I didn't even realise I was doing it most of the time, I just said it I guess out of curtesy. There was something, but I knew it was a mix of good and bad, and I didn't want to be manipulated or tricked, so I closed off from them all.

I remember one night, my boss called me to the office to ask why I hadn't kicked everyone out. I said: "boss I have?" He showed me the CCTV of a man sitting at a table with his hand resting on his face. I went to the front of house, and no one was there? I was like he is freezing the CCTV surely. I went back to the office, and the picture was still there, so I sent my cousin up to the table, and he put his hand straight through the anomaly. I was in shock; panicked that this was a ghost? I couldn't explain it. I felt compelled to let the entity know my cousin meant no harm - A very bizarre feeling.

In another pub I worked in, it was full of activity, and I knew of a malevolent entity in the cellar. I was constantly in a mix of emotions, wanting to not let anything show, but the curiosity of what if was always there?

But my fear was so strong that any little sniff of paranormal, spiritual, or anything I shut off and blocked straight away. Amazing how our minds can condition us to believe things.

In 2015, I gave birth to my beautiful twin girls; they were eight weeks early. They arrived in August, my little Leo's. I suffered severe post-natal depression. I wanted to help others so they didn't feel how I did, but I was just slowly unravelling. I still believed I was bad luck too, as no one had ever told me otherwise.

Late 2015 I suffered a major breakdown. That I think was masked by the happiness of our beautiful girls. Then when they arrived, and the trauma both myself and my fiancé had, I just fell apart. But every time I tried to find happiness, I just dipped lower and lower into a spiralling depression. I had heard about the amazing benefits of Reiki and looked into it and how this amazing holistic therapy could help with how I was feeling.

I contacted my friend who had offered many times to come and see me, but every time I declined; I was scared. What if I don't know; maybe what if it didn't work or was it just a fad? I just could face people. But I still kept looking into it and how it all worked. It intrigued me.

At the end of 2017, myself and my fiancé parted ways.

I remember just feeling lost. But I started to see number sequences. At first, I just thought it was a coincidence, but I didn't realise they meant more. I would see the same sequence over and over again, everywhere; 111 and 1111. I tried to brush it off, but it just showed itself more.

I have always had an interest in numbers as we know from earlier on, believing I was bad luck. So, to me, I could only assume that 111 must mean something awful. In fact, it was the opposite. I found out I wasn't bad luck at all.

I used to speak to my dad all the time about ghosts and spiritual bits. He had told me many times he did palmistry, but I didn't know what it was, so I dismissed it. He later told me I had to find my own path; he couldn't force me to find my path, as it had to come naturally. I will always respect my dad for that. I told him about the number's id see, and he would just smile. I would get so annoyed and be like "for the love of God, why are you smiling." I later found out he wanted me to learn what they meant.

I started to learn what these numbers meant and how they came into my life. I learnt that in actual fact, they were angel numbers and meant positive things. It's amazing how different you look at life when the glass is half full. I also started looking into numerology and the understanding of these numbers too.

I decided to book my first reading with Tina Pavlou in January 2018, and wow, it opened my mind so much I started to believe I wasn't bad luck and in actual fact, I had a lot to offer the world, I just didn't realise it. Tina didn't know me. She had never met me or knew anything about my life. I have never been drawn to having a reading before until this time. I used to study astrology, understand the star signs and what they meant for us. But I had never wanted someone to tell me my future. It didn't seem right. But when you are at rock bottom, and you are so lost, it's amazing the signs and guidance you get.

That year I started to learn more about mindset, meditation and how these things can help with our mental health. See, I had been going back and forth to the doctor for ten years about my mental health and just got pushed aside. So, I tried to look for natural ways. I was enjoying finding new ways and learning about spirits and how you feel when they are around you. My best friend Lottie took me under her wing and showed me that it's okay to open up spiritually and that in fact, I had guides and angels looking out for me and my twins. It was finally like someone had clarified to me everything I had thought as a child. I can't tell you how happy this made me and how I believe it helped me on my spiritual awakening path. I will always be grateful to her and Tina for helping me envelop these feelings.

That year I knew I wanted to just open up and keep learning about everything spiritual. Now I say this, but I still held back. I guess I was scared of the unknown and scared that if I open up fully whilst not being in a stable state of mind, would that mean I would be susceptible to the evil side of spirits? Everything I researched and learnt meant I would always hold back, not fully knowing I was holding back, due to the fear of not fully under-standing the spiritual world.

2018 was a tough year; my mental health was really testing its limits. I still didn't fully know what was wrong with my mental health; by this point, I was beginning to just think it was me. I found solace in meditation and crystals at the time. Learning and understanding the uniqueness of what such beautiful stones hold and how they can play such an important roll in our lives. I decided to take my twins or as I refer to them, my lion cubs, to a crystal shop. My twins are amazing, they wanted to learn to meditate with me, and they were always picking up my crystals and wanting to know their names. They would sit and hold them, and so I thought, why not let them choose a crystal of their own.

So, we went to our local crystal shop, and we looked at all the beautiful crystals. I asked them to see which ones they liked the most. Then they would pick up the crystals, and I would ask them which ones made them happy. Ava picked rose quartz and opalite, and Emily picked up lapis lazuli and amethyst.

The gentleman behind the counter asked if the twins wanted to know what their star sign crystal was? I said I knew their birth month, but I'd love to know what it was as I wanted to get it for them. The gentleman then politely told me their stone was the tigers' eye. I just stopped in awe at the fact this was my first ever crystal. I couldn't stop smiling.

As 2018 continued, I tried really hard to remain positive, but I just felt I was going on a downward spiral again. I wanted to do something I should have tried a couple of years previous, reiki. So, I approached my friend and contacted her about receiving reiki.

It was a surreal feeling. I remember lying there thinking of how this would go. I remember thinking is this just going to be a load of tosh, or does it actually work?

I laid down and closed my eyes. I remember lying there and just falling into a beautiful calm state. It felt like all the pain, angst, and worry was melting away. I could feel tears rolling down my cheeks and a sharp stabbing pain in my chest. It just felt as though I needed to release some energy. I needed to release all the hurt and pain that I had kept inside of me.

I then felt a cold rush of air go from my feet, and up to my body. It was like someone had put a fan at the base of my feet, and it was blowing up my body; it was so surreal.

I then awoke, and my friend spoke to me about my chakras and also what she saw. She saw my power animal, a lion. My throat chakra was hurting, and I had been coughing badly for a while. She then explained to me what this meant and that I needed to open up and speak my mind. Funnily enough, this was always something I struggled with as I never spoke up, as I didn't want to upset or hurt anyone. I couldn't handle upsetting others, so I just kept it in. This was bad as you should always be open and speak your mind. You shouldn't be malicious or nasty but if you need to communicate with people or if people have upset you, then speaking out to resolve any disagreement, is always better than staying silent.

I realised I was the master of my happiness, and to be happy, I had to let go of anything or anyone that no longer served me to the higher good.

I was intrigued by reiki. I felt a release and felt that it had done me wonders.

I booked again to see my friend, and at that time, I was in a very bad way. I felt like I had hit rock bottom or thought I had. I went to see my friend and I was just constantly in tears; I couldn't stop. My life just seemed to be unravelling in front of my eyes, and I didn't know how to stop it or resolve it. My friend was brilliant. As daft as it sounded, I always knew that you had to release the negativity before you could rebuild and truly be happy. But when it comes to yourself, you don't tend to listen, do you? I lay there and just couldn't stop crying throughout the whole session. Now I know that I was letting go, but to me, I just thought I wasn't strong enough for this amazing therapy. See I had never been to any form of therapy so to me the hard part was letting go, crying, being angry etc.; the part I just couldn't get my head around, was that it needed to be done before the healing begins. I just thought I was weak and broken. Isn't it amazing what we tell ourself and our limiting beliefs? So, I didn't return and spent my Christmas upset, alone in a crowded room and full of resent.

I wanted to learn. I have always found ways to beat the black dog or put it at bay, so to speak, and this time was no different. I was more determined. I wanted to understand more and more about reiki, how it works and how it heals people and animals. But I just couldn't face having a session again and being so vulnerable.

I started reading and doing reiki courses, understanding the origins, energy and vibrations. I just couldn't stop learning. I was also starting to feel like myself again. I had started therapy with a councillor, something I had put off since my mother's death, and something I knew I needed to do. Why I had put this off for twenty years, I will never know, but we find strength in the most peculiar of ways.

I then learnt and understood the energy of chakras, meditations, just saying positive affirmations and being grateful for the little things. These small changes were bringing me out of my shell. I spent 2019 studying and learning to love the voices again, the visions, the chills and learning to be positive. I learnt everything from Usui Reiki, crystal reiki, animal reiki and many more amazing subjects including Feng Shui, meditation and numerology. I just wanted to learn as much as I could about anything I could. I was like a spiritual learning sponge. I felt so alive.

My best friend was my guide, and she would help me learn that my angels were guiding me. I started smiling again and decided I would go back to reiki.

Wow, what a transformation; I saw and felt so much more and spoke to my good friend Marie who I always say was, and is, another beautiful soul that helped me on my path and worked with me to find my spiritual path and happiness.

I told her that I was learning animal reiki and what an amazing therapy that it is to be able to heal and work with such pure and innocent souls. My friend simply smiled and told me that I should consider working with animals. I then told her the story about how I wanted to work in a zoo when I was eighteen and work with animals but got scared of going to college, so I never followed the path.

Marie smiled and said she thinks I would do amazing at working with animals, so I thought what a magical gift that it is to work with animals.

I finished my reiki session and just felt like I was on the right path. But then it hit... I started going downhill; I can't explain how or when it started, but it just seemed to have hit me full on like a bat out of hell. Maybe it was the stress of selling my home that triggered the downward spiral; I have no idea. I would drop the twins off to school, and I would lay in my beautiful conservatory with my dogs and just sleep. I would have the doors open and listen to the sounds of the trees outside. I just needed to shut off to the world, but it wasn't enough. I started to self-harm again. I hadn't self-harmed since I was fourteen and was in such a bad way that I needed a release. I would cut my arm with my lion on so that others couldn't see. The one thing that kept me going was the love I have for my twins and how I had to find my way as I was not losing them, they are and always will be my light.

I called the doctors surgery and made an appointment. For the first time, I went to the Drs and just bared all. Whenever I went to the doctors previously, it was always in a depressive spout, so naturally, it was always depression that I was told I had. I dismissed the manic mania stages I have as that was just being me. Why would I question the hyper happy side of me? I confessed to my doctor about self-harming myself, and we made progress in realising, it was in actual fact, severe mood swings. And that was, in fact, the reason why one moment I was happy and the next I would drop, and never fully understand why I was never getting better.

Now I knew it was more about personality I felt like I finally had clarity. I felt like I finally knew how to help myself, so in turn, I can help others effectively.

Now I understand I will be on medication for life, but this was the first time I accepted this. I have never wanted to be on medication, who does? But instead of listening to those that have doctorates, I thought ah I'm happy yeah, no more meds….. No!!! I was wrong, as soon as they came out my system BAM, I dropped again. So, this time around, I stopped and became sensible. I also decided that alongside the medication, there are natural ways that can help me. So, I performed Reiki on myself, and I would meditate daily. The great thing is I'd meditate with my dogs. They had to touch a part of my body, and they wouldn't leave me during this. I'd meditate with the twins too. I'd say positive affirmations and believe them. I would accept that it's okay to rest. If I needed to sleep and the world seemed too much, it would be okay to take the break.

I also found solace in performing reiki to people, distant and one to one. But the best part for me was working with animals. Now I have no background in animals, so to me, it helps me with my reiki as I'm not going into the session thinking on a veterinarian level of could it be this or this; instead, I was just going in as a Mum wanting to let the animals know I was here to help.

It was magical from learning distant animal reiki and having these majestic animals in my visions, to seeing people's animal spirit guides and telling people what these beautiful animals meant.

I also started to learn what our animal guides were and why we'd say we would see a robin pop out or a fox run past us. What did this mean?

I just kept learning, kept seeing more and more beautiful animals and healing more and more animals. My heart was starting to fill.

But then I just seemed to stop? It was bizarre I just stopped and pursued coaching instead, but this didn't fill the void that working with animals did. I tried pushing it, but every time I did, I could feel something draining from me. It was like I was trying to please everyone else and not me.

I would be stuck on wondering what my spiritual path was and what direction I should go? I knew I didn't want to be a medium because that wasn't me, but I kept seeing more and more, and it was more the question of, what do I do? Deep inside, I was worried that if I let negative in, it mimics well. I didn't want to do that. I kept picking up reiki and putting it down again due to being so confused about what I should do. My dad was a palmist, should I follow that? He told me that I was not allowed to do tarot, he said that wasn't my gift and was very strict on me not doing it. I love my dad, so when he said things like that, I listened. Plus, I never wanted to do tarot reading; it didn't appeal to me. It amazed me when others did it, but I didn't wish to do it.

I was still seeing beautiful angel numbers, and they amazed me, but I must admit I was mischievous and didn't always listen to them, but numbers fascinated me, so I looked more into numerology to understand it better and learnt more on how it worked. It helped me to understand different people, their life paths and all the way through to what the year held for them. All this from a number, how amazing is that.

My journey of self-healing was a long one, but to me, it seemed a million times quicker knowing how to help myself and the different ways to battle my emotions than what I already knew. Mentally I was on a path to assess if I had bipolar. I learnt to accept this, mainly because it had always been with me and always will be, but now, I can learn to understand it and work with it.

I also saw this as a way to help others too. My logic was, if I go through many different emotions, especially going through business, what better way to adapt what I use to manage my triggers than to help others who are going through stages such as limiting beliefs and self-sabotage too.

I started learning more on the importance of morning routines and how they have a positive impact on our lives in business and daily life. I started to meditate daily, do affirmations, as well as write in my gratitude journal and ensure I was doing yoga in the morning and evening. I also wanted to make sure I was adding the spiritual twist into the mix of things. So, I added a mix of reiki, law of attraction, numerology and Fengshui to my day. This worked really well for me and helped me to keep my balance, as well as order in my studies.

My confidence was growing, and I was starting to feel alive again. I was starting to feel like myself again, and I loved it. I had a huge journey in front of me, but I was grabbing the bull by the horns and owning my life.

I knew I needed to get healthy and work on my physical and mental being. Once I started to love number one, I could then help others love themselves too.

I continued to work on understanding more of my spiritual ability and came across a few stumbles on my way. I would pick up attachments and not know how or even that I had them. But thanks to my amazing circle of friends, I learnt how to ground myself more, how to not let it get to me and what to do to rid the attachments if I got them.

Once I felt at a point, I could feel myself becoming more confident and myself again. I created a business to have a mixture of self-love, care and mindset as well as bringing a spiritual element too. I wanted to ensure I used the amazing spiritual things I had learnt and use them to help others. I wanted to be a happiness coach with a twist. I wanted to bring happiness to people's lives as I have always done, but I wanted to add a little twist. I wanted to add the spiritual side of things to the mix. Why? Because thanks to unleashing my spiritual side, it helped me to learn a lot about myself and my body. It helped me to release the pain I had carried around for years. It helped me to push past fears and barriers. I will always be grateful for everything I have learnt to this day. Without it, I wouldn't be the person I am now.

I still want to learn palmistry. I want to always keep learning, keep evolving and keep teaching my children to embrace and be their true selves. They are after all my saviour, my strength and my guidance. I will always be indebted to them both. I'm one lucky mummy. Thank you, Ava Elizabeth and Emily Rose. Thanks to you both for loving me, caring for me and being my strength when I felt weak. I promise to always guide you. xx

ABOUT THE AUTHOR

LIZZY ADAMS

Lizzy found her gift when she was about four years old and WOW; Was it about to blow her mind?

Lizzy has qualifications in Reiki, Meditation, Feng Shui and Numerology and is self-taught in many other spiritual practises.

Lizzy is a Spiritual Happiness Coach which means in a nutshell; she helps bring a bucket load of positivity into people's lives and works with amazing souls on their spiritual awakening journey.

Whether you feel lost or struggle with knowing the direction you want to go in spiritually. Lizzy works with you to find your path. In this chapter, you will find out just how Lizzy stumbled across her gift and the bumpy road that was ahead. Enjoy.

Contact Lizzy:

www.spiritualhappinesscoach.com

Email: lizzy@spiritualhappinesscoach.com

LYNN ROBINSON

I was born the youngest, the only girl and on my beloved dad's birthday; 'Daddies little princess and the apple of his eye'. When I was 6 months old, I contracted German measles in my throat and was very poorly. The doctor was worried that it was so severe that I may go deaf or blind, which fortunately wasn't the case. It was my dad that looked after me even though he was at work all day; he would come home and care for me whilst my mum slept. Under the stairs, he placed my cot, and he put a blanket up to stop any light coming through. Due to this disease, whenever I get run down, tired or ill, it always goes straight to my throat. Apart from this, I was a healthy child who was always outdoors; cycling, swimming or at gymnastics. In fact, when I think about it, whenever I was ill, it would always be my dad that looked after me.

I worshipped both my brothers; they were my heroes. Mum used to get them to take me to the park with them and swimming etc. They moaned excessively about it, having to drag their little sister along with them, damaging their street cred. My middle brother hated my guts at the start, but when I was about 6 or 7, we used to go caving at the beaches in Thanet armed with ropes, torches and lunch. It was one time after he'd had the 'birds and the bees' talk with my Dad, and he experimented on me to see and feel what it felt like. He told me not to say anything about what had happened, or he would do something nasty to me. I was petrified and cried all the way home. However, until my father died, I did not tell anyone, apart from my husband. When I eventually plucked up the courage to tell my mother, I got told that I was a stupid girl, because I should have told her when it happened. I didn't know it was wrong until years later when I was older, and he was in the RAF by then. I asked what, if anything, she was going to do, "I'll definitely see him in a different light now, but there was no need to do anything now as it would just open a 'can of worms' and it's just my word against his"!! I was dumbfounded.

Being the only girl wasn't much fun as I was expected to do loads of chores every week from a very early age. I was also a 'latch door kid' because my mum had gone back to work when I started junior school, so I had to let myself in after school with the spare key under the mat at the back door. I would put the lights on, pull the curtains, light the fire and make my own tea. As I had school meals, it was just soups, sandwiches etc. Mum would usually get home about 6.30, and I would have had to have cleared, tidied, and washed my plates before she came home. I was never allowed friends' round or never allowed to have sleepovers etc. When I was 11 years old, I became a 'woman'; two weeks after starting secondary school I came on my period; therefore, my Mum made me do all of my own washing and ironing.

I was 15 when my parents decided to separate and divorce. I felt stuck between the two of them pulling me from pillar to post, both wanting me to be with them, so when I was 16, I decided to go to London. Whoever I chose would be upset – that's why I applied to have a job in London, so I would not upset either of them. My brothers were eight and nine years older than me and were both in the Army, and the RAF, so they were not there to witness all the arguing and the sniping that my Mum used to do towards my Dad.

At school, I was the mother hen, agony aunt type; everyone would always come to me with their troubles – but who could I go to for mine? When I was 15 years old, I started to self-harm as I overheard my dad say to my mum years ago that "if it hadn't been for me that he would have divorced her years ago". I used to bite myself and pull my hair out as I felt like it was my fault what my Dad had to go through with my mum – I was so angry with my mum and used to get so angry with how she treated him. I felt that if it hadn't of been for me, my Dad would have been happy, and if I hadn't come along, he would have been free from her. Now, as an adult, I realise it wasn't my fault I just loved my Dad so much. I miss my Dad terribly. We had such a wonderful relationship, and I still feel so strongly connected to him now, even though he passed 16 years ago. He is always with me.

Unfortunately, this was not the case with my mother. I now know that she was jealous of the relationship I had with my father. My middle brother hated the fact that he had been pushed to the middle by a girl. He tried his best to get rid of me; he was found putting a pillow over my face as a baby in the pram and would put his scouts' scarf around my neck, tightening the woggle. My older brother was the opposite, he lived away at boarding school, and when he would come home, he would take me out in the pram. He didn't care what his friends thought of him; he loved the idea of having a little sister.

I first got into my spiritual journey by reading the autobiographies of Doris Stokes. I really resonated with her and loved hearing how she helped people. I was about 16 years old and used to be up at 4am in the morning to travel to London to work as a receptionist from the Kent coast, so I had plenty of time to read.

My manager used to drive us up to London, and he told me that he had been to see a lady who was a 'medium.' The story he told me was quite profound, so I asked for her phone number. About three months later, I was at a crossroads in my life, and I needed guidance, so I phoned this lady late one Friday night after finishing work.

The telephone box was just around the corner, and I dialled the number and put my 2p in to speak. I said to the medium 'Can you help me?' and the first thing she said to me was 'you sound very young' I got a bit narky about this – I was 16 and felt older than my years so defended myself and said 'what's that got to do with anything' – good old teenage hormones! She proceeded to tell me that she saw me walking through large rubber doors, along wide corridors and up and down stairs and that there was an elderly lady in the family who was nearing the end and to expect the worse and as for the crossroads everything would turn out okay.

I ran home and asked both Mum and Nan if they were okay and they were; so, I forgot about the rest and enjoyed my weekend. On Monday at work, I received a phone call telling me that my Aunt, who was 92 and lived in Hackney, was poorly and could I go and see her as soon as possible. My manager drove us there from my workplace in Silvertown, and when I entered the house, my Nan gave me a letter that I shoved into my pocket, and I went and sat with my Aunt.

I spent the next hour talking about good times with my Aunt, and when I got up to leave, I said 'I'll see you later Auntie', and she said "Goodbye Lynn", and I knew then that was the last time I would see her alive. About 4pm that afternoon, Nan rang to say that Auntie had passed peacefully. I was allowed to leave work early with my manager, and whilst crying in the car I went to get a tissue out of my pocket and came across the letter that my Nan had given me earlier.

When I opened the letter, it was for an interview at Hackney hospital, for a Clerical Assistant. I got the job in medical records, looking for patients notes for clinics and just as the medium had predicted I ended up walking along long wide corridors, up and down stairs and through large rubber doors. After that, I was convinced there was more to this spirituality stuff and needed to know more!

Whilst working at Hackney hospital, I needed to have a small operation, and while I was waiting to go down to theatre a lady on the ward called me over, explaining that she could see things. She asked for my hand and read my palm, telling me that the man I was with, was not good for me and that I would lose a lot of money and heartbreak if I stayed with him. At the time, I was absolutely besotted and in love with him, my then 1st husband, and made the excuse that she must be talking about my previous boyfriend who had cheated on me. I asked if I would marry this man and sighing, she said 'yes'. She then proceeded to tell me that I would find the person of my dreams and have two children and that they would be the same sex, but she couldn't tell me if they were boys or girls. I thanked her and went and had my operation. This reading came back to haunt me on numerous occasions, especially six years later, when my first husband spent all our money on buying a new motorbike and hiding it from me in a neighbour's garage.

I was 18 when I met my first husband who was a police officer in Hackney; he was 12 years older than me and had been married before, and he had also travelled the world being in the Army. Looking back, I think I looked upon him as a father figure; it was a whirlwind romance we were married within a year. I realised shortly after marrying him that there were a lot of things that he started to control about me. For example, I wasn't allowed to wear trousers or leggings, red nail varnish or red lipstick. We had three dogs, and I used to have to take them out in a skirt and wellies in Epping forest. When we used to go to friends' houses, he told me what to wear. I realised he was very mentally controlling, and when I became manager of Laura

Ashley, he didn't like that either. He could have been an inspector, but the only reason he stayed as a PC was so he could be on the front line. He resented me for taking the position of Manager even though he had the same opportunity in his career to progress too.

Working in the hospital led me to go into my nursing qualification, which was in May 1983 at Whipps Cross hospital, Leytonstone. I loved learning all about the body and how we did procedures, but I didn't feel comfortable – I felt like I was a square peg in a round hole. All my other fellow students seemed to slot in nicely, but I didn't, and I spent more time crying than doing the nursing side; feeling helpless that I couldn't help everyone – this is when I realised that I am a sensitive soul and an empath.

I also couldn't understand when someone died where their soul went, and no one could give me the answers that I needed. So, after 18 months of training, I left nursing and went to work in retail. I went to work for Laura Ashley Ltd, a British premium home furnishing and garment company. This was a complete contrast to nursing, and it took me approximately six months to stop calling customers' patients. I loved working for LA and progressed all the way to Manager by the age of 24. It was hard work, but we had fun and laughter, and I met lots of people, including the Ashley's children who worked within the company. At Managers conferences, they would come and sit with us at mealtimes and ask how they could make things better within the shops, which is a rarity now.

In our third year of marriage I had to have the coil taken out, and the options for him were if we were to have sex a) he would wear a condom b) he wouldn't wear one, and I get pregnant or c) we don't have sex at all. He decided on, no sex at all because he didn't want children and didn't want to wear a condom. If I had of known this, I wouldn't have married him in the first place, as I was desperate to have children. I really took all this to heart and would eat to make me feel better, I had put on nearly three stone after we married, I was just so unhappy, so in 1989 we separated, and I moved back home to Thanet; then 18 months later, I met my current husband, Paul.

What a breath of fresh air Paul was and still is. He is my rock and always has been. When we first met, I tripped him up on purpose to buy him a drink, we got talking, and the rest is history. He is so supportive of me, doesn't control me and allows me to be who I am. Paul is loyal and reliable and steadfast and has been an excellent husband, father and grandad to our family. Paul's parents were wonderful and very supportive of us too. I am forever grateful that this wonderful man and his family came into my life.

In 1989 I also suffered my first major breakdown due to my first marriage dissolving and ended up coming back home, to Thanet. Laura Ashley were great and kept my job open for me for over 6 months, but I knew I couldn't go back as I had nowhere to live and three German shepherd dogs to look after – my fur babies at the time. It was a year or so after separation that I met Paul, my now-husband.

I did a couple of jobs to make ends meet and eventually got a job as a receptionist at Margate hospital which only lasted six months as I then found out I was pregnant with my first son.

I managed to get a part-time job at Ramsgate hospital after three months of having him and stayed there for two years until I fell pregnant again with my second son. After six weeks, I started back at Margate hospital as a clerical officer to the Medical records manager. I worked there for seven years until I became a foster carer in 2000.

We fostered a young boy for two years, and he was part of our family. As far as I was concerned, I had three boys. He called us Mum and Dad and fitted in well, then one day social services moved him away to be with his siblings up North. We were all gutted and missed him terribly. After that we had troubled young teenagers from countries such as China and Bosnia; the language barrier was difficult for them and us, so I decided to give up being a foster carer, feeling that I couldn't help them as much as I would have wanted to.

Eventually, a new vacancy arose at Margate hospital as a private patient administrator organising theatre rooms, supplies and staffing. I was surprised to get this job, as at this time, I didn't feel that I deserved it. I worked here part-time for 4 and a half years, then my local church took me on part-time as the assistant manager of their new centre. After having a disagreement with the vicar who judged me over something that I hadn't done, he then told me the position was no longer viable and asked if I would relinquish my position and go down to 10 hours a week. I always saw myself as a good Christian girl – I attended church regularly during the week and at weekends, and after this experience with this vicar, I never went back to the Church again. This shook my world as I always felt very safe at the Church, but after this experience of being completely misunderstood and judged for something I hadn't done, I stepped back.

This was when I started reading Sylvia Browne books; the veil dropped, and I suddenly started seeing the truth. It was as if I was opening up and suddenly realising all the questions I had asked previously in nursing; I was finally getting the answers, such as where does the soul go? Are our loved ones with us? Are they present? She really helped me understand that they are always around us; they are with us and are supporting us throughout our lives and our journey, you only have to ask for their help.

In 2007 I started working back at Laura Ashley Ltd in a new shop in Broadstairs as Assistant Manager, it wasn't the same company that I worked for before due to Bernard Ashley selling it on, it was all about profit and sales, which was a shame, but I loved the products so enjoyed my time there.

When I turned 50 years old, I started a habit of drinking more. I used alcohol to suppress any problems or upsets, being the sensitive soul that I am. I went from drinking three bottles of wine a week to two bottles of wine a night. We had the sad news that Paul's mum passed away this year only to have the good news that we were now grandparents to a beautiful little girl. My son and my granddaughter's mother are not together, and my son now lives in Australia, but this special gift they blessed our family with, I will be forever grateful. My granddaughter is a joy and pleasure to be around and is also a sensitive soul, just like her Nana. We spend most weekends together, which I cherish so much as she lights up our lives.

About four years later, I had a wobble at work and ended up being off sick for four months due to alcohol addiction. After Christmas, I had an epiphany and decided I needed to do something about this addiction; that was when Arbonne came into my life. I needed to put back into my body the nutrients I was lacking, which after having a gastric bypass in 2010, I was lacking Vitamin B12.

I needed to replace the alcohol with the vitamins and Arbonne being vegan and plant-based, it gave me the opportunity to do the 30 days to Healthy living programme and to stop drinking. I went 33 days with no alcohol and felt fabulous. Through signing up as an independent consultant with Arbonne, I got to meet my up-line Natalie who although originally from Thanet now lives in Perth, Western Australia.

Natalie also wrote her chapter in the first book of When the Goddess Calls and the book was being launched in March 2019. I was asked if I would go and support her at the launch along with one of her friends as she couldn't make it. We went to the launch, and this was the very first time I met Tina Pavlou and the other sisters of The Goddess Rooms who had also written chapters in the book. I sat quietly listening to what Tina was saying then she looked at me and asked if she could scan me. I agreed, and she told me that I had a lot of pain in my stomach –

I said it was probably due to the drinking and she said NO, I was using drink to suppress the pain.

She said I needed to see her when she got back in June and to make an appointment with her which I did. At the appointment in June, the cards were shuffled, and one sprung out – this was saying divine intervention. I was meant to be there. She asked me to come back that night to Angelic reiki share which I did, and I haven't looked back since. This was the best decision I have ever made. Since then I have done Angelic Reiki 1,2, 3 and 4 and become an Angelic Reiki Master. I have also attended Theta Basic, Advanced and Dig Deeper courses and will be doing more later this year. I feel I have found my calling surrounded by beautiful soul sisters and a wonderful gifted leader.

I am also a Young Living oil distributor; these oils as far as I'm concerned are the purest in the world and can be used in a variety of ways. I raise my vibration on a daily basis with mantras and meditation. Throughout the lockdown of 2020, Tina did a daily mantra which helped support me through all the emotional challenges we all faced through this time. This accompanied with these beautiful oils has kept my frequency high, enabling me to be there for myself and others.

My granddaughter also loves the oils and is always asking me to massage them into her back and feet. I also use these oils on my clients for my treatments that I offer from home. I specialise in Angelic Reiki facials helping people to raise their vibration and lift their mood.

Try looking for the rainbow in everyone, and if you cannot find their rainbow, YOU be the rainbow for them. You never know what impact you may have given them.

 'Just Be The RAINBOW'

 'To see a World in a Grain of Sand,

And a Heaven in a Wild Flower,

Hold Infinity in the Palm of your hand,

And Eternity in an hour.'

— (WILLIAM BLAKE 1757-1827)

Lynn Robinson is an Angelic Reiki Master and Theta Healing practitioner who lives in Margate, Kent. Lynn is married to her husband Paul, and they have two boys and a beautiful grand-daughter who they adore.

Lynn's story shows that she has faced adversity in her life yet still has a wonderful sense of humour and ability to light up a room with her smile. Lynn embarked on a journey of self-discovery, and even with everything that she has been through, she has the strength to help others feel good about themselves and empower people to step forward into their best lives. She attends The Goddess Rooms regularly for Angelic Reiki shares which help her with ongoing addictions, which she is overcoming.

Lynn is an Arbonne Independent Consultant offering her clients a way to use vegan nutrition, skincare and makeup to support mind, body and skin; looking after themselves from the inside out.

Lynn also is a distributor and strong advocate for the Young Living essential oils which have helped support her through some of the toughest times of her life and increased her vibration to that of pure love.

Lynn also offers Angelic Reiki Facials and Theta Healings at her home or at The Goddess Rooms in Ramsgate.

You can contact Lynn below:

Email: lynnmargate@aol.com
Website for Arbonne:
www.lynnrobinson449343961.arbonne.com
Website for Young Living essential oils:
https://www.myyl.com/lynn-robinson

facebook.com/lynnrobinson
instagram.com/lynnrobinson449

NICHOLA DREW

$\mathcal{W}$here do I begin? I'll start at the beginning; I've always been different.

I've never felt like I belonged or fit in, even with my family.

I didn't really look like them, I mean I had the same hair colour and eye colour as my dad, I had my mums laugh and wicked sense of humour, but I never really felt that I belonged there with them.

It was like I was dropped off at birth and abandoned by my real parents.

I always felt like I came from somewhere else or was meant to be somewhere else.

Even as a child, I used to pretend to be a witch, or a fairy, or a mermaid. I never wanted to be here; On earth or be human; I always knew there was more to me than just me, I spent more time in an imaginary world than in the real one. I even used to 'cast spells' to make my fantasy worlds real.

Even from a young age, I could sense energy and see things or know things that people hadn't told me. As I got older, these experiences got more and more intense to the point my bed would shake at night, and I would feel something ominous standing in my room waiting for me. The house I grew up in as a child scared me, there was something there, and I knew it. I can still see my bedroom; I can still feel the dark energy of that house even now, and that's over 20 years ago. That house was the beginning of the end for my family, my parents got divorced, and we finally moved out of that house. My parents' divorce had a huge impact on my life, as that really was a turning point for me and the way I saw myself, it was also the beginning of a new chapter of emotional & mental abuse from my father towards me & my sister. He became an alcoholic and began the slow descent downwards into nothing. His angry rages where he would shout and swear at my sister and me and call us things no child should hear, set my foundations for my feelings of unworthiness. I watched him hold my mum up at knifepoint, I heard him call my mum names, and he told me things no child should know. He was punishing my sister and me because my mum finally left him to be with the love of her life. And to make matters worse, during all of this, I fell out with my group of girls who I thought were my friends but who then, for two years, became my torturers. So not only was I in the midst of my family breaking down, my mum dedicating her time to her new relationship and my dad drowning himself in alcohol and possibly drugs; I was left with nothing and no one.

So there I was, a sad, scared and lonely 12-year-old with no friends and no support.

It was just me alone with my thoughts, my thoughts of fear, my thoughts of worthlessness and my feelings of sadness like I'd never known. I became completely numb to the world, just plodding along. Existing. Life became nothing more than a cycle of getting up, going to school, trying to hide from the bullies as much as I could, going home, reading all the death threats from the kids at school and people I didn't know, and then crying myself to sleep wishing I would die and then I would be free. But no, every day, I woke up and would go through it all again. I tried to talk to my mum, but I was told to get on with it, I tried to talk to my dad, but he was too self-absorbed to hear, I wanted to talk to my sister, but she was trying so hard to be strong for the both of us that she didn't know how to help. So I went to the one place I felt safe, the one place no one would hurt me, the school chapel.

I sat in the chapel and cried, I asked God to take me away, and I heard the words 'No. You have work to do my child,' I looked up and above the altar was this beautiful being. I knew it was Mother Mary. I saw her for nothing more than a split second and then she was gone. That's it I thought, I've really lost my mind now, and that was the first night I cut myself.

I don't know why but I did, I just wanted the pain I felt to be physical, so I had something to see, to represent my self-hatred, but all it did was sting like hell and bleed.

Fast forward a year, I made it through the bullying, I had made new friends & I had my first boyfriend! Things were looking up, and I was starting to feel good about myself. Little did I know I was about to have my first dance with the devil. This event was the first day I truly believed in and saw evil, and it was also the first time I believe I was saved by the angels. My dad decided to move back to Blackpool, his hometown, so being the daddy's girl I was I offered to help...the whole thing was an awful experience, and I'm lucky to have made it home alive. At some point on the drive home my dad snapped, he was driving down the motorway at 100mph screaming, shouting and swearing at me and trying to reach across the seat to hit me. What had I done? Nothing. He just turned on me out of nowhere when I asked how far we were from my home. This tirade went on for an hour, and I've never felt so scared for my life. At some point I blacked out. All I remember was hearing the words 'sleep my child; we will keep you safe, close your eyes, you will get home safely', and when I opened my eyes, we were back in Rickmansworth after the 6-hour drive from hell. I tried to talk to my dad about what happened, but he claimed he had no idea what I was talking about and just walked away. On the way home with my mum, all I kept thinking was why me? Why did he attack me? It wouldn't be a good 10 years until I would learn the answers to this.

Fast forward 6 years to when I turned 18 and I could finally drink! Now between the age of 12 and 18 I had begun to believe and feel there was so much more to life than just going to school and going to work; I hated school, I felt it was pointless and the day I left I was so happy! But I left school and spent the next few years flitting between college courses, desperately searching for something that resonated with me. It was in this time I had started to see, hear and feel things more intensely than ever. To the point, I would force myself to stay awake at night as I was too afraid to go to sleep, as whilst asleep I would see and feel things I just couldn't explain and would often experience sleep paralysis. Alcohol was the first time I experienced being taken over; I used to have a few drinks and blackout. I would lose total control over my body, mouth and mind; I would do things, say things and wake up in the morning thinking how the hell did I get home? What happened last night?! This became a regular occurrence whilst drinking. I even began to talk in different languages! But I didn't stop because I was on a path to total self-destruction and the more I drank, the deeper down the rabbit hole I went. When I turned 22, and after many years of partying, experimenting with drugs, sleeping with people I didn't know, and getting pointless piercings or tattoos; life gave me a huge shock. I suffered a miscarriage with my partner at the time, who I had been with for 4 years and was engaged to. This was a huge turning point for me in my life, I had never wanted to have children, but after finding out I was pregnant something in me changed, I couldn't believe this tiny thing inside me was growing and it's the first time I truly believed in the miracle of life. But it wasn't to last. The baby decided it wasn't ready for Earth and its spirit left. I was woken in the middle of the night to a pain I'd never felt before. I looked down to see I was covered in blood and began to scream for my mum, I had only found out two days before that I was pregnant, and now the baby was dying. I phased in and out of consciousness and the next 24 hours were a blur. My baby was gone; I was heartbroken and angry. I blamed myself, I blamed my body for failing me but most of all, I blamed my partner because just that day he had told me he didn't want it and I was to have an abortion. So the spirit took matters into its own hands and left. This set me on the path to healing, to find out why all of these things were happening and had happened to me, and how I could heal them and myself. And I discovered Usui Reiki. I found a fabulous woman near to me and booked my appointment for my first healing, on the day I was so nervous. I had no idea what to expect, but something deep inside me told me this would be the beginning of something amazing and to just go with it. I had my reiki session & I felt and saw things I didn't know I could! I knew I had to learn how to do this and the lovely lady gave me the number for her reiki master; it took me a week to pluck up the courage to ring this lady, and when I did, it genuinely changed my life.

I did my reiki 1 and my world changed! Within weeks of me doing my reiki level 1, I had joined a psychic development group, I had split up from my boyfriend of 5 years and I had met someone new! Life just went so fast, I went from knowing nothing about angels or spirits to learning how to channel, how to read tarot cards, how to connect to the spirit realms; the list goes on. My world was opening up and life was amazing! I was getting really good at reading tarot cards; I was even taking them with me to work to do readings for people. One day I was sitting at my desk when my dad rang me and asked me to do his cards, he had a huge business deal that week and wanted to know if it would go through. I quickly drew 4 cards for him and took a picture with the intent to read for him, but I got distracted and forgot about the reading. It wasn't until the next day I remembered to do my dad's reading and I sat and channelled. I sent the reading and decided to ring him to talk about it later.....we'll later never came. I never got to speak to him because the next day he died. I was driving down the motorway and I felt this awful feeling of distress and then a feeling of total peace just washed over me, the whole time I couldn't breath and I knew something wasn't right. I immediately tried to ring my dad and he didn't answer. Half an hour later whilst at work I got a phone call form an unknown number, it was my grandmother ringing to tell me my dad had just been found dead in the shower.

I was in shock. I went into autopilot and drove home. I sank into a deep depression and couldn't stop crying, I was so angry at him for dying and I was devastated I never got to say goodbye. In the days that followed myself and my sister returned to Blackpool to pack up my dad's belongings.....little did I know that I had in fact predicted the event that were to follow my dads death in his reading, it was his girlfriend at the time who re-read the reading to me and the reality of it all sank in. I had predicted my dads death and that's when I stopped reading tarot cards. I blamed myself, and I hated my gifts. So I stopped. I stopped everything to do with anything spiritual. I was done with my gifts.

It was during this time that I had already signed up to learn angelic reiki, as I had already booked and paid for the course I decided to go; it was exactly what I needed right at that time when I had stopped believing in myself; id always believed in and felt angels but angelic reiki took this to a whole new level. The energy and healing that took place during the course gave me the renewed sense of life that I so desperately needed right at that time and after 5 and half days I walked away an angelic reiki master and ready to take on the world. I also walked away with two of the most wonderful friends and mentors I could have ever asked for, who are still in my life now.

Not long after this I found out I was pregnant with my first son; it was like a gift from the angels in a time when I needed it the most. However becoming a mum wasn't the amazing experience I thought it was going to be and after a traumatic C-section which left me in so much pain I thought I was dying, to not having that instant love connection with my child; I was depressed and day by day sinking lower into my black hole, until one night I couldn't cope anymore and I seriously thought about taking my own life; when I felt an overwhelming sense of love and protection towards my son, I couldn't leave him he needed me and I needed him. How little did I know at that time, that becoming a mum would be the making of me and the kick start back into my spiritual journey. Two years later, after lots of stress, depression, job losses and financial struggles, I fell pregnant with my second child. I was not ready to be a mum of two, but clearly the angels and creator had other plans for me. My second birth was again another c-section but this time I was prepared. During both operations as I was having the epidural done, I felt such a sense of peace & calm, I knew I wasn't alone and that someone was watching over me and my child, waiting to welcome the tiny human into the world. I knew it was an angel. At the birth of my first son I clearly saw and felt my dad by my side, but I chose to ignore him as I was still angry at him for leaving me; he was there again at the birth of my second son but again I ignored him as I still wasn't ready to forgive him for dying.

Over the years I struggled with being 'just a mum' I felt like I was here to do more, so I would start up my facebook page advertising tarot readings and angelic reiki and I would get nowhere; so I would give up and feel depressed about being a failure. I used to sit and cry and ask the angels what was the point in having these gifts and not being able to use them. I would go from course to course, searching for more, searching for something that would lead me to my answers. It was during this time that I first met Tina, I instantly liked Tina she had the most amazing energy about her, her smile lit up the room and her confidence was mesmerising. This amazing woman one day would be the start of a whole new beginning for me and was the key to the answers I had so desperately been looking for.

2019 was a hectic year for me, I made a lot of choices that affected me greatly, both personally and financially. I bought a business that I would eventually hate, would almost cause the end of my relationship, I was almost made homeless and financially was at rock bottom. But somehow I always got through it and came out the other side unscathed. Someone was looking out for me. After the house move from hell and the end of 2019; I decided 2020 would be my year, the year I finally would step up and start living my true path and start teaching others and growing my business. So in March 2020 I went to Glastonbury and re-did my Angelic reiki masters, it was the most wonderful experience and I felt totally renewed and ready to take on the world again; however the day I finished the course was the day before the UK went into total lockdown due to the Corona Virus.

Lockdown started and it really was a true spiritual awakening for me. At first I was so angry! Angry at the fact I was now locked in my house, unable to see my family and unable to fulfil my goals of starting my business. Even more so I was hugely concerned for my children's mental health after all the upheaval and changes we had been through in such a short space of time; how would I explain to a one year old and three year old why we can no longer see their nanny, or why we can't go to the park or to the soft play!

I was furious at the world and the depression reared its ugly head.

As the days and weeks went by I was getting sadder and angrier; and the one day I was scrolling through facebook and I saw that Tina was live in her Goddess group doing something called mantras in pyjamas, something told me to tune in and see what it was all about. There was Tina in her pyjamas looking all glamourous with her essential oils and talking about Lord Ganesh the remover of obstacles. She got out her mala beads and began to chant. After a few minutes I decided to join in and I felt like such an idiot, I wasn't getting the words right but I could feel the energy, and I carried on chanting. I started doing it every day, along with the Theta clearings and radiation energy clearings she did every day. And I felt amazing! I felt clear and in alignment for the first time in my whole life. I even got up one morning and decided to start going for walks, which turned into running. I signed up to train to be an chakra dance facilitator, and the crazy thing was the first chakra we worked on was the base chakra of which Lord Ganesh is on of the deities!

Things were falling into place and it felt amazing. I did however begin to realise that my relationship was no longer working for me, and it hadn't been working for a long time but I'd never had the strength to stand up for myself and say enough was enough.

I signed up to be a young living rep and the more I used the oils along with mantras in pyjamas the more I grew, mentally, emotionally, and spiritually. For the first time ever, I knew I was on the right path and was ready to see where it would lead me. One day on one of my runs I knew I had to go home and end my relationship, I wasn't happy any more and it wasn't working. So I did it. I ended it, and as I knew it would things turned unpleasant between me and my partner. He threatened to take away my children and refused to leave the home. So after days of this awful atmosphere I caved and decided to give us another go. But deep down I knew I deserved more and was ready for more. Lockdown carried on, mantras in pyjamas carried on, I kept using my oils and then I started to get busy. I was actually beginning to get readings for the first time in my life and I was making money from helping people. It made me feel alive and worthy for the first time in my whole life. I felt like I was more than just a mum and I knew I had to learn how to do Theta. Towards the end of lockdown I kept on messaging Tina asking her when Theta Basic would be being taught and then one day the message came! I was so excited, but I didn't have the money to pay for it, and then a miracle happened I woke up one morning to find a council tax refund I didn't even know I was due in my account and I booked onto the course immediately! It was like the universe wanted me to go and I was going no matter what! Time dragged as I waited for the course to come around and eventually it did! I had no idea what to expect but it genuinely was the most sensational, amazing and life altering experience; I cleared beliefs I didn't even know I had, I made genuine friends and I finally felt like I was home. I had found my tribe.

Theta and Tina made me realise I'm worth so much more, and that I have the ability to create the life I want, I just have to ask for it. I'm ready now to move on with my life, clear my limiting beliefs and create a meaningful and successful healing business.

I'm ready now to achieve my full potential and become the best me I can be not just for me but for my kids as well.

I'm going to do my Theta advanced in September and I know it'll be the next step in my chapter; and thanks to the angels and divine timing I would never be where I am now, I wouldn't be writing my story if it wasn't for Tina and creator.

Never ever think your unworthy of greatness or being the best you, you can be because you are. Never settle for less because we all deserve the best in life.

Don't ever give up on your dream because your just one decision away from a totally different life.

ABOUT THE AUTHOR

NICHOLA DREW

Nichola Drew is a full-time mum to two beautiful boys, both of whom are light-workers in their own right.

She has big dreams of one day living by the beach and owning her own healings rooms.

Nichola is trying to build her spiritual business around being a mum, it has taken her a long time to get to where she is now, but the journey has been well worth it.

As without Angelic reiki and Thetahealing, she wouldn't be the healer & medium she is today.

Nichola tried to do everything in her life with her children's well-being and happiness at the forefront of her mind; she wants to show them that they can be anything they want to be in life and that they don't need to settle for anything less than their dreams.

The corporate world of work was never for Nichola, and she knew this from an early age, from working in a bank to working in office's she felt the corporate world drained the life from her soul and she knew there was more to her life than being an administrator.

This deep knowing and longing have always been the driving force behind building her healing business and one day she knows she will be able to support her family financially whilst doing what she was put here to do....which is to help heal, guide and teach others how to live their best and most amazing life; free from limiting beliefs and filled with love & power of the angels and creator.

Nichola is a natural born medium & clairvoyant, from a long line of ancestors who were gypsies and witches.

She reads Tarot and Angel cards, is an angelic reiki master and Theta practitioner, amongst many other things.

Her goal is to eventually be able to help and guide other mums of highly sensitive children, to help them to understand them and how they see the world, with the support of crystals and essential oils. She would never be the healer she is today if it hadn't been for becoming a mum and she wants to be able to help and support other parents in order to become the best and most emotionally supportive parents they can be to their little light-workers.

Email - angelsheavenandhealingwithnikki@outlook.com

facebook.com/angelsheavenandhealing

instagram.com/angelsheavenandhealing

NIKI MCLAREN

J was born Nicole Annette Norton in Sydney, Australia, on 2nd August 1969, at Princess Margaret Hospital in Darlinghurst. After 36 hours of labour, I eventually arrived. My slow entry into this realm was certainly not an indication of how I would grow up. On the contrary, I did everything loud and fast. Like a true Starseed, I am strong-willed, a freethinker, a headstrong non-conformist; a passionate truth seeker and when you combine those traits with intelligence, high perception, intuition and a wicked sense of humour, you get a heady combo of emotions, passion, strength, determination and wit.

I realized around the age of 5 that I was not like the other kids. Having visions, knowing what people were going to say before they said it and feeling the presence of spirits and how people felt was not something I shared. Keep in mind this was the '70s and people who had a disability were mocked and ridiculed, gay people were bashed and killed in broad daylight, and anyone with a pink mohawk was called punk and assumed to be a drug-addicted misfit. So, a kid who says they hear a voice and feels and sees spirits, well you can just imagine how that would have turned out.

I was baptized a roman catholic and attended catholic primary school in Sydney's eastern suburbs. Part of the curriculum was to attend mass every week. I found this extremely difficult because I couldn't sit still, I couldn't chat, it was cold and drafty, but most of all, it all sounded so farfetched to me. So, at the ripe old age of about 6, I decided that Catholicism was not for me, and the catholic explanation of religion seemed sketchy and was full of questionable unproven data.

I was witnessing all around me the disaster, death and destruction that was going on in the world, and it was simply unbelievable that a benevolent God existed. I felt it was impossible that if He was indeed all around us, and was a 'miracle worker,' then why did all these bad things keep happening. This was all especially confusing, considering this was the time I experienced my first of 3 sexual encounters that were unwanted and not consensual. It was from that moment that I started looking for more in this world, questioning authority, not taking no for an answer and basically being a pain in the butt with all my determined truth-seeking.

I was always asking questions that no one could answer, but mostly my question was "why?". My mum and dad were usually the ones who were cornered for these interrogations, although I do remember catching the odd grandparent, aunt and uncle off guard. This questioning was followed by a long explanation from the prey, I mean person, which was then followed by "but…. why? This was usually when exasperation set in, and the adult said, "I don't know why, that's just how it is," made an excuse and quickly ran away. Sometimes they answered my questions adequately but, for the most part, I was left wondering and having a conversation with myself in my head about how dumb or unbelievable their answer was. When I started school, I found all of the subjects boring except for science, human biology and cooking. They were the only subjects that kept me engaged for a solid 55 minutes. I distinctly remember approaching my science teacher and asking her "what is a dense molecular structure?" She had a puzzled look on her face and said, "where did you hear that?" I told her I had just been to see the new movie at the movies, Superman and that's what he is made of. I was about 9yrs old. I've never stopped asking questions and much to the relief of my family and friends, we now have Google.

Growing up, my family moved back and forth between Sydney and Perth quite a number of times. My brother was born in Perth in September 1970, so as a 13-month old, I was in the back of a car trundling across the Nullabor. My dad's family were all in Sydney, and my mum's family were all in Perth, so back and forth we went. I started school in NSW and went to 4 different primary schools. I attended the same 2 high schools which I left, went back to, left and went back to…hang on is that right?? I think so. Anyway, I've always considered this to be a wonderful experience as it taught me to adapt and make friends very easily, which is where my sense of humour came in very handy. Unexpected situations and meeting new people became very second nature to me.

When I was about 11 years old, my dad and my uncle took my brother and me to a motocross event at the Sydney Showgrounds. It was awesome! The bikes were going over jumps, there was dirt flying everywhere, and it was LOUD. I loved it. This was where the 2nd sexual encounter occurred. I was alone, at the fence that surrounded the arena, a sort of viewing area, and the crowd was all around me. There was a man; he was right behind me. My heart began to race, as I realized that he was getting close to me. Then he was actually in my personal space. I remember feeling scared and shocked. He had me pinned against the fence, and I froze. Then the fear built up so much that I told myself to move my legs and my arms. I pushed my way out and turned to look at his face. He glared down at me with eyes that were black. I felt a darkness around him, and his eyes were pure evil. He even had the slightest smirk on his face. I ran back to my dad and stayed by his side for the rest of the night. A few weeks later, I plucked up the courage to tell my mum and dad about what had happened. They were upset that I hadn't said anything earlier. As a parent, I now know how they were feeling that evening. The guilt and anger would have been all encompassing. Guilt and anger are the first place's we go to when things happen to our children. They had an argument that night. About a year after this, they separated and then divorced. My dad went to Perth to live. I don't know what caused their marriage to breakdown, but I do know there was a lot of things going on at the same time as what happened to me.

At about 13, my high school days were filled with the usual teenage stuff. Music, famous people who we read about in glossy magazines. I started reading Tarot cards and did a bit of palm reading as well, at school in our lunch breaks. My friends were always blown away at how I 'knew stuff'.

I began looking in the mirror and comparing myself to what I thought was 'the ultimate female.' During this time, my self-esteem plummeted. I started using food to control how I felt about myself and cope with growing up. I was anorexic at 14. I grew fast between 12-16, so I was about 175cm tall, and my weight was well, let's just say that if I turned side on, you couldn't see me. There was no internet back then, just TV, movies and magazines with girls like Elle McPherson and Claudia Schiffer on the cover. The world idolized the Super-model, the famous actors and the trophy wives. They were tall; great I can tick that box, I'm 175cm tall. They were thin and athletic; crap can't tick that box. So, I started going to the gym every day and eating less. I was doing aerobics classes and circuit classes after school. I certainly became quite fit, but I still didn't look like them. This was when the 'black cloud' appeared in my life. I became depressed, very depressed. It was around this time I started to have visions. At totally random times of the day, I would be walking home from school, smelling some-one's roses or patting someone's dog through the fence and then boom! Amongst many, I saw a bus crash over the side of a mountain with people screaming and dead bodies everywhere with other people injured. When the vision went away, I remember thinking well that was weird. I also had a vision of a plane crash with people dead everywhere and smoke billowing up from the wreckage. Both these visions became a reality after seeing them on the news. These were just a couple of what I was experiencing. When I realized these visions were prophetic, I started to tell my mum. Just between you and me, I think she was freaked out. She went white the first time I told her about them. This made me feel uneasy and that perhaps it was wrong to have these abilities and then even worse to speak of them. So, I started to ignore these visions, feelings and the voice that told me things about people and places. The voice was always the same and never told me to DO things; it just popped words into my head which would then start a thought process. This thought process was where I came to 'know'. For a long time, I didn't trust it and tried to ignore it. I was scared of what might happen to me as there were movies like "One flew over the Cuckoo's nest" around and people spoke about schizophrenia as "hearing voices". I decided that I didn't want to end up like Randle McMurphy. So, I never spoke of any of my visions again.

A few years went by, and my brother decided to move to Perth to live with our dad. It was just mum and me for a long time. We moved to the Southern Highlands in NSW and travelled to Sydney by train every day to work. The country is beautiful there, and we were renting a cottage on a working dairy farm. It was so nice to wake up to cows mooing every day. We made some lovely friends in our country neighborhood. A lovely couple who I returned to visit for a holiday allowed me to stay with them. That holiday turned into a year. I got a job and lived with them for a few months on their 10-acre hobby farm. I learnt to drive a tractor and bale hay. I moved out and got a flat with a friend. I got a job working in a Café in the main street of the small town. I bought myself a little car, so things were great. I had a close friend who I went out with to cafes, bike rides and over to her house to just hang around chatting. She was so much fun; we had the same wicked sense of humour. This was also the time of the 3rd sexual encounter. I knew the man; he was not a stranger. He was a shop owner two doors down from the Café I was working in, and that's why I let him into my flat that late afternoon. We were chatting and laughing, and after what felt like seconds, things went wrong. At the time, it felt surreal. I was floating above myself, looking down on what was happening. It was like watching a movie. I now know this to be an out of body experience. I told no one about this for years. I felt so much guilt, shame and anger. I did a lot of reading in those days to try and quell my curiosity about the world and answer my continuous stream of questions. It was after reading some books on sexual abuse/assault that I realized; this was rape. It wasn't long after this I returned to Perth and went back home to my mum. I was about 21. My depression got worse and worse. I ate to make myself feel better. I didn't care anymore about anything. Food made me feel good, and it was like a reward system for me. My weight skyrocketed. My self-esteem dropped down lower and lower. I was in the depths of despair. I didn't want to live anymore. I felt like my life was dark and that I was inside a black cupboard with no way out. I felt like I had no control and that the spiral down was gaining momentum. I decided that while mum was at work, I would end my life. I got the sharpest knife I could find from the kitchen. I held it across my wrist, sobbing my eyes out, I pushed down and started to cut. Then suddenly, I had a vision; it was my funeral. Like I was there, but no one could see me. My mum, brother and my dad were all crying. I could literally feel their pain. I sobbed and sobbed. I looked down at my wrist, and there was nothing there, not even a scratch or a dent. It was at this moment that I realized that I was meant to be here. I decided then and there that I needed to do something with myself and my life. I needed to heal myself. I went to my doctor and asked for help. He referred me to a psychiatrist. My psychiatrist then diagnosed my depression. This was the beginning of a lifelong journey of self-healing, self-improvement and searching for answers.

I read books, books and more books. I did courses, lots of courses. I tried naturopaths, chiropractors, so many different medications, herbal remedies and supplements. I tried diet after diet, eating plan after eating plan. One month it was macrobiotic, the next vegetarian, the next raw, I was the queen of fad diets. My weight went up and down, up and down according to how well my antidepressants were working and if the particular one I was on wasn't giving me nasty side effects. One day, I was wandering around my favourite health shop looking at all the goodies, and a book jumped out at me. It was about essential oils. I had a quick flick through it, and then I bought it. I had seen essential oils for sale in various shops but didn't really know much about them. This was when my passion and never-ending love of oils began. I was about 22 and went to see an aromatherapist for a massage and a consultation. We had a long discussion about how I was feeling and about my depression. She made the most amazing blend, especially for me. I felt so special and the oil blend smelt absolutely fantastic. The massage was one of the best I have ever had, which for me, is a big claim.

I estimate I've had well over 500 in my lifetime. I used the blend she gave me, and it truly changed my life. I felt a deep soulful connection to these plant oils, and I have had them in my life ever since.

My twenties were a mix of pubs, clubs, drugs and booze. So, some of it is a bit hazy. It was also a time when my weight was down for a while. During this time, I had a few boyfriends. I look back now and realize I was trying to make myself feel better about myself by making them happy and always being a "yes" person. I was working in various roles doing reception and secretarial jobs, but I was unfulfilled and unhappy. On a deep level, there was a piece of me missing.

I went to a party with my girlfriend one Saturday night, which is where I met my future husband and the father of my children. He was quiet and not very talkative, which had me intrigued. At that time, I was a vegetarian, so I had brought my own dinner to put on the BBQ. It was sliced sweet potato and pumpkin that I was having with a salad. Anyway, he was in charge of the BBQ, doing all the cooking. I approached him and asked him if he would cook my dinner for me. He looked at my vegetables and burst out laughing! We both looked at the BBQ, and then both burst out laughing. There was no room on that BBQ; it was covered in slabs of beef, chicken and of course lamb (he's a kiwi). Anyway, he made a special spot in the corner and cleaned away all the meaty bits and cooked my veggies beautifully. We were together after that for about 10 years.

I was unhappy at work, and I saw an ad in the paper for a course in Phlebotomy. I thought, Yes, that's me! I'm doing it. I finished the course and got a job as a phlebotomist (specimen collector for a pathology centre). I did that for quite a few years, and it was a great job. I was able to go part-time when I was pregnant and then increase my hours in between my pregnancies. When I left to have my second child, I was yet again, unfulfilled and feeling like there had to be more to life and what was I doing here on this planet? Where was I supposed to be and who am I? All this time I'm still soul searching and looking for my purpose. I was talking to a friend about my job, and she told me about a course that was running at TAFE (like a college). It was how to be an Anaesthetic Technician. It's a highly skilled job that requires the person to assist the Anaesthetist in the operating theatre. We are their right hand. The Anaesthetist relies on us to be up to date with resuscitation skills, equipment knowledge, anaesthetic machine operation and troubleshooting. To be able to pre-empt the next move, we need above average pharmacological knowledge and emergency lifesaving procedures, but this is just some of our skills. It was a 2-year course which I passed. It's a job I still do to this day.

During that time, we had two wonderful children and got married. Yes, in that order. Whilst working as an anaesthetic technician, I soon realized that if I wanted to do more in the theatre environment, I had to have more skills and knowledge. So, I decided to do my bachelor's in Nursing at Notre Dame University in Fremantle with fulltime contact so that I got it completed in the 3 ½ years. By this time, I had 2 kids under 10 years old, and I was working fulltime. I cut some of my hours back and took on extra 'on-call' hours to cover the loss in my hours. As some marriages last a lifetime, ours didn't. I had just started my 3rd year at Uni when we separated. It was really hard to juggle the kids, work and Uni, but I persevered. Even when I couldn't face another shift or another lecture, or the 5 weeks of fulltime unpaid practical nursing that we had to do twice a year, I still got out of bed. Thankfully, my mum was always there for us. She picked the kids up from school and dropped them off. She also took them swimming and ballet and was always there to support me when I felt like giving up. My mum is a living earth angel.

We had lots of amazing moments and holidays together as a family, and I learnt so much about myself and life. For that, I am eternally grateful to my ex-husband and friend for life. We remain close and band together to support our children.

After the separation, I went on working as an RN and anaesthetic technician full time. I had a good social life, going out with Uni and work friends. I was going through a slim stage, so I was happy with how I looked, but I wasn't happy on the inside. That yearning, deep guttural feeling of something missing that I couldn't put my finger on kept coming up and going down, up and down. Something was always guiding me and showing me where to step next. I had this conscious knowledge that I could have a conversation with myself, in my head, about what was going on around me. The voice had never left me. It was always there and is always there. Sometimes, it would yell at me to get my attention which worked! It always made me stop in my tracks. I knew then that I was not paying attention to what was being presented to me. It's then that you realize the Universe has everything planned right down to the nanosecond.

After we relocated to a rural area with the boyfriend I had at the time, I transferred my job and continued working in theatre at a local hospital.

My daughter came home from school one day and asked if she could go to her friends for a while. I said yes, so we went over to her house. As soon I walked in the most amazing smell overtook all of my senses and I shrieked "omg essential oils". I soon became friends with her friends' mum Sam, and that was the first step walking down this path with an essential oil company I had never heard of but clearly had the best oils I had ever experienced. I became a member of a very special group of people. People who, like me, want the best for their family and themselves. People who believe in service to others, honesty, and being the best, they can be. Through the network of knowledge, I heard about a course that was being run at a local venue in November 2018. The course was a full 2 days and involved using the oils for emotional release. It was being run by a lady named Artemis. My friend told me she did a lot of work with animals and oils and had a vast amount of knowledge. That pricked my ears up straight away. I went along to the course, not really knowing what to expect, but if it involved the oils I was there! Those 2 days were unforgettable. I laughed and cried, learnt how to read auras, learnt how to perform a mini emotional releasing technique that gave me my first astral travelling experience. I learnt information about the essential oils that changed my life permanently. I was now in a unique position where I had people all around me who had the knowledge and skills I not only wanted, but as the Universe knew, I needed. This was the beginning of my awakening and journey to enlightenment. I got as much knowledge from those around me as I could; my curiosity never diminished. My love of essential oils was always with me, but it was now a major part of my self-healing journey. I wanted to do courses and learn how to perform other techniques using these amazing oils. A few months later, I heard about a course that needed people for the students to work on, and it was going to be held not far from me. I put my name down to experience this amazing technique. I read about it before I went and thought it sounded fantastic. I went along, and as this session was for the level 2 students' assessment, they needed actual people to perform the technique on as part of their assessment. It was all so professional. I was very impressed. The time and effort put into gaining accurate information through discussion with the client was top level. After our chat, the student tailored the session to me specifically. It was amazing! I felt rejuvenated, calm and relaxed. I slept like a baby that night. A few days later, I was a bit teary and fragile. I rang one of the course facilitators and told her about it, and she explained I had an emotional release from the session. Wow! I was blown away. I had to do this course. I enrolled straight away for the next course that was being run, which was a few months after that student day. I completed Level 1 and 2 in the Raindrop Technique and received my Practitioner certificate.

Whilst I was doing the course, I heard about another course that was only run by Artemis. It was held once a year, in Byron Bay, and there were very strict numbers. That's it; I had to do it. It specifically focused on using the oils to assist with emotions, and that really appealed to me. For some reason, I was drawn to that course. Something told me I had to be in this place at this time. It was run over 5 days by Artemis. We stayed in a retreat which only had the students there. Over those 5 days, I learnt things about myself I never knew. I laughed, and I cried. It was tough. Artemis has extremely high standards, so I had to stay focused. So many emotions and feelings came up from a place I never knew existed. The power of these oils was phenomenal. While I was at this course, I met a beautiful soul, Nicole. I instantly felt at peace being around Nicole. Her whole being is serene and gentle. She doesn't walk, she floats. Nicole and I were chatting, and she mentioned ThetaHealing®. ThetaHealing® is a process of meditation that we believe creates physical, psychological and spiritual healing using the Theta brain wave. While in a pure Theta state of mind, we are able to connect to the Creator of All that is. Theta is designed to teach people how to harness their psychic abilities through spiritual awareness. The 7 places of existence give us the conceptual framework for understanding how and why creation works on the physical and spiritual levels, and how it relates to us on all levels of our being, mentally, spiritually, physically, psychically and emotionally. The 7 planes of existence are the philosophical guide to the art of ThetaHealing®. I asked Nicole about the courses, and she told me she was coming to Perth later in the year. I enrolled in the course, Basic DNA ThetaHealing®. I feel blessed to have met Nicole and have her in my life. Before Theta, I thought working with essential oils was phenomenal. After I did the first Theta course, I practiced the theta techniques on myself with the oils. No words! My psychic abilities went through the roof, my intuition took on its own 'autopilot', and I was literally feeling all my chakras. I enrolled for the next course, which was the Advanced DNA that was running in Perth scheduled for a few months after that. It was being run by a lady named Tina Pavlou. The other people I did the basic course with had met Tina and were telling me about her and her gifts. I couldn't wait to meet her. Well, Tina blew me away. She knew things about me that I had not told anyone else. She knew how I felt, what I saw. It was Tina who told me I am a Shaman. When I researched Shamanic healing, customs and cultures, I instantly felt a connection deep in my heart. Feeling and hearing spirits are guiding me to help people, and it felt right to me. It felt like home. It felt like a warm blanket around me. When the spirit speaks to me, I listen.

Since I met Tina, I have joined her group When the Goddess Calls "The Temple". Every day Tina does mantras with the amazing essential oils. I have learnt so much from Tina. She is so honest and truthful about how she feels - having someone like Tina as a mentor gives me the strength to keep walking my path.

Over the last 10 months, I have been through one of the most difficult times of my life. The health of several family members has been affected severely, and in one case, it was life threatening. I have been pushed to my absolute limit. I worked through C19 on the frontline in one of Perth's busiest tertiary hospitals. My relationship broke down with a man I had been with for 5 years. This was the most betrayed I had ever felt in my entire life. As the saying goes, "you think you know someone". Each challenge has taught me more about myself, and how my faith in the Universe holds me strong. I feel my gifts are getting stronger and stronger. I feel my consciousness and vibration rising every single day. My awareness of the earth's energy, the balance of nature, planetary cycles and the transformation of the matrix has expanded exponentially. I am able to focus and change in and out of realities at will. Together with Creator, I have helped clients and their animals heal and move through difficult times of their lives. I feel humbled and privileged to be able to share my gifts, and I consider every client to be sent to me by the Universe for my benefit as well as theirs.

Over the last 3 years, I have met some truly inspirational people who have guided me on this path.

To Tina, Nicole and Artemis, it is my honor and privilege to know you and be able to learn from you.

To all my Theta sisters who are always there to lift me up when I have a bad day, who have allowed me to 'enter their space' and have all celebrated my wins wholeheartedly and sincerely, I truly love you all.

To my fellow Young Living friends who share their time and knowledge so freely, I thank you and salute your passion.

To Emma, thank you for taking the time out your busy life to always be my friend. I know I can rely on you for your absolute honesty, integrity and support.

To my mum, who has never let me down, ever. You are truly the wind beneath my wings; I love you more than you know.

To my children who I absolutely adore, thank you for choosing me to be your mum again. You have taught me so much in this life and in all our previous lives together.

I consider my current life a gift, and I hope to continue guiding, healing and coaching people and animals from now, and through all my reincarnations and lives.

ABOUT THE AUTHOR

NIKI MCLAREN

Niki is an RN, a mum, a sister, a daughter and a friend.

Born in Sydney Australia, Niki now lives in a rural area about 1 ½ hour's south of Perth in Western Australia. She has two amazing children, a boy, 19 and a girl, 15 and 6 fur babies (2 dogs and 4 cats).

Niki is a Shaman, an empath, a clairsentient, a clairaudient and a Seer. She was born a Starseed (also known as an Indigo child which is a 3rd dimension phrase) and is 6th generation Chinese on her mother's side. She has always been drawn to water and feels at peace in and around water. As a Leo, she is a fire sign and feels connected to her shamanic self when around open fire. This connection enables her to shift from her ordinary reality through a shamanic state of consciousness into a non-ordinary reality where she is able to connect with her guides and messengers. She is at home and most comfortable among trees, flowers, and the silence of the forest but mostly with animals.

All of these abilities assist Niki with her healing practice which is to be of service. Through self-healing and learning new techniques, Niki is able to help her clients. Niki feels it is her Universal purpose and a privilege to guide people on how to heal themselves through honest, authentic storytelling about her life experiences and sharing the messages she receives from Creator, her spirit guides and totem animals.

She is a certified practitioner of Theta Healing®, Angelic Reiki, Egyptian Emotional Clearing Technique & Raindrop Technique which use natures gifts, and the very best therapeutic grade essential oils which Niki is also a distributor.

Niki has been reading Tarot since the age of 12 and has recently started reading Viking runes and oracle cards. She practices meditation, mantras and uses crystals and essential oils daily to enhance her practices. Her home is full of plants, animals, Chinese art, antique furniture and lots of love. She is an avid upcycler of old furniture and has just recently started doing macramé to explore her creative side and plans to hold some workshops. Her garden is her special place where she revitalises and grounds herself. She is a keen cook and is renowned for her baking.

A self-confessed professional student, she is always just finishing or just starting a course. Her next course in November is Theta Healing Dig Deeper.

Contact:

mclarenniki@gmail.com

Young Living Distributor: 14755028

facebook.com/nikimclaren1

14

NUALA O'BRIEN

s the journey continues, I put ink to the paper and begin to write and share some of my story to help others do the same for themselves; to become aware, enlightened and heal through their trauma and pain.

Ever since I was young, I knew I had a gift to share with the world and that I was different and unique in many ways, not understanding what, where, when and why?

At school, I was called a witch....me? A witch? Sure, a witch has long black hair and long nails and here's me with long blonde rat's tail hair and bitten nails. I was bullied and ridiculed for this and my upturned nose, which I now love about myself. Funny how what others found offensive, is now a unique gift to me. The reason why was I was called a witch was because I used to say things and thought everyone had an awareness like I had as I was able to see and feel other's emotions. I was able to read and connect with other people's emotions and knew things before they happened.

We moved from my grandparent's home to our new home on the 23rd of March, 1973. Mum and Dad were only 36 and 37 and were excited about moving into their new home; then this almighty tragedy struck their lives and ours. My sister Mary had an accident on the 8th of May, 1973, at the tender age of 4.5 years, she was a petite bonny wee child, full of life and very quiet, with bright blue eyes and blonde hair. The accident was at 2.15pm, on the way home from school, on a lovely sunny Tuesday afternoon, while this happened at the top of the lane, Mum was watching from the bedroom window and saw Mary's physical body fly up into the air; she ran out the back door and up the lane. Mum went into the hospital with the man that knocked her down, holding Mary in her arms, thinking she had only broken a bone or two. While staying by her side, Mum saw Mary's spirit leave her body that same day at 5.15pm. I didn't realise my mum had this gift until years later when she spoke about it while I was in my early twenties. She also explained where she had seen spirits while she was out cycling home from a "Ceile" when she was in her teens. A few years after Mary passed, Mum had seen her spirit at the bottom of the bed. Deep down, I know Mum blamed herself for not saving my sister at the time, although there was nothing she was able to do.

Going through the passing of my younger sister, Mary, in that tragic car accident was a very traumatic experience in my life. I remember that day as strong to this day as ever, as I was at school when it happened and when I came home, I remember one of my aunties coming down the lane in floods of tears shouting she's gone, she's gone...! There was an emptiness in the air and so much sorrow and shock around the home.

I remember my dad sitting in the corner in the hallway on his honkers, knees bent and crying; it was a deep painful hurting cry like I'd not seen him cry like before. I went over to him and hugged him and asked him:

"What is wrong, why are you sad?" he said, "I hit my thumb while using the hammer to put nails into the wood."

As our house was in the final stages of completion and work still had to be carried out, he was still trying to finish it while going through the devastating trauma. Even at the young age of 6.5 years, I knew Dad was in a deep state of grief.

When I turned 20, still feeling like a teenager at heart, I fell pregnant. I left Ireland to go to the UK, with fear in my blood as my Dad had said he would put a shotgun to my head if I got pregnant before marriage. Which we later spoke about, and he expressed his sorrow for these words, and I forgave him fully. My partner's family wanted me to have an abortion, yes I will admit I looked into it and thought – *"no way"* – this child is a gift and I am the one who got pregnant, so I left and went to the UK. Off I headed with my partner into the unknown.

While I was living in London, I remember going to the toilet one day, and the pain was excruciating, there was a huge blood clot; it was a foetus, and I didn't know what to do. I had lost a child there and then and thought, oh I'm not pregnant anymore. As the days passed, I got bigger and bigger and realised I was still pregnant and that I'd had a miscarriage (one of a set of twins). At this stage, I hadn't been to see a doctor since the day I was told I was pregnant. I didn't even have a scan done, or any bloods checked as I had moved to a new country in the middle of it all and hadn't quite gotten around to signing up with a doctor. I went on to have my beautiful, healthy daughter six months later.

My Mum travelled to London to meet my newborn baby. While I was holding Kelly-Marie in my arms and with my mum sat to my right-hand side, she said

"Would you not give her up for adoption?" And I said, "Why on earth would I do that?" and her reply was "I did when I was 26".

That was the moment I learnt that I wasn't my mum's firstborn child and the reason why we hadn't got that mother/daughter bond as strong as I had with my father. What a time to find out I had a half-sister, called Debbie. Mum went on to explain that she had a child before she met my dad and that she gave her up for adoption and that Dad has known since they met. Oh my – you must be joking, after all the pain and the experience I went through – no way. At that moment, my emotions from having a newborn baby and finding out I wasn't my mum's oldest child all made sense. I looked down at my child in my arms and promised her that I would never lie to her and that I would be honest, open and true to her from that moment on and I have kept that promise to both my children from that day forward.

Eight weeks later I moved back to Ireland, with my new bundle of joy in my arms. We rolled up at my Mum and Dads home in a taxi, lights flashing and my nerves rocking with excitement and fear at the same time, as I was surprising them with our arrival. I had never seen my Dad in his underwear in my life, until this day. He saw the taxi and realised it was I that was in the car with my daughter Kelly-Marie, he ran out to greet us and lifted her from my arms. He fell in love with her at that exact moment, and all was forgiven. He took her in his arms, and I could see he was overjoyed with love and joy.

My partner at the time joined the army, and we set things in motion to get married to him in his army uniform. I wanted the 24th of September although this didn't happen as the date was taken. You see my daughter was due on this date and it was my sister Mary's birth date. Anyways, my partner didn't get to complete his army training due to his asthma. Three weeks before the wedding my Dad asked us not to get married and I said: "No it's too late, all of it is booked". We went ahead, and on the morning when everyone left the house and Dad, and I got ready to go to the church, we never spoke a word to each other, "the unspoken words." We sat in silence all the way to the church (if he had asked me then not to not get married, I would have said ok). I pulled up at the church, and there was the red carpet all laid out in front of me, I had forgotten all about purchasing this item, and Dad had got it for me. I broke down in tears and knew I was walking into something that I wasn't ready for. It didn't feel right at the time, and I knew I was going against my gut instinct. Have you ever seen a bride walk up the aisle in tears? Well if you were at my wedding that is exactly what you would have seen. I walked that whole aisle in tears. The funny thing was that years later my ex-husband told me that his brother had been nudging him up at the aisle saying it's not too late to change your mind. We laughed about this later on in the years.

My partner and I stood by each other, yet I always felt that there was always something missing. We struggled on and set up three businesses together over the years. We moved from Ireland to the UK many times, splitting up and getting back together again over and over in those years. We had many happy and many sad memories; yet none I regret, as all these experiences made me stronger and determined to help and serve others. Though all the moving around, cheating and non-communication within our relationship and another beautiful child, I left the marriage in 2009 and got a divorce in 2010.

Mary has been by our side watching over all our family since her passing. I remember walking across a double pedestrian crossing with traffic lights in the busy London traffic when I was in my 30s, and the lights were green for me to walk. I walked ¾ over the first lane and felt this massive push on my back that sent me onto the next lane. *"What was that I asked?"* as I turned to see what it was, there was a car speeding through the red light on the lane I was previously walking on. What a gush of wind there was when the car flew by, it was a really sunny hot day in London and no air to be had. That for sure, was my sister saving my life!! I'm so grateful for the love from above and so blessed. Thank you...my guardian angel Mary, my sister.

While still in London, I recall the night of my daughter's first Holy Communion; I had what I believe to be my first encounter with an entity. Whereby I went upstairs to lay on my bed; at this time, my husband, Dad, brother and aunty were in the sitting room below. I lay on the bed, body down and face to my right; I could feel this dark energy press on my feet, the weight was intense as it reached my shoulders, I was stiff with fear and terror. It was making its way slowly up my body and was getting heavier and heavier as it reached my shoulders. I felt like I was pinned to the bed and wasn't able to move. I was stiff and afraid and thought what now, so I plucked up the courage to shake and move it off my body, to free myself. I lay there in shock and dismay for what seemed like an eternity. I eventually put my nightgown on and went back downstairs to the sitting room where my husband, Dad, aunty and my brother were chatting. My brother and husband asked me what the loud thud was in my room about 15 minutes previously. With eyes wide open in disbelief yet relief, I was delighted that they had heard the thud, that was confirmation enough for me, that they had heard it too.

Both my children had seen a dark entity in the house over the 13.5 years that we lived there. We openly spoke about these sightings and shared experiences between us. I noticed Kelly-Marie often talked with spirits while she interacted with her dolls and tea set. (Which brought back memories of when I used to do the same when I was little). Around this time, my husband had consulted with a medium, and she had mentioned that I had gifts like her.

I realised my children were also blessed with this gift. Sometimes, the entity hovered above in the hallway, and sometimes it was peering at the door while I was in the kitchen. Eventually, I understood how to clear the entity and did so one night months later when it appeared at the right-hand side of my bed. This time it was getting bigger and bigger, I sent it to the light there and then and it never returned. My fear turned to love, and it left our home from that exact moment, never to return. Our home felt lighter and more positive from then onwards. Even my children had said that the house felt better and they had never seen it again. Thank you. It was like it needed help to pass over and I wasn't sure how to do this sort of thing back then, yet I had done it. Since then, I have learnt to rid spirits and help them cross over. We moved out to Essex a few years later.

I always wanted to be a nurse or a teacher when I was young and left school early so this didn't happen as I imagined, although with my love for healing and caring for others I went on a different path whereby I studied alternative medicines, aromatherapy, herbs, crystals feng shui and all-natural products. I used their properties and applied them to my family and my daily way of living, opening a new avenue into the world of holistic and complementary therapies.

My sister-in-law who was an avid born again Christian bought me a bible, and it sat in the cupboard for many years later, I delved into it reading it on various occasions, understanding it at a deeper level each time. At the same time, I was also studying many other religions, and spiritual teachings; including Jehovah Witnesses, the Koran, Buddhism, Taoist and Hinduism, all this understanding helped me to come to my own conclusion that each religion in itself teaches the same thing...LOVE.

Eventually I went on to study everything esoteric that I was able to source. Our home was fully arranged to bring in positive chi with feng shui and crystal placement throughout, and the aroma of essential oils, diffusing them and making healthy meals with the knowledge gained from their properties and benefits.

I was always intrigued by tarot readings from my early teens. I myself started to use playing cards when I was around 15 yrs old to do readings. I told my Dad that someone younger than him with red hair in his family was going to die within the next 6 months, and then his brother died. He rang me and confirmed what I had already told him in the reading. This is the first time I had seen something like this while doing a reading, as other readings were about relationships and careers. I later advanced onto tarot, angel and oracle cards. I visited many spiritual places of interest; churches, historic buildings, holistic fairs and events. I was learning as much as I could.

From a young age I had a fear of dogs, I remember when I'd be out cycling my mum would say, hurry past this house as there's a dog in it. We would cycle past hell for leather! So when my children were 16 and 12, I got two wee Westies, Joey and Angel. They never left my side; they sat on my knee every evening and followed me everywhere. My love for dogs grew daily, and my fear was subsiding. After two months, wee Angel became ill. She was walking into the walls and dribbling lots. I didn't know what was happening, so I took her to the vets, and the vet also didn't have a clue. He suggested that we put her down, OMG, I was in floods of tears, as I held Angel in my arms. I wouldn't let her go; we stayed in the waiting room of the vets for four hours,

I was in tune with Angels pain and she with mine. I eventually let her go, and my heart broke into tiny pieces, yet through that heartache, my love and connection with dogs has grown to a deeper understanding, and I have lost all fear of dogs. A few months later, there was work being carried out at our home, and the workman asked; "are any of you getting headaches, feeling tired and sleeping a lot?" Yes of course we were, it turns out that there was carbon monoxide that was leaking from the old boiler. The workman nailed our windows ajar and put in a new boiler. You see wee Angel was spending most of the day in the kitchen and she had died of carbon monoxide poisoning to save our lives. Everything happens for a reason. As for wee Joey, he lived on till the ripe age of 14 and died of cancer in my ex-husband's arms on a beautiful summer's day.

When my Dad was ill, in 2012, I was able to sense the pain and his anguish, while I travelled from the UK to Ireland and back every second or third day to be by his side. According to the Mayan Calendar, the world was to end on the 21/12/12. Part of my family's lives ended the following night as we lost Dad to the other side at 11.27pm. Dad's spirit had come to visit me that very night, at 3.20am when the rest of the family in Ireland had left his side in the hospital. As I lay on my bed, I looked up to the corner of the room, and this beautiful white and pink cloud appeared, it opened up, and a set of white golden stairs fell to the floor from the cloud. I saw a hand wave as if it was beckoning me to walk up the stairs and with my faith in the creator of all that is – I did just that. I was able to see my physical body on the mattress, yet I was climbing those stairs. Oh my heart was beating and at peace, as I walked slowly/ more like floated and what I saw inside that cloud will stay will me forever. I saw the most magical experience ever; there was my dad, looking younger, like in his 40s and he was healthy and smiling. Standing beside him was my sister Mary (who had passed 40 years earlier). Both my grandmothers, grandfathers, my aunty and OH MY – millions of angels and mystical creatures in their majestic forms; all were floating around and intermingling with each other. I felt a sense of calm and peace wash over me as I felt my soul glide back down those stairs and into my physical body once again. At that moment, I felt my Dad brush my hair on the left-hand side of my face and say "sleep now my love – you have much to do on this earth and in this lifetime; listen out for the signs – use your intuition, and we shall guide you". He is my hero and my first LOVE, a treasure for ALL eternity.

When my Dad passed, I was devastated; I went into myself and was at an all-time low over the next two years. I remember waking up in the corner of the shower almost blue in colour and shaking with the cold water trickling over my body. My tears flooded like the water in the shower. I didn't know how to go through this grief on my own at that stage. I thought I had known grief when my sister passed and my grandparents, especially my mums mum but was I so wrong. My dad's passing shook me to the core.

While going through my separation, divorce, dad's passing and moving home many times, I came to a realisation that life goes on and does get better and easier. I delved into more self-development, crystals, angel and tarot cards, and reading tons of books on spirituality, personal development and all things holistic, improving my wellbeing in all areas, mentally, physically and emotionally.

It was in those years above on my search for enlightenment and purpose; I met Tina at a charity event in Colchester. Tina sat to my right-hand side that day, and I knew from that moment that she was going to be prominent in my life from that day forward. The love emanating from Tina/The Angel Lady back then; is still as strong and beautiful now as it was that day. We chatted a little throughout the day, and she introduced me to Louise Hay and her book; "You can heal yourself". This book helped to awaken me deeper on my journey and showed that we can heal ourselves.

I also was given a lovely book around the same time by Dale Carnegie, and my personal journey deepened even more and more; since then I have read over 600 books on personal and spiritual development and have been doing lots of work on myself ever since. It's a journey that will develop over time for us all and deepen more each day. I believe we learn something new each day, and that is a gift for us all to open up to. My search and meaning for purpose and healings took off to another level.

I came across Reiki, and it blew me away; the power behind the healing and what I saw in the body. I saw grey matter in areas that were diseased, and I was able to sense and feel the pain of my clients. I didn't fully understand this at the time. Since coming back to Ireland, I completed my course in complementary therapies, which gave me a deeper meaning to it all; this is where I learnt Anatomy & Physiology, all about the physical side of the body, the mind and the soul, Reflexology, many Massage Modalities and Aromatherapy. To finally doing my course in Executive and Life Coaching and Train the Trainer. I was gaining my qualifications in healing, caring, guiding and teaching. My dreams were starting to take form in a totally different way than I expected in my youth. So out of the many experiences and paths took on my journey to date, my true self and miraculous purpose has been revealed in a unique a wonderful way. In this time, the bond between my mum and myself has healed and has deepened.

What I put out I get back. How I see others and the beauty of the world is who I am, my perception of reality is true to my beliefs and values in life. I am true to myself when I am showing up as my true authentic self. I am here to heal and help others better themselves by being true to myself and leading by example. I found that people perceive what they have deep within their hearts. We are all connected, just on different stages of our unique journeys. It's my purpose, to share my expertise, knowledge and wisdom with others, so they may do the same. I stand up for myself, my perception, beliefs and values with every breath I breathe. Working with my Vision and Mission statements are my goals and purpose. Building an empire for others to also shine their true authentic selves; by being the best I am, they can be too. I'm going to turn my dreams into reality with patience and perseverance and working daily to achieve the bigger things in life.

I reconnected on a deeper level with Tina, again many years later, doing Mantras in Pyjamas. Oh my, what fun and wonderful times these were.

Every time I go to delete my social media accounts, someone comes along to stop me in my tracks; by stating and saying what they read, or having spoken and opened up to express themselves to me, saying I have saved them from doing something stupid or that I have inspired them to keep going. I believe I am being channelled to help these people to be true to themselves and be their unique and authentic selves. We are all channels of love and just need to see it for ourselves, and that's what light-workers are here to do.

I feel blessed daily to have this gift to help others awaken from within for themselves. It is by no means an easy job to do the inner work, although it is so worth it, and by doing so, you are then able to do the same for others.

I believe that tarot, angel, Lenormand and oracles cards have wonderful messages and inspiration to help awaken the inner beauty to guide us through our journey. With these and a positive attitude and inspiration, I have gained a strong connection with the divine love that is within myself and others. We are all mirrors, each of us has our own demons to face, and it's something we need to accept and love about ourselves to allow life to unfold and to forgive ourselves and thus forgive others to be able to see the divine light we all share. We are all born in love and are a collective oneness; it's the side of ourselves that we feed that grows.

Over the years, I have helped many to overcome pain and to give them guidance on how to unlock their own blocks and to move forward in their lives. I have helped them change their medication, give up drink, drugs and to stay on this earth as they have a purpose of healing, loving themselves and then sharing with others to do this for themselves too. We all have a part to play in this lifetime.

Since I was young, I was always able to turn a negative into a positive – which I have been told that I do naturally without even realising I do it. I believe love is within us all; it just needs to be found and expressed.

I have helped many with emotional trauma, growth and expansion, and to gain belief in themselves to help them move forward

My vision is to inspire others to feel alive, liberated and carefree, loving and fully expressing their true inner beauty.

My mission and how I actually do it is I automatically feel and unconsciously understand a person's need. Intuitively I respond appropriately by accepting or adjusting what 'exactly' is required; I agree a plan of action, unlock the blocks, and then intuitively I guide them onwards while supporting them within their unique journey

I believe if we learn something new every day – no day is wasted. To live each day and touch the heart and soul of another is a unique and wonderful goal to achieve and be a part of their journey by encouraging and inspiring them.

Recently, I was given the opportunity to learn Tai chi and incorporate music into my energy healings with the aid of tuning forks. I have learnt through all the traumas, pain and hurt, we each have our own demons to face and as Susan Jeffers says in her book "Feel the fear and do it", you will become stronger. Over the years and through all my experiences I've grown, matured and come to realise that we all have to grow in our own time, and we are all unique.

I meditate daily and have learnt the value of what it brings to my life by silencing the mind and the chitter-chatter. The more I trust my intuition, go with the flow and be in the moment, the more at peace I am in my life. We are all connected through the oneness of love and to appreciate the beauty of nature and the simple things in life is what we strive for deep within. We have the strength and the determination to change our perspectives to one of positivity and truth. My love for words, music and movement has been my lifeline; a source of enlightenment and peace that I hope to share and experience.

The journey to self-love, is long, challenging, empowering and an ongoing process and doing "THE WORK' works; it's so liberating, beautiful and is a never-ending cycle of awakening and enlightenment. Everything is energy.

I am a qualified Life, Executive and Spiritual Coach; Meditation and Energy Management Tutor.

Here's to lots more learning, sharing, caring, love and alignment.

Miracles do happen in life – they fall like healing rain from the creator above on a dry and dusty world.

Be confident, believe in yourself, have faith in the unknown and trust your inner tutor.

Love and light Namaste Nuala x

ABOUT THE AUTHOR

NUALA O'BRIEN

Nuala O'Brien is a daughter, sister, mum and Mamog (Irish Granma). She has two children, a girl and a boy and two grand-children, also a boy and a girl.

Nuala channels messages through psychic readings, her intuition and mediumship. She is a clairsentience first and foremost, meaning she feels other's feelings and connects with their energy; then a clairvoyant, clairaudient and claircognizant. She feels, hears, sees and knows without knowing how she knows, she just knows and trusts the journey.

She is a Reiki Master, Meditation Tutor, Spiritual Coach and Aromatherapist. She has been studying Theta Healing with the intent of doing her courses with Tina at the Goddess Rooms. Nuala had always taken time out to meditate even when she was a child, although she didn't understand what it was at that stage in her life. Coming from a large family, she required the time out from all the chitter-chatter in the home and would sit by the beach or out the back of her home behind the sheds, just to get some quality "ME" time. She always felt she was different and unique.

Nuala was reared in the beautiful countryside of County Meath in Ireland and moved to London and Essex for 27 years, to return to her homeland 6 years ago.

Nuala is friendly, bubbly and great fun to be with. She is an old soul with amazing insights and wisdom. She is down to earth, helpful, and has positive energy. She is unique, not like most people, engaging, inspirational, very spiritual, well connected, generous and a free spirit.

Nuala has a zest for life, self-growth, and health; and by sharing her gifts with a wider audience, she hopes to instil this in others so they too may believe in the power of themselves.

Nuala makes people feel at ease, focusing only on the person she engages with at any one given moment. She is open, direct, honest and says it how it is, and OMG does she speaks her mind! When Nuala allows her intuition to flow, she is more powerful than she realises.

Nuala is a naturally gifted healer, who radiates a warmth that lifts people's confidence and inspires their creative energy. Nuala is an avid reader, always learning and trying different avenues, giving her an extensive holistic insight. She helps others to look at the bigger picture, to step out of their own way; to see things clearly or from a different perspective and to believe in the unknown. She believes that the body can heal itself by letting go.

Nuala's vision is to help others better themselves and to be presently living in the moment. She helps others understand their physical, mental and emotional pain; sharing how she managed to attain this for herself and show them the light to a brighter future; to heal and grow to be our true authentic selves. With her ability to listen, she aspires to aid others to live to their full potential.

Nuala loves the outdoors; she walks by the beach and through nature with the trees and woodlands, practising meditation and Tia Chi. In her spare time, Nuala writes songs and poetry, as her love for music and words excel in this area along with positivity and motivation for the soul.

 "To inspire others to feel alive, liberated & carefree, loving & fully expressing their inner beauty".

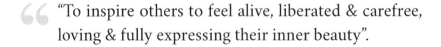

Contact: Nuala O'Brien

Email: nualas22@live.co.uk

Facebook & Linkedin : Transform into your uniqueness

facebook.com/groups/2211928029125409

Young Living Essential Oils Distributor

15

SARAH PALGRAVE

A year or two ago, I would have hesitated to write this chapter. The unworthy part of me was saying, 'who would want to read my story?!' But we all have a story, all are worth telling, and it's through storytelling that we can relate to one another and share common experiences and inspiration. I've made a lot of progress throughout my life, more so in the last four years, even more in the last year. I've always known that love was the overwhelming force in this Universe, and love was the only answer; but I allowed fear to dominate my life, emotions and therefore, my experience. Waking up to that fact and the effect it had on my behaviour, feelings and relationships has been like a light switching on.

There are only a few memories I have in this lifetime that do not include the feelings and expectations of others. I noticed from a young age that I had a preternatural ability to understand emotions and situations I had no previous experience of. I was blessed to have loving parents; I believe I chose my parents as I needed a solid foundation to transform fears and beliefs I've carried for many lifetimes. I can remember being in my own bubble as a toddler, untainted by the conditioning and programming we receive from others. In this bubble, I could be whoever and whatever I wanted, and I saw no obstacle between myself and my desires; I remember that feeling of Oneness. From primary school onwards, I found human experience could be quite painful. I was super sensitive and absorbed the energy around me. I quickly learned by the reactions of others what was acceptable and desirable, and what was inappropriate or weird. I was always wise beyond my years and sought deeper levels of understanding the world around me. I absorbed the energy of others and dimmed my light accordingly. I wanted to be accepted and to fit in. I had no comprehension of what it is to be an Empath; what this meant, how it felt. I went through my young life soaking up the world around me, which was often uncomfortable; I always *felt too much*.

Although I didn't realise it at the time, my first spiritual experience was around the age of 5 or 6; we had just moved from my birthplace of East London to a seaside town in Kent. I don't remember exactly how I was feeling at the time, but I had a repeated experience just before I went to sleep in which I recall feeling in awe of, rather than frightened. I was at the top of the house in a small single room, the bed facing the window and the door on my left opened out onto the bed by my side; I couldn't see out of the open door. Each time, I would start to smell a pungent smell, akin to animals in the zoo, like when you walk past the big cat enclosure, and it's hot and musky. The smell became increasingly stronger as if a big cat were approaching my room, coming up the stairs towards me. I could sense the animal's presence and feel the heat, but it would never actually come into my room. I since discovered through different meditations that my spirit animal is a tiger, and I believe the universe was sending me strength and comfort.

I was a sensitive and intelligent child with no siblings, and by the age of 9 or 10, I had started to hold a little excess weight. I was using food as a comfort even though there was no apparent reason why I needed to. I used to love role play of being a teacher, but I remember jokes made at my expense about being bossy, so I stopped this expression. I started to play small, which would become a self-sabotaging pattern. I can remember playing down my intelligence at school, so I wasn't seen by my classmates as a geek. I also convinced myself I wasn't academic. I later challenged that belief when I successfully studied for a degree at 28 years old, and continue to break through other barriers of belief by taking further studies way into my 40's. I had a safe and loving home environment and remembered having a classmate whose parents were getting divorced; this was not as commonplace in 1985. I can distinctly remember thinking when I was 10 years old that would never happen to my family, yet within 2 years, my parents told me they were separating. It came as a huge shock, and I never really had any explanation of why, which I understand now was just a result of my parents trying to cope with it and protect me. This did, however, affect me in a big way, and I can remember feeling lost as if the foundations of my life had been pulled away. My mum took me to America just afterwards to visit her sister, and I sulked the whole time complaining that I wanted my dad; I hated it and probably made it miserable for my mum. Somewhere after this, I started to feel dissatisfied with life, and I made a conscious decision to find stimulation and gratification outside. I can remember gazing out of my bedroom window with the overwhelming feeling that there is life and different experiences out there. From around the age of 13, I was going out searching for something. I wanted to expand my world and discover what life had to offer. I started smoking cannabis and getting into music, stopping round older friend's houses, feeling experiences. During my mid-teens I was bunking school, taking other drugs and going to raves by the time I left school. Although this did create a habit of self-abuse in the long term, there were some pure times of unadulterated joy. The music scene at the time was about taking the drug Ecstasy, but also about feeling a sense of connection and belonging. I felt like I had an identity that I could control, although I had started to create a shadow by trying to fit into an image of how I thought I should be. I learnt a lot about mental processes in that time, and I always say I am lucky to have come out the other side; a lot of people I knew at that time ended up as addicts or dead. It was difficult to go to a 'normal life' after those hedonistic rave days; it was such an intense experience. I lost weight and sought attention and gratification outside of myself, although it took years to shed the image in my mind of being a fat, undesirable kid. I'd always had popular friends but also knew what it was like to be bullied. I was soft, sensitive; this was often treated as a weakness, so I decided this wasn't how I wanted to appear to the world, so I sought to construct a different, tougher version of myself. I separated from my true self and then wondered why I was never happy and felt alone. I was often too 'deep' or intense for those around me and dulled down my senses to fit in. I struggled with the question of what my purpose was and often envied those who never seemed to be troubled by life. As I got older, I jumped from job to job, course to course and changed my mind frequently about the next thing I wanted to do. I was always drawn to help others, but the traditional roles of a social worker, teacher or nurse didn't fire any passion within me, and I battled against anxiety and social phobia. I've now accepted that working in 'The Matrix' is not in alignment with who I truly am, the structures and systems of our society in the West have never resonated with me; it never felt easy.

Two things happened in my late teens; my first spiritual awakening and a drug-induced experience triggered my first experience of depression. I took LSD and thought I saw all the evil in the world in people that night, (by sharing I am not condoning drug-taking; it's just a part of my story). This energy looked like a fluorescent green vapour lingering around people's auras. There were very few in that rave who didn't have this energy around or within them. It was a frightening experience which left me bereft and depressed for a few weeks. At that time, I was doing work experience in a primary school and remember sitting at the back of class crying, thinking about the kind of world we're passing onto these children. The teacher must've noticed and wondered what the hell was wrong with me, but she didn't say a word. I had the weight of the world on my shoulders, and I didn't understand how to process the information coming into my senses. After this experience, I went inwards and started to read anything I could lay my hands on to do with mysticism and magic. I studied an A-Level in Psychology and started to meditate; I found I could easily visualise light coursing through my blood. I constructed my birth chart somehow in detail and attended a world peace group meditation in London, where I experienced the feeling of Oneness. I loved it. The energy around this resonated with me, and I felt more in alignment with happiness during this time. But still, I felt very much alone in this practice and didn't grasp the concept of self-healing and the work required to carry on. I also still felt a burden of pain; I can remember feeling mass consciousness suffering acutely to the point where I couldn't watch the news or child abuse or violent issues in the media at all without becoming overwhelmed with sadness. With desperation, I asked the universe, 'how am I supposed to make any difference here?' and Spirit spoke to me very clearly, 'the difference we make to each other is enough'. I recall feeling a little underwhelmed with this response as it was hardly an earth-shattering revelation or an epiphany! But it's true nonetheless; we start to feel love with ourselves, and this ripples out to those around us and the Universe. It took me many years to really grasp the meaning of that message from Spirit.

Into my twenties, old programs and patterns took over, and I chose unsuitable boyfriends and behaviour, which re-enforced my feelings of unworthiness. My mum became gravely ill and was in hospital in London for months; it was the only time I ever argued with my dad. I was consumed by my thoughts and feelings. It took me years of getting into situations that had a negative effect on my life for me to admit that my life was totally out of alignment. People who needed healing and love were naturally drawn to me, and I somehow thought it was my responsibility to fix them. By my mid-twenties, I started to reject this pattern just by withdrawing from others who I didn't feel completely comfortable with. I always felt an undercurrent of something missing from my life, an unfulfilled potential. Knowing what I didn't want anymore was enough to steer me in the right direction, or at least away from trouble. I stopped partying (which had become empty and boring), stopped drinking, taking drugs and started to turn my life around.

I fell pregnant with my only son when I was 25 and knew instinctively what was required of me. I've always had an overwhelming sense of what is right and wrong, and a heightened sense of conscience even though I had chosen at times to ignore it. My mother is a good woman and parent, and I knew I had to step up; I was ready to put somebody else before myself. Looking back, I took this too far, went to the opposite extreme and tried to be 'perfect' whatever that is! But hindsight is a wonderful thing, and I know I did the best I could at the time. I loved my son's father deeply, but we antagonised and triggered each other, and I had unrealistic expectations of him and the situation we were in. I accused him of not communicating with me, but I was not speaking my truth either. I issued ultimatums, and neither of us were great at managing our emotions, so we broke up when our son was about 3 years old. I'm a very independent spirit and figured I would be better on my own. I never guessed the scale of heartache this would bring me, and it took me years to get over the emotions the situation brought up. I've since realised I had a lot of lessons to learn because of that experience, taking many years of healing. Becoming a mother changed my life, gave me a focus and a renewed purpose. I've never felt so serene and whole as when that little baby was resting in my arms. I still say my son has been my greatest teacher. When he was born, I took one look at him to see if he was healthy and well, and his fierce little eyes told me he was strong. I remember thinking he was an 'old soul'.

Depression crept back after I split-up with his dad, and I felt overwhelmingly angry and sad. This bout lasted longer, and I was medicated for at least 3 years. I had a lot of guilt buried deep within me and was determined to be both mother and father to him, keeping everyone happy. I went back to employ-ment, and it depressed me, so I enrolled at University on a whim when I was 28 and studied for a Degree in English Litera-ture and History for the next few years. I think my motivation was to keep my brain fed, and I did it for pleasure; it was amaz-ing, my confidence was boosted when I came out with a 2:1. I was proud of myself as it was the first thing I had committed to and actually completed. I found my academic flow and started to realise how much my lack of self-belief was holding me back. Over the next couple of years, I slowly weaned myself off the medication after realising my circumstances were now differ-ent. I felt like the tablets weren't really having a positive effect anymore. Around the same time, I developed a nerve condition in one foot, and then the other, called Morton's Neuroma. This was extremely painful, resulting in an operation in 2010, which didn't work long term. I later felt that this painful condition manifested as a result of my fear of moving forward; I was still yearning to be looked after and had yet to learn that my happiness would not come from outside of myself. This situation did, however, lead me to take up yoga to regain my physical strength and balance. This was to change my life and lead me back onto my spiritual path.

Although focusing on the physical benefits of this wonderful practice, I was taken aback to find myself crying in classes and releasing a lot of emotion during relaxations. I didn't expect this or understand it, but I was blessed to have a teacher who focused on the holistic approach to yoga and the spiritual benefits and techniques. I became addicted, and my life started to feel better. The breathing techniques and philosophy behind the teachings really resonated with me, and I learnt about mantras, different traditions, and the power of focused intention. It really improved my life, and I started to feel good and started to love my body. When I turned 40, I decided to join the yoga group on a retreat in the Kent countryside, also making a pledge to myself to do this or something similar for myself each year from then on. It was a turning point in my life; I sent an intention to the Universe. I was starting to work on myself and devote time and resources to intentional healing. The retreat was wonderful, and Oxon Hoath is in my heart with its history, beautiful surroundings, and the biggest most magnificent trees! I went consistently for the next 3 years. It was the start of my journey to re-connect to myself and Nature. During a reflexology treatment on my first visit, the therapist told me she sensed I would have to say no to something soon and that I already knew what that was; this was the start of me consciously listening to my intuition. I was in a relationship that wasn't bringing me joy, and I knew wasn't right for me; he bought me lots of things and although it's nice to receive gifts, I felt deep down this was his control method, something that goes against my nature. He proposed marriage just after this, and I ended the relationship a short while after.

On my second visit, my chosen treatment was Angelic Reiki with Tina Pavlou. I was so excited as I'd never experienced Reiki healing before. Tina was also doing a workshop on the Angels. It was magic, as she stood at the front of the studio with passion oozing from her voice when she spoke of the Angelic Realm. Tina led a meditation, telling us she could see our Angels standing beside us; before she could say so, I raised my left hand, sensing a presence next to me. The Reiki session blew me away. We were outside on the grass, and I felt like the earth was holding me. I heard Spirit telling me that I needed to develop a daily meditation practice to advance with my practice and deepen my connection within. It was the end of the year, and this was my intention for the new one. I was then working in Mental Health services after wanting to try this career for a long time; one of my close friends lives with a Personality Disorder and complex PTSD, and she inspired me to do the job. I knew I would be good with people in this situation as I had empathy and understanding, and I really enjoyed it.

The following year was 2016, a time that was a huge turning point in my life. During 2015, I'd started to feel depressed again and mentally out of control. This time, the trigger was my inability to take control of my son's behaviour and happiness; he was a troubled teen and rebelling against life. I knew he was making bad choices but, like me, would not be told anything and did the exact opposite of what anybody suggested. I felt like a failure and experienced a desperation and loneliness I'd never encountered before. I noticed my experience of depression got worse each time; the pits of despair got deeper. I realised I wouldn't be fit to take care of anybody if I went under; this powerful thought, combined with my new spiritual practices saved me. I was determined to make good of this situation and start to work with the lesson's that life was presenting me with.

Synchronicity happened in early 2016 when my yoga teacher announced she would be focusing her monthly workshop on each chakra, combining the postures, breathing, seed mantras and intention to clear and tone each one from the root upwards. At the time, we also had a wonderful sound therapist come in and do a sound bath for us at the end of each workshop, focusing on the frequencies corresponding to each energy centre. I used this at the start of each month to work with my chakras in turn. In between the workshops each month, I used daily practices of meditation, mantras, affirmations, colours, crystals, and focused intention. It's amazing what comes up when working deeply with intention, and I was thrilled to discover the power of sound therapy, including my own voice with mantras. I spent that year working daily on this process, chanting 108 repetitions of my mantras in my car to and from work, meditating daily on a Sri Yantra symbol and getting massages and Reiki with all my spare cash. I discovered from this process how important it is to feel safe in day to day life, and that our culture is counter-productive to this. It took me most of that first month with my root chakra and my daily mantra, 'I am safe, I am peaceful, I am grounded', for the feeling of safety to really filter through to my emotions. We are blessed in the UK to be safe and have our basic needs met, so what was all this about? Most of our fears are imagined in western culture, which is as real to our body as a physical threat. Our lives are stressful as we are taught to validate ourselves through the eyes of others, and unworthiness and competitive judgement are reinforced by the media. We are basically stuck in survival mode, with fight or flight responses firing off in the body most of the time, which makes it difficult to feel well and content. I started to become aware of the concept of 'The Matrix' and that all is not as it appears. I started to wake up. Once I realised that fear was underneath my negative thought patterns, I visited Clifford, a fantastic sound therapist for a one on one session. He gave me a personal mantra in Sanskrit to say daily, and it blew me away. I had to stop two weeks in as it triggered me badly, and I felt worse. I messaged Clifford and asked him what was happening, to which he asked what I was thinking about when I was chanting. I was focusing on the fear as the thing I was trying to get rid of! The power of mantra. From then on, I focused my mind and feelings on the OPPO-SITE of fear. Wow, this was intense and a big learning curve; pay attention to where your focus is. Where your attention goes energy flows, regardless of your *intention*. I found I had to spend nearly 2 months on my throat chakra (not uncommon to be blocked here in our oh so polite, "sorry, sorry" culture). There were a couple of months in the year when the workshop didn't run, and these always corresponded with times when I needed more patience to work on the chakra I was focused on. I started to observe and love the way the Universe worked for me.

I experienced more and more synchronicities in my life; I found it magical. These were signs from the Universe showing me I was on the right path. My massage and Reiki therapist said to me one day that she felt I was already attuned to Reiki, and I thought, 'what am I waiting for?' I booked a Usui Reiki course online after some research, finding a course taught from St. Josephs Hospice in Hackney, close to where I was born. I absolutely loved it, and my first experience of distant Reiki was so powerful, I can remember thinking 'this is the future'. I did a lot of inner work in this time, dealing with whatever emotions and beliefs the whole process brought up. I realised parts of me were like a frightened little girl, and I was making decisions based on fear and insecurity. By the end of the year, I had a real sense of needing to go deeper; I felt like I had come as far as I could on my own, digging out trauma and experiences that had formed negative beliefs from as far back as I could remember. But there was more, and I could feel it. I felt like a different person, healthy and strong, learning ways to manage my emotions as I progressed. I felt blessed to have my practices which were like a delicious secret to me at the time; I hadn't found my sisterhood to share with yet or realised that my purpose was connected to this wonderful world of energy and healing. I was sending out positive and life-affirming thoughts to the Universe, asking what would help me further, and my intuition told me I needed to understand past lives. I read and studied lots and bought a book on the Akashic Records, and then in our November workshop, Tina came to yoga, and I thought to myself, 'there is the soul to guide me'. Thank you, Universe!

That year ended in conversation with Tina; her adding me to her Facebook group, which would later become 'When the Goddess Calls'. By January 2017, I'd enrolled on Angelic Reiki 1&2 courses with Tina and started going to the Reiki shares and meditations she was running. It was the beginning of something wonderful. Tina talked about and used Theta Healing, and I found this modality really resonated with me; it appealed to my ability to access the root of a problem, an argument, an issue: where and how did this start? My Angelic Attunements were over a weekend at the end of January, just after my son's birthday, and it was very snowy with ice everywhere. I recall the feeling of trudging home under the wintery sky with the snow glistening and me feeling as high as a kite. I was so happy I'd found this feeling of natural connection. By the time the course finished, I was experiencing flu-like symptoms and ended up taking the following week off work. I felt awful, but I knew I was having a bit of a healing crisis; I'd read about it, and Tina had warned us this was common when your vibration rises. Sometimes our bodies resist but having the knowledge of what was happening and starting to look at physical illness energetically, helped me not to go into the mental resistance. I can remember lying in bed that week in a trance-state, with a vision of a bare empty wooden room with one window, being swept out by one of those old-fashioned brooms made with sticks tied together, vigorously sweeping into the corners. A male voice said to me clearly, 'you're clearing out all the shit so your vibration can raise'. It made me laugh as Spirit was so down to earth. I was away with the Angels that week. I much later read 'The Tibetan Book of Living and Dying', which relays an identical story as one of the allegories used by the monks to teach. For our vibration to rise, we must clear our being of all the old stagnant energies and distortions; the shit has to go.

Throughout 2017 and 2018, I threw myself into courses and study, completing Theta Basic, Advanced and Dig Deeper. I also trained in massage as a nice way to combine treatments. I took further Theta courses, Access Consciousness Bars courses and finally, completing my Angelic Reiki Masters, which was phenomenal. I was inspired, uplifted, energised; it felt great, and I could start to share my skills with others. I worked hard and dedicated all my spare resources to my self-development, and somehow the Universe managed to provide me with any shortfall money I needed. Tina opened The Goddess Rooms, and it was wonderful to witness her success and her dreams being realised. I committed to assisting Tina and The Goddess Rooms wherever possible; it's a joy and a privilege to be part of this, and the Divine Feminine philosophy behind Tina's work resonates deeply with me. So much of our emotional baggage as women stems from our genetic and ancestral trauma; it's important to embrace this within healing to embody who we truly are. As I worked deeper and deeper within myself, I started to notice real shifts in my self-worth and self-belief. My thought processes became clearer, and I was able to remove and shift a lot of my blocks to attaining peace of mind and balance. I had come to terms with acceptance in life and the fact that we have no control over others or outside events. I found peace with my son regardless of his behaviour, and our relationship improved. I started to heal patterns of people-pleasing, self-sabotage and to overcome the fear of being seen and heard.

Miracles happened. As a Goddess group, we went to Glastonbury for the weekend and made wonderful memories, shared
our vulnerabilities and received healing. I'm blessed to have
found a group of women so open, loving, honest and courageous. It's beautiful to find no judgment and love with other
women, and within that space, you find yourself expanding and
growing. I started to work daily with the energies of the
Goddesses and Ascended Masters and asked Kali (a powerful
Hindu Goddess who embodies Shakti feminine energy) to help
me move forward into my full potential. Then came 2019.

At the beginning of 2019, if anyone had told me what was going
to happen, I wouldn't have believed them. Details are unneces-
sary, suffice to say it was the most turbulent and traumatic year
of my life with family and home events. The Universe picked
my life up and shattered it into pieces over which I had no
control. I spent a few months in shock and self-care, but I knew
there was a greater purpose to what was happening, and no
matter how upset I got, I always had a feeling that old and
unhelpful patterns were being brought to an end. It took me a
while to get myself together and remind myself that every
ending is a new beginning. I had to focus on accepting and
building something new from the rubble. I kept going over
recent events in my mind: this is what you've asked for, this is
what the last 5 years have led up to. Thanks, Goddess Kali, even
though you were a bit brutal! The mindset I'd worked so hard
on in the years previous helped me to tune into deeper levels of
acceptance and forgiveness, and I started to apply my will and
attention together consciously. I wanted to manifest something
good from this. What followed was the most wonderful and

transformational chain of events. I reunited with my son's father, John, (something I'd previously sworn would never happen!) And my son started to repair his relationship with his dad, which had become strained. This wouldn't have happened if not for the traumatic events of the year. Through a series of events, I ended up taking a trip alone to Glastonbury for peace and healing, where I had the most amazing Shamanic healing. I received a message during the healing which confirmed what I already felt; I had to start to prioritise my emotional needs, and that meant living in alignment with my true purpose. I had thought for a while about how wonderful it would be to do something that lights you up for a living; I had never found this level of fulfilment in any of my jobs. I started to tap into what lights me up and immediately knew this was healing, energy, yoga, learning and teaching; I had always seen myself as a teacher, even in my childish role-play, but lacked passion for any of the standard curriculum subjects. Once I had made this admission to myself, I then started to work through the blocks that came up as a result. Could I really work as a healer? What if I fail? What will other people think of me? On and on. I delved deep into this with a lot of honesty and the support of Buddhist teachings and my Sisters; this was just my ego and all the subconscious programming. Theta Healing helped me to clear and release my blocks around fear, abundance, success, and worthiness.

I had an overwhelming feeling of misery in my job after everything that had happened. It was like the veils had dropped, and I struggled with the corporate masculine energy of work. I was back in an office with a good salary, but I just couldn't do it anymore. Each day became more like torture; it was like every-thing in my body was screaming to get out. The trauma of the year had a physical effect on my body, and I desperately needed a rest, I felt exhausted. I booked to join Tina on a retreat she was running in Bali in November 2019; I had dreamt of travelling to Bali, and I was so happy to be going, although I'd never flown that far before. I decided in June of that year that I was done with work, in a job that made me feel so confined and handed in my notice. People did a double take when I said I didn't have a job to go to, that I needed a rest and I wanted to work as a healer. My colleagues were so lovely when I left work and presented me with two beautiful bracelets as a leaving present. It didn't feel real, but I was certain it was the right thing to do. The very next day, I was lying on the sofa in my living room looking at the garden and listening to the birds singing, and I felt mentally free. I clearly heard, 'how did you ever expect to co-create your reality when you were crowded with the thoughts and wishes of others for 9 hrs a day?!' I found the confidence to start to write and speak online about subjects that I am passionate about; energy healing and mental wellness.

Bali was one of the best experiences of my life. Quite simply, it was transformational. I needed the healing after the year I had, and still, I had a lot of anxiety coming up as I'd also decided to move away from my area and make a fresh start-up in Durham where John already lived. My son refused to come so I had the obvious concerns of leaving him although he was 19 and my parents would still be close by for him. Apart from having the most amazing time generally, laughing, crying, meeting new Sisters and more members of my soul family, Bali taught me a lot, and I was meant to be there. I met some amazing healers and experienced a type of Shamanic healing which I had never seen anything quite like before. This resonated so deeply with me. I realised I was very drawn to this type of healing. I felt strongly that the time was now, and no amount of pain, trauma, loss or sadness is worth your sanity. This place touched me deeply. I asked our guide what the Balinese was for Soul; he told me it was Jiwa. I set up my business page Jiwa Healing that evening. I left Bali with my heart full, my head clear, knowing I would return.

We came up to the North East of the UK at the end of January before the world went into lockdown. My flat was rented out just in time, and my things went into storage. My only agenda when I first arrived was to relax and sleep when I felt like it (a luxury when you're used to an alarm going off at 6am for nearly 20 years). I was poorly for a while and thought about the events of the last year. I knew this all needed to settle, so I decided to focus on the good parts. I pondered over the fact that a year ago I'd been single and very distant from John, as was my son, and now we had healed relationships, and things were different. I'd left the corporate world and stepped in the direction of my true calling and purpose. I had started to remember who I am. I hadn't had the means or resources at the beginning of the year to do this or to go to Bali; it had all just manifested, one thing after the other in magical ways I would never have imagined. My life had cleared out the old to make way for the new, and although it'd been painful, it was wonderful, and I was grateful. I now know why Creator brought me here, to the hilly windy Moors! Apart from being so peaceful, I've discovered the most wonderful and deep connection to Mother Earth, which has accelerated my healing and studies. I've committed to a Shamanic Apprenticeship and enrolled at Newcastle University to study for an MA. I have embraced my sense of self and am grateful to have overcome my personal blocks to happiness and success. I've expanded my comfort zone to embrace the pure abundance of life and own my potential to be of service to others and assist transformation. As Martin Shaw says, "Identity comes not from what you claim is your innermost self but from the myriad ways you reach out and touch the world." *(Scatterlings)*. There are so many wonderful possibilities for the future once you love and commit to yourself. Know that you can. You are unique and so worthy! If you wish to, you can transform your life.

ABOUT THE AUTHOR

SARAH PALGRAVE

Sarah is a mother to one beautiful son, a Multi-Dimensional Healer, and Self Development Coach.

After following a deep call to heal herself and create change in her reality, Sarah has answered the call to serve others and be a conduit for Divine Light energy. Currently located in the North-East of England, Sarah works in adult Mental Health services and is a passionate speaker and advocate of Mental Wellness.

After turning 40, Sarah dedicated her life to the path of personal healing and connected with Tina Pavlou in synchronicity; at a time when it was apparent that deeper healing and ancestral issues needed to be processed in her life. The support and guidance of Sisterhood enabled Sarah to heal, learn and grow on multi-dimensional levels, remember her gifts and step into her Light.

Sarah is now a Theta Healing Practitioner, Angelic Reiki Master Teacher, Access Bars Practitioner and Therapeutic Masseuse. She combines energy healing with practical coaching on Mental Processes and is currently participating in a Shamanic Apprenticeship. This journey has led Sarah to cast off the shackles of low self-worth, self-hatred, judgement, and resistance to life.

Sarah now owns her purpose as a Lightworker and teacher in service to helping others connect to the power of their true Being and purpose, and she envisions a world where we are taught about levels of Consciousness at school and in the workplace. Always keeping her spiritual toolbox topped up, Sarah believes that possibilities for our future are expanding and are limitless as so many more people connect with the energetic reality.

Sarah is dedicated to the path of personal development and healing and is now working to help others to realise their self-worth and transform their lives.

Connect with Sarah:

sarahpalgrave@yahoo.com

f facebook.com/Healthofyoursoul
instagram.com/SarahPalgrave

16

STACEY ANNE BERNADETTE

Firstly, I want to let you know something. I see the magnificence in you!

I want to tell you why it's so bloody important to say a BIG FAT YES to opportunities.

Yesterday I had the most profound healing experience. I said yes to writing these words, and as I type them this very second – I am releasing years of regurgitated trauma. An old self-limiting belief, a story that has held me back many times. I was given this opportunity and finally ready to reclaim my power. Well, maybe not initially, my first thought was "SHIT", followed by the inner critic "I can't do this". Hello ego, my first reaction was fear – a deep-rooted fear of being heard. "I am not ready, I have nothing to share, no one will want to hear what I have to say". Can you believe I said I needed to sleep on it! Like seriously? I had just been given a massive opportunity to share my message with the masses, to have my words published on paper that will outlive me, a legacy for my daughter Harper, and I was saying I had to think about it?

I knew I was responding from fear. I have learnt over the years not to resist fear; it holds us back. However, meeting fear, shaking its hand and becoming besties has helped me to move forward.

As I lay in bed, I closed my eyes, placed one hand on my heart and took a deep nourishing breath. I dropped from my cranial brain, from the fearful thoughts into my heart, asking for guidance. What am I to do here? Well, the answer came fast, loud and clear with no emotion attached. YES, YES, YES! And here we are.

Today I spent hours receiving new energy. By saying yes to the universe, I was saying yes to the next uplevel version of me. My whole being felt totally overwhelmed with emotion. Emotions were erratic; jumping from overwhelming joy, freedom, pain, excitement, sadness. The inner child part of me - the wounded, scared child who did not think she was good enough - who believed she was less than - who did not deserve to be heard. She was jumping with joy saying thank you, thank you, thank you. Saying yes, released her from a padded prison of safety, safety that felt suffocated, chocked and in chains far too long. Breathe in freedom little one.

I was given a message "allow yourself to let the tears flow". In that moment I purposefully sat alone on my sofa. I gave myself permission to feel all the feels, the full intensity. The gut-wrenching knots and twists, the heaviness behind my eyes. In that moment I invited the feelings in, like I wanted to hangout with them, like I wanted them to be there. The tears flowed carrying out pain, loneliness, anger, abandonment, guilt and grief. Memories from childhood flashed through my mind. I felt the energy move through me until there was nothing but joy and excitement for this next chapter.

Let me take you back on my timeline.

I am just an ordinary girl from the best council estate in Stockport, following her dreams, doing what she loves.

I lived with my mum (Marie) and two brothers Dean and Jake. My dad left when I was two years old. Thankfully, I come from a long line of strong women.

We did not have much money growing up, but we were abundant in so many other ways. I remember the fun times of cooking bread on our fireplace to make toast. We didn't have a toaster. Holding the bread against the fire with a knife, oh so carefully in hope not to tear the bread. It was always annoying when the crust tore. The fire could be used for so many things. Dry your clothes and hair after a bath. I Remember sitting so close to it that my back would go scaly. My mum shouting for me not to sit so close. There was something comforting by sitting close to it. Plus, the UK is bloody freezing.

I was six years old when myself and my family first experienced grief and loss. My beautiful innocent cousin Kelly died in a road accident. We were the same age and in the same class at school - a gaping hole left in our hearts. As a child, I would visit and sit by her headstone, sometimes with our school friends in the pouring rain and just chat away with her. I knew she could still hear me.

I was drawn to all things mystical from a young age. I was the kid on a school excursion who instead of buying sweets or a toy would buy a piece of pyrite with the few pounds mum had given me - carefully placing the crystal on my desk or under my pillow before I slept.

There were many great times in my childhood. I was a daydreamer who had a wild imagination and adventurous nature. I loved being outside, playing in amongst mother earth, climbing trees in the woods with my friends, making dens. There were also many things I used to wish I could forget, that my eye could unsee, my ears could unhear, and my feelings could of unfelt.

Parts of me did not feel they belonged as I struggled to find a place to fit in. Parts of me felt unloved, and those unloved parts meant I was unlovable. Not good enough. Mentally, I constantly backed this up with evidence comparing myself in school. I gave it the confident joker approach, but inside I was hiding. I now understand ALL my experiences had meaning. They lead me to this point. To equip me with the tools to help others heal and choose their own narrative.

I was never academic in school. If one thing that reinforced the belief you were not good enough, it was being placed in the lowest grade of your class and it being called 'bottom set'. I found it super hard to concentrate at school. I had other things playing on my mind. I remember receiving an 'F' for a subject in my final exams. How the fuck is that possible? I thought I would be the last person headed to university.

During my teens, I moved in with my grandparents. The first father figure in my life, my rock, Joseph Kelly. My beautiful, inspiring nanna Anne Kelly (now resting with the angels) - She was a character. The never-ending cups of tea. No one made toast quite like you. How you would bribe me with a pack of 10 cigarettes if I went to the shop and got you some and not tell grandad. The stories you would tell me about your childhood and escapes in Ireland. You felt like home to me. You always told me "make sure you travel the world".

Game changer! My nanna passed away. I was studying business and had a heavy feeling in my heart; this was not the path for me. I was never going to have my own business (little did I know). I was feeling a huge nudge from the universe. I was an empath. I learnt this skill as a child, tuning into other people's emotions to read what mood they were in. Everyone would come to me with their problems - even much older people. I had an air of openness, where to be honest, nothing phases me. I had the ability to meet people where they were at, which built trust, and they felt understood. I was drawn to counselling and fell in love! This course was the start of my personal healing and growth.

I missed my nana so much, and I wondered where she was. After she died, I was sat on the sofa downstairs, and I got a whiff of her unique musky nana smell. As soon as it came by my nose, it was gone. I just knew she was with me and she always is. I remember going to see a clairvoyant. I was always drawn to the intangible. A clairvoyant told me I was psychic, but I brushed it off at 21 years old.

I woke up one day feeling a shadow of myself. I was hiding bruises on my arms. I felt broken inside. I did not recognize who I was. I was drenched in shame. The shame of staying in an abusive relationship too long. I was angry, hurt and frustrated. I felt alone. I don't think I had ever cried so much in my life. Uncontrollable. No one really knew how I was feeling. I kept it hidden. I had created a belief from childhood that it was unsafe to talk about my feelings. To be vulnerable meant I was weak. For a long time, I struggled to cry. I used to try and make myself, but instead, I would get angry and lash out. Anger was a familiar emotion. The rule was I could be angry, but I could not be hurt or vulnerable. I felt ugly, unwanted. I remember thinking I was fat, eating and then making myself sick.

I was in and out of failed relationships. Looking back now, the pattern is so clear. I created a belief my biological father did not love me; therefore, how could any man love me? I entered relationships with either men who were untrustworthy, or I would self-sabotage the relationship. I always ended it before they left, because men always leave, right? Well, so I unconsciously believed. I had no awareness of the subconscious patterning.

We are energy first. Right? Well, I first experienced Reiki at the start of my counselling studies. Our tutor was an extraordinary woman. She was a Reiki Master, one of the wisest women I have ever met. She introduced me to chanting and dancing (like nobody's watching). I remember being sat in class with women who were nearly ten years older than me training to be a counsellor, thinking I have no life experience. This was not your normal patriarchy class; we all sat in a circle. One day my tutor explained the chakra system and how sound is used to move energy through the energy centres of the body. She began chanting, and I burst out laughing so hard I had to leave the class. I was totally in my ego. I was worried about what others thought, fear of being heard, of being me. I did not know then, that ten years later, I would be sat facilitating my own women's sacred circles chanting OM. My intuition was trying to guide me to learn more about Reiki, or maybe it was creating the seed within me.

At 26 years old, I graduated with a Bachelor of Arts with Honours in Person-Centred Counselling & Psychotherapy. This was a proud moment! The mix of overwhelming emotions! Joy, gratitude, freedom! The proud moment was walking up those stairs to receive the final piece of paper, knowing my grandad was watching. He had been there through the blood, sweat and tears. I achieved my dream.

The positive for creating a self-limiting belief that I am not good enough is that I was on a constant achieving mission to prove to myself I was good enough. My masculine energy in overdrive! This served me for a long time before I burnt out and realized nothing external determines my worth. If I set my intention on a goal, the odds could be totally against me, and I would find a way. A close friend once told me I am like a cat, falling from the tallest building, always landing perfectly on my feet. I always took that as a compliment. Of course, I did! I had a team of angels behind me. I had a fire in my belly lead by intuition that just knew. Knew where to go.

It was around this time I reconnected with my biological father and extended family – I gained more understanding of who I was and my roots, which was another healing experience for me.

As a child I dreamed of travel, teaching English in a foreign land and somehow working for the Red Cross. Part of me wanted to run away, but the other half knew I needed to remember who I was -Beneath a self-sabotaging ego. I had an around the world ticket, my independence, a blue Berghaus rucksack and I was off. I met the fear of going solo and did it anyway. First stop Thailand.

Ever travelled to a place which totally feels like home? Or have felt the gravitational pull to a foreign land and unsure why?

I still feel the humidity and distinctive smell getting off the plane, the hustle and bustle of Bangkok and tranquillity of the islands. I was blown away with beaming sunsets as I travelled around South East Asia, Australia, New Zealand, and LA. Being from an industrial town, I had never fully embraced a sunset until this point.

I was blown away by the vast array of culture. I was expanding my current level of thinking daily. I was learning the true definition of presence. To be fully present and unrestricted by the social/work pressures of life that I had previously known. I did not require an alarm (only for pre-booked tours). I was absolutely loving life. I felt free, and I learnt more about myself and the world every day.

Travel opened me up to my mystical side. The world is expansive and magical, yet also intrinsically connected. The places that I have travelled, the wonders I have seen and all the magnificent people I have met - you really cannot put a price on experience. As I ended up in Perth (Australia), and it felt like a home away from home.

It was on this epic adventure that I was introduced to my shadow. Those darker parts of ourselves that we do not wish to admit. The parts that we deny and distort. The thing is you cannot run away from yourself, no matter how far you travel. Part of me was still wearing a mask. I did not feel confident in who I was, the underlining belief of I am not good enough. I did not feel like I belonged; I felt the odd one out in every situation. I felt social anxiety going on a night out. I would use alcohol to feel more confident when, in fact, I would be losing my inhibitions and feeling worse. The guilt and shame that came along with it. Looking back, I was on a downward spiral, but I thought I was living the dream. And in so many ways I was, but a lesson was on its way.

After two years of travelling and working around the world, I surprised my family and was happy to be home. A few days later, I was not feeling well. My stomach felt so sick. I visited the doctor who took some tests and told me I had damaged my liver. WHAT? I felt so scared. My liver was not functioning properly. I spent a few days in the hospital as they pumped me with all the good stuff to flush out any toxins. I felt so weak and sick. My family and friends visited, and all I felt was the shame of feeling like everyone can see, I do not have my shit together. This was the first time I realized my body was a temple, and I was abusing it. Obviously, this was happening to wake me the fuck up. I had taken a detour; it was time to get back on the aligned path. I went home a few days later and prayed, something that I had not done for years. I prayed to my nana to help me heal my body. I went through a cleanse, joined the gym and started meditating. Three weeks later, my liver was back to normal. The doctor could not believe how quickly I had recovered.

I could not settle in the UK. Australia was calling to me. I booked a one-way ticket back to Perth. This was the start of a huge transformation.

I achieved another dream working for the Red Cross. Community is one of my top values, and the universe guided me into a community support worker position. I wanted to up-level, so I studied internationally to train in Community Coordination. I moved into a team leader role - my passion of early intervention for young people.

Talk about rocking my world. In 2015 I met my love and absolute bestie. The one person I can sit on the sofa and cry to, especially if I am on my menstrual cycle, who will put his arms around me while he eats pizza. Who I feel totally safe to let my guard down and be me? I do not have to be the makeup-wearing good girl or people pleaser. I can just let it all hang out and still feel loved. We began on an amazing adventure together.

Surprise, baby on board! Falling pregnant for me is how many people like to describe, an awakening. I would not say I woke up. We are all awake. Rather deepening into what is already there, another layer of awareness that we all have access to. My senses exploded! My surroundings seemed brighter and louder. Like someone had turned the dial up. I started to know things that were beyond logic, beyond our 3D reality, certainly not tangible. Hello claircognizance. Now I understand everything is energy, including our thoughts and feelings. We can read whatever is energetically in a person's space, hashtag superpower.

Finding out I was pregnant was terrifyingly exciting for me. Harps was a total surprise, and it took a hot minute for me to overcome the shock! I had always feared I would not be a good mum, especially to a girl. The mix of emotions got me all anxious and overwhelmed.

After a couple of weeks, the excitement kicked in! I've got this! The day we found out that we were having a girl, fear set in again. I did not feel equipped!

As soon as Harps body flopped out, I reached down to lift her up. Those big wide beautiful eyes touched mine, and my heart burst open with unconditional love flowing through my entire body. Every ounce of fear I had dissipated from me. They say love conquers all and in this moment that was exactly what happened.

I remember going through a period thinking WHO AM I. I didn't feel prepared for the transition from maiden to mother. I felt I'd lost all sense of who I am. Then I realized Harps was a gift given to me to help me rediscover more of who I am and gain the confidence to shine my light into the world (even if I didn't know what that light was yet). I was not losing anything; I was gaining transformation. I was becoming unstuck. Not only was I birthing a beautiful little human, but I was also birthing a new reality.

I woke up one morning and realized I had heard the call for a bloody long time. I was ready to answer. I completed Reiki Level 1 attunement and what a profound experience. My hands started to heat up. It was my turn to carry out a healing on a lady who I was paired with. I started on her head. Pearl white liquid flowed like a fountain from my head, down my shoulders, arms and to my hands. She said she could feel a fountain or waterfall pouring over her, exactly what I imagined. Her head felt dizzy, which she replied she had lots going on in her head. I suddenly felt tight in the chest; I could not breathe. This lady confirmed she had heart problems and has had surgery. Before the op, she was tight in the chest and breathless. I was also drawn to her stomach. My hand went red hot, tingly and sweaty. I felt a strong urge to touch her stomach and not move. Later on, she found out she had a stomach infection.

Talk about opening pandora's box! It was like a door had just opened; I walked through knowing there was no turning back. The world just became expansive.

I sat at my kitchen table with my love. I was at a crossroad. Looking back at a life I was over. I felt stuck working in the matrix. I was trying to make a difference in the world, feeling restricted by numbers and figures, under micro-managed patriarchy system. I was not this anymore. I felt anxious because whatever was next was so uncertain. I said to Ben "I don't know what to do". He grabbed a piece of paper and a pen and said, let's brainstorm. I wrote words from my heart on a piece of paper that would be the start of my epic transformation. Everything begins with a thought and thoughts become things.

June 2018, I had created Holistic Journey Perth. This was the start of deepening into my intuitive intelligence. I began practicing Reiki and other healing modalities. I was introduced to Tina by absolute fluke. I was drawn to go for a reading and learn more about Theta Healing, and I became an Advanced Theta Healing Practitioner. I healed mother and sister wounds by jumping out of my comfort zone to create women's circles. It took me a while to realize I had an extraordinary gift, working with energetic bodies and identifying the root cause quickly. I was also an epic manifestor. If I can think it, it will happen! I spent the next few years refining my craft. I started off with one client per week, which has built brick by brick to working with hundreds of client sessions. As I helped others heal, I was healing myself.

2020

We booked to go travelling on a family travel adventure to India, UK and Europe. Our main purpose - to visit family. We handed in our notice for work, confirmed our rental lease end date and arranged for our home items to be collected for storage. In March 2020 they closed the Australian Borders due to the COVID pandemic. Be the calm in the chaos. We took a great big lean back and thought okay, we could take this day by day and TRUST it will work out. I kept asking myself what if this was happening for me? One of my core-drivers is adventure, which means I am okay with uncertainty, my partner, on the other hand. Remember I am like a cat? Well, my job kept me on. We extended our lease and cancelled the storage service. We got credit for most of our flight. Universe what is next? Show me.

For years I have talked about becoming a life coach. It has been a dream, but the fear of being heard and being seen kept it at arms-length. I was sat in a nice comfort bubble practicing Reiki, Theta and other modalities. The universe was nudging me. You are not done yet. One evening I received a message from a lady I had not spoken to before. We follow the same FB groups. She said, "I noticed your comment about coaching courses. I am starting one tonight, you should check it out". This course spoke to my soul immediately. I was feeling the fear. That old story of I am not good enough. The fear of being heard and seen. My ego shouting so loudly, you cannot afford it, you are too busy, you do not have time. The saboteur in action. Shut up ego! As I became the observer to my thoughts. I needed perspective. Ben was working away – 'FIFO LIFE, FIFO WIFE'. I waited for his call and explained the opportunity. Bens simple straight reply "stop talking about it - GO FOR IT".

SO HERE WE ARE BEAUTIFUL.

I continue to live my dreams! We live in Australia by the beach. I have a beautiful family and a little gorgeous two-year-old daughter, Harps, who is the greatest teacher of my life. Harps is here to help me break a tribal cycle. I realize it is not just about me anymore. No way I was going to pass down to this little one the same destructive patterns. Harps has taught me to push myself to my edges and beyond, how to be confident, how to be heard, how to feel and express myself authentically. How to laugh, be silly and dance around my kitchen. How to let go of worry and live for the here and now. Time is precious; life is precious. Watching kids grow is like watching a flash of lightning before our eyes, showing us not to waste time in our thoughts. To take empowered action towards our goals and dreams. That is what I want for you, dear girl.

I have the willingness to meet the fear of being heard and seen because my purpose is much greater than hiding in the shadows. I realized part of me was still hiding. I was hiding behind Holistic Journey Perth. It is time to switch things up and for me to wholeheartedly step out as me, Stacey Anne Bernadette. I am doing what I love every day. Coaching women to be the best version of themselves and balancing the flow of the masculine and femme energies within them.

I gained the courage to rewrite my story, realign my energy and rework my confidence. When the GODDESS CALLS, you answer. When you answer, you can overcome all that holds you back. These past few months have given me the opportunity to reconnect to who I am and the values that drive me. I have spent time going through my timeline, defining how I got to this epic point in my life.

How did I overcome all the obstacles in my life? Here are some of the greatest lessons that have helped me become the visionary in action.

SELF-BELIEF

You got this! Always back yourself 100%. This is one way of loving and respecting yourself. Believe you can and you will. Self- belief is like a magic key that opens a better and more inspired delicious future. A future of doing all the magnificent things you have dreamed of even if you do not know how to do them yet. Comparison will only hold you back.

BECOME BESTIES WITH FEAR

First, realize that fear is something we have created to keep us safe and comfortable. Instead of resisting fear, what if you became friends with it? Inviting fear in instead of resisting it, feeling all the feels, shaking its hand and doing the thing anyway. How awesome do you feel when you have done the thing that scared the shit out of you? You feel damn good.

THE DANCE WITH VULNERABILITY

Learn to open your heart by being open about what you have been through. When you have been hurt, and the trust has been broken, make the choice and have the willingness to jump back in again by letting your guard down, by being yourself.

SELF-RESPONSIBILITY

Take radical ownership of your own thoughts, feelings and actions. This is one way of reclaiming your power. No one is doing it to you. NO ONE CAN DO IT FOR YOU. Take your life by the reins and show them how it is done; people will follow by example.

BELIEF WORK/INNER CHILD HEALING

You have the power to bring conscious awareness to self-limiting beliefs and change them. Just as you have the power to create, you have the power to uncreate. Get to know your inner critic, what does she sound like. How and why is she trying to keep you safe? Listen to the inner child and what she needs from you now.

RELEASING THE SHAME

Learning to accept and love unconditionally, all parts of yourself. Shadow and light. Refusing to let the past define you and remove the labels you have given yourself or that have been passed down on your ancestral line. Shame becomes internalized as a lack of self-worth. That little voice, I am not good enough. Turn off victim mode and acknowledge your higher self. When you acknowledge your higher self, you can be yourself. Feel all the feelings and express yourself. Have the courage to talk about whatever you feel in a safe space. Repeat after me – I AM WORTH. You do not need validation from anyone, or anything outside of you. You are WORTH, your birthright and infinite abundant essence of who you are.

REMOVING THE OBSTACLES

Deliberately and carefully build your own belief in free will and know you have choices. Nothing is ridged, only if we create it to be. Its all perception. We can all get caught in the problem, ruminating, catastrophizing. What if you became the shit hot problem solver?

TRIBAL CYCLE/ANCESTRAL BREAKTHROUGHS

You will know when you break through a tribal cycle when you break the pattern of behaviours of those before you. You can heal the emotional imprint of these patterns and begin to create your own path of new cycles. You control your choices. Find the root pattern and call it out. You may notice it already as you feel triggered by it. If you do not forgive the actions of others and yourself, you cannot move past it.

BOUNDARIES

Having clear boundaries allows you to protect your energy physically, mentally and emotionally. It is simple! Make a list of what is okay and what is not okay. What are your non-negotiables? Remember, you can always say an assertive 'no' with love, even to yourself. What are you giving energy to right now that is draining you? Saying no to that which drains you means you can say yes to that which nourishes you.

CONFIDENCE IS A SKILL

Know that we are all not born with confidence. It is a skill that EVERYONE can deepen into - Like waking up and being ready for the challenge, a willingness to act. Confidence is to have a deep trust and belief in yourself. When you step out to rock life, own that shit! Know that confidence does not mean you will not fail; it does not mean that you are in a constant state of happiness. It does not mean you will never experience happiness or self- doubt. Confidence is to try new things and be willing to meet the fear and still doing it anyway. Confidence is staying true to who you are in a chaotic world.

SURRENDER

Relinquish any beliefs you have where you can control the outcome. Stay present, the only reality you have right now is reading these words, right here, in this moment.

FINAL THOUGHTS

You are a visionary! Be courageous to take actions towards your dreams. Know what your values are and ask yourself, are you living in alignment right now? Trust your heart and let it guide you. When making choices and decisions in life, ask yourself, "Am I choosing this out of love or fear?" Stay present! Spend less time worrying and more time doing the things that light you up. You are here to vibrate your beautiful essence in the world. Keep your head held high, be seen, be heard, be felt.

ABOUT THE AUTHOR

STACEY ANNE BERNADETTE

Stacey Anne Bernadette is a 35-year-old visionary in action. She was born in a small town in Stockport England, and is now living by the beach in Perth Australia.

She is a passionate life and confidence coach who has taken herself to the deep depths of personal soul work and continues to do so.

Stacey graduated university receiving a Bachelor of Honors degree in Person-Centred Counselling and Psychotherapy with a strong calling to help people overcome obstacles to live a fulfilled life. At 23 years old, she was working as a counsellor for an alcohol and drug service, providing 1-1 sessions facilitating art therapy and pre-detox groups for 25-year-olds and over.

A love of knowledge and adventure lead to further training, completing teaching English as a foreign language certification. Stacey trained in Thai Massage at the Siam Healing Centre in Koh Phangan, Thailand. She was continuing her adventures to Perth, Australia, becoming an international student and achieving a diploma in community coordination.

One of her top values is Community which she has worked in for the past 9 years – from separation and mediation counselling services, developing co-parenting programs, disability services, out of home-care services, and supporting young indigenous children in child protective services.

But the universe had other plans.

Stacey's healing journey and soul work guided her to master the art of energy work – the main purpose of working holistically with the whole person, mind body and soul. She is an intuitive empath who can sense what is going on with a person on emotional, physical, mental and spiritual levels. She is a Usui Reiki and Advanced Theta Healing practitioner.

In 2018 Stacey gained the courage to step out of the matrix to create her own healing practice after the birth of her daughter. The unexpected transition from maiden to mother and the realisation she carried her sister and mother wounds spurred

Stacey to create women's circles. The power and transformation of women coming together to share stories.

She has met the fears of being heard and seen, reclaiming her power by taking empowered action to and beyond the edges of her comfort zone. She is a serial manifestor who continues to smash her dreams by taking life by the reins and investing in her personal growth.

Stacey's mission is to help other women realise their goddess energy and become the leaders of their own life. To rewrite their story, realign their energy and rework their confidence. Stacey teaches women how to believe in themselves, expanding their current level of thinking of what is believed to be possible to even more possibilities - Igniting self-worth, and turning dreams into reality.

Stacey is supported by her number one cheerleader in life, her love and soul mate, Ben.

Drop her a DM – Stacey would love to hear from you.

Contact: Email: info@staceyannebernadette.com
Website: www.staceyannebernadette.com
Facebook Group: Visionaries in Action

instagram.com/staceyannebernadette